W9-AEJ-838

*The
Women Who
Reconstructed
American
Jewish Education,
1910–1965*

The
Women Who
Reconstructed
American
Jewish Education
1910–1965

CAROL K. INGALL

Editor

BRANDEIS UNIVERSITY PRESS

WALTHAM, MASSACHUSETTS

PUBLISHED BY

UNIVERSITY PRESS OF NEW ENGLAND

HANOVER AND LONDON

BRANDEIS UNIVERSITY PRESS
Published by
University Press of New England
www.upne.com
© 2010 Brandeis University
All rights reserved
Manufactured in the
United States of America
Typeset in Miller and Block
by Passumpsic Publishing

University Press of New England is
a member of the Green Press Initiative.
The paper used in this book meets
their minimum requirement for
recycled paper.

For permission to reproduce any of the
material in this book, contact Permissions,
University Press of New England,
One Court Street, Lebanon NH 03766;
or visit www.upne.com

Library of Congress
Cataloging-in-Publication Data
The women who reconstructed American
Jewish education, 1910–1965 / Carol K.
Ingall, editor.
    p. cm. — (HBI series on Jewish women)
Includes bibliographical references and
index.
ISBN 978-1-58465-856-6 (cloth: alk. paper)
— ISBN 978-1-58465-855-9 (pbk.: alk. paper)
1. Jews—Education—United States—
History—20th century. 2. Women
educators—United States—History—20th
century. 3. Jewish educators—United
States—History—20th century. I. Ingall,
Carol K.
LC741.W66   2010
370.8992'4073—dc22   2009047978

*This project was published with
the generous support of the Lucius N.
Littauer Foundation.*

The author is grateful for permission to
use material from the following sources:
Eric Zinner of NYU Press for material
    that originally appeared in Shuly Rubin
    Schwartz's *The Rabbi's Wife* (2006).
Taylor and Francis for material that
    originally appeared in Miriam Heller
    Stern's "Ladies, Girls, and Mothers:
    Defining Jewish Motherhood at the
    Settlement House," *Journal of Jewish
    Education* 69, no. 2 (2003): 22–34, and
    Carol K. Ingall's "Anna G. Sherman:
    A 'Benderly Girl'?" *Journal of Jewish
    Education* 70, nos. 1–2 (2004): 32–39.
Patrick Dunn of Taylor and Francis for
    allowing the reprint of Carol K. Ingall,
    "*Hava n'Halela*: Tzipora Jochsberger and
    Her Vision for the Hebrew Arts School,"
    Journal of Jewish Education 71, no. 2
    (2005): 201–17.
The following archives also gave permission
    for use of their material: American Jewish
    Historical Society, New York and Newton
    Centre, Mass.; Hadassah, the Women's
    Zionist Organization of America, Inc.,
    New York; Jacob Rader Marcus Center of
    the American Jewish Archives, Cincinnati,
    Ohio; Judah L. Magnes Museum,
    Berkeley, Calif.; Western Reserve
    Historical Society, Cleveland, Ohio.

5 4 3 2 1

TO MY GRANDDAUGHTER,

Shirley Michaela Hoffman-Ingall

Contents

Foreword

From 1881 to 1924, when millions of east European Jews were pouring into the United States, it often seemed that the primary educational challenge to immigrants and their children was learning how to be American. However, by the end of the period of mass immigration, it became apparent that if Jewish culture were to be transmitted, Jewish educational institutions would be needed to facilitate that transmission. Jews had to create "new institutions and new educational models." Thus, it should come as no surprise that Carol K. Ingall dubs the period between 1910 and 1965 the golden age of American Jewish education. As she says in the acknowledgments, it was a time "when the regnant progressive pedagogy of the day . . . was molding the teaching of Hebrew language and classic Jewish texts." New educational movements, ideas, and initiatives were being formulated that were essential to keeping the American Jewish population interested in sustaining Jewish life.

As Carol Ingall writes in her introductory chapter, the men who were influential in shaping American Jewish educational trends are often the subject of scholarly interest and popular awareness, but much less has been written about the unsung heroines in this book who "kept Hebrew and Hebrew nationalism alive through education, not only in the Talmud Torah schools and in the first decades of the suburban synagogue schools, but also in children's literature, camps and youth groups, adult Jewish education for women, and cultural arts programs for all ages." These are extraordinary achievements, and they should be acknowledged and appreciated. Moreover, in discussions of the roots of Jewish education in the United States, the following names should regularly appear: Ethel Feineman, Grace Weiner, Jessie Sampter, Rebecca Aaronson Brickner, Libbie Braverman, Mamie Gamoran, Sadie Rose Weilerstein, Anna G. Sherman, Temima Gezari, Tzipora Jochsberger, and Sylvia Ettenberg. Each of these women made a mark on an aspect of Jewish education, whether in arts, camping, textbooks, or adult education.

The eight contributors to this book trace the evolution of Jewish education in America not only in terms of the dynamics of Jewish organizational life, but also in ways in which Jewish education was influenced by important education theorists. As Carol Ingall notes, these immigrants had to create their own pathways to becoming Americans while ensuring that they and their descendants would remain Jews. The formidable nature of the task facing Jewish education is underscored by the fact that, despite the efforts to professionalize the field, much work remains. Even today, when asked about their Sunday and Hebrew school experiences, some Jews assert that they learned nothing, that it was a waste of time, that Hebrew school was merely a training ground for bar or bat mitzvah or a holding pattern for children who were not going to Jewish day schools. According to these complaints, some Jewish schools may have been responsible for departure from, rather than retention in, the Jewish community. How extraordinary, then, are the accomplishments of the women who are this book's heroines. They battled impressive odds and often managed to transform educational practice in a difficult environment.

This book will not answer the question about what went wrong, but it will describe what went right in the period from 1910 to 1965. The eleven women singled out in this book were ahead of their times. Their belief in what Jewish education might accomplish is an inspiration to those who look to Jewish education to energize contemporary Jewish life. We are pleased to have *The Women who Reconstructed American Jewish Education, 1910–1965* as the latest publication in the HBI Series on Jewish Women, supported in part by Dr. Laura S. Schor. The book looks at a significant Jewish institution through the lens of gender. Ingall's book should be read and discussed as we continue work in Jewish education. And one should remember that it is only with the advent of a women's studies approach to history, including Jewish history, that we are able to identify these eleven heroines (and others), to understand why they made the choices they did, and to offer them the respect, even if only in hindsight, that they deserve.

SHULAMIT REINHARZ

Foreword

Acknowledgments

This book is a very personal endeavor. As a child growing up in Boston, I attended the Dorchester Mattapan Hebrew School, housed in a synagogue, but open to any Jewish child who lived in the neighborhood. The school met five days a week, four afternoons and Sundays. I attended Sabbath services as well, as did many of my classmates. I studied the Hebrew Bible and prayer book, and Hebrew literature (in Hebrew), and I learned about Jewish history, Jewish music, and how to celebrate Jewish holidays. Far from being a burden, Hebrew school was a welcome alternative to the Boston public schools, where even a goody-two-shoes like me might be singled out for the "rattan" for a minor infraction. ("Rattaning" consisted of the teacher whacking our open palms with a ruler, the post–World War II upgrade from a piece of cane.) The stern, unsmiling women who struck fear in my timid heart in the mornings were very different from my afternoon and Sunday teachers at Dor-Matt, as we called it. My Hebrew teachers were almost always women, young and kind-hearted graduates of local schools of education, teachers colleges, or normal schools. Unlike my teachers in the Boston public schools, my Hebrew teachers could marry without fear of losing their jobs. One of the highlights of my Hebrew school years was being invited, along with my classmates, to the wedding of the glamorous Miss Stein.

Although many remember religious school with the same fondness as visits to the orthodontist, most of my classmates and I, students during the late forties and early fifties, looked forward to school. Our teachers were passionate and energetic in their teaching; they were committed to Hebrew language and culture, to Zionism and the new State of Israel. We learned through music, art, and drama. We were taught to speak Hebrew, and learning a second language made us feel special and accomplished. About half of us were coached for the entrance exam to the Prozdor, the high school division of the Hebrew Teachers College, where our teachers had studied. My pleasant associations with this Talmud Torah (communally funded school) transferred to Jewish studies in general; I chose colleges around schools that either offered serious study of Judaica or were in proximity of institutions that did. I chose Jewish education as my profession. My educational biography, in Ellen Lagemann's felicitous phrase, was shaped by my childhood experiences.

Only as an adult did I realize that I was part of the golden age of American Jewish education, when the regnant progressive pedagogy of the day (which seemed to have leapfrogged over the Boston public school system) was molding the teaching of Hebrew language and classic Jewish texts. I am grateful that this book gave me the opportunity to study that period, to help me understand why my fond memories of Hebrew school are so different from the bitter ones depicted in many American novels, memoirs, and short stories. I am delighted to have shared this journey of discovery with some of my colleagues, contributors to this volume whose research informs this period through the creation of portraits of women who accomplished so much and are so little recognized. I have benefited enormously from the friendship and wisdom of Ofra Backenroth, Alan Bennett, Lisa Grant, Jonathan Krasner, Shuly Rubin Schwartz, Miriam Heller Stern, and Rebecca Boim Wolf.

I thank the archivists who helped answer questions and provide invaluable resources: Sean Martin of the Western Reserve Historical Society, Kevin Proffitt and Camille Servizzi of the Jacob Rader Marcus Center of the American Jewish Archives, Ellen Kastel of the Ratner Archives of the Jewish Theological Seminary, Gennady Yusin and Lizanne Hart of the staff of the Kaufman Center, and Lara Michels of the Judah L. Magnes Museum. I must single out Susan Woodland, the archivist of Hadassah who has been so supportive of this endeavor, for her unflagging energy, diligence, and responsiveness.

I had the good fortune to have all sorts of technical support from David Kraemer, librarian, Hector Guzman, and other staff members of the Library of the Jewish Theological Seminary, as well as Edna Nahshon, Jordan Killam, Rosemary Raymond, Sam Spinat, Andrew Ingall, and Ruth Page.

This book benefited from the input of its anonymous outside reviewers, the contributions of Sylvia Barack Fishman and Shulamit Reinharz of Brandeis University Press, the close reading of my good friend and colleague Shuly Rubin Schwartz, and Marjorie Ingall, one of the best writers I know. I acknowledge my profound gratitude to the University Press of New England (UPNE) for introducing the women in this anthology to a wider audience. I thank Lori Miller, my "manuscript boss," Amanda Dupuis, Anne R. Gibbons, and in particular Phyllis D. Deutsch, editor in chief of UPNE, for her confidence in this project, her patience, and her incisive advice.

In the twelfth century, Judah ibn Tibbon counseled his son "to make books your companions . . . for then your will shall be restored and your spirit will become beautiful." This book has been my companion for more than six years. I hope its publication can, in some small measure, inspire those who follow in the footsteps of these women, restoring their will and beautifying their spirit.

Contributors

OFRA ARIELI BACKENROTH is the associate dean of the William Davidson Graduate School of Jewish Education of the Jewish Theological Seminary, where she teaches courses in Hebrew language acquisition and using the arts to teach Jewish studies. Along with Shira D. Epstein and Helena Miller, she wrote "Bringing the Text to Life and into Our Lives: Jewish Education and the Arts" for the *Journal of Religious Education* (Fall 2006) and is the author of "What Do We Know about Art Education Research" in *What We Now Know about Jewish Education*, ed. R. L. Goodman et al. (2008). Backenroth has contributed a chapter titled "The Arts and Jewish Day School Education in North America" to the *International Handbook of Jewish Education* (forthcoming).

ALAN D. BENNETT, executive vice president emeritus of the Jewish Education Center of Cleveland, has been a frequent contributor to the *Journal of Jewish Education, Religious Education*, the *Journal of Jewish Communal Service*, and *Reform Judaism*. He wrote "Effective Use of the Central Agency and Professional Networks" for the *Jewish Educational Leader's Handbook* (1998) and *The Vision and the Will: A History of the National Association of Temple Educators, 1954–2004* (2004).

LISA D. GRANT is associate professor of Jewish education at the Hebrew Union College–Jewish Institute of Religion, New York. Her research and teaching interests include adult Jewish learning, professional development, and the role of Israel in American life. She is the lead author of *A Journey of Heart and Mind: Transformative Jewish Learning in Adulthood* (2004) with Diane Schuster, Meredith Woocher, and Steven M. Cohen. Along with Helena Miller and Alex Pomson, she is coeditor of the *International Handbook of Jewish Education* (forthcoming).

CAROL K. INGALL is the Dr. Bernard Heller Professor of Jewish Education at the Jewish Theological Seminary and the author of numerous articles in research journals about Jewish education. She is the author of *Maps, Metaphors, and Mirrors: Moral Education in Middle Schools* (1997); *Transmission and Transformation: A Jewish Perspective on Moral Education* (1999; winner of the 1999 National Jewish Book Award); and *Down the Up Staircase: Tales of Teaching in Jewish Day Schools* (2006).

JONATHAN KRASNER is assistant professor of the American Jewish experience at Hebrew Union College–Jewish Institute of Religion in New York. He is working on a book about the Benderly boys and the history of American Jewish education that will be published by Brandeis University Press.

SHULY RUBIN SCHWARTZ is the Irving Lehrman Research Associate Professor of American Jewish History and dean of Albert A. List College of Jewish Studies at the Jewish Theological Seminary. Her most recent book, *The Rabbi's Wife: The Rebbetzin in American Jewish Life* (2006) won the 2006 National Jewish Book Award in the area of modern Jewish thought.

MIRIAM HELLER STERN is director of curriculum and research at the Fingerhut School of Education at American Jewish University, where she teaches Fundamentals of Teaching and Learning, including social foundations of education, curriculum development, and practitioner research. She received her PHD at Stanford University in the history of education; her dissertation was titled "Your Children, Will They Be Yours? Educational Strategies for Jewish Survival, 1916–1944." She has written articles on the history of American Jewish education, including the history of informal Jewish education and a reexamination of Samson Benderly's work in the Progressive Era.

REBECCA BOIM WOLF, a PHD candidate in Jewish history at New York University, is working on a dissertation titled "Selling Hadassah: The Shifting Images, Icons, and Impressions of the Women's Zionist Organization of America." She has taught modern Jewish history at New York University and the Jewish Theological Seminary.

*The
Women Who
Reconstructed
American
Jewish Education,
1910–1965*

Introduction

CAROL K. INGALL

The *Women Who Reconstructed American Jewish Education, 1910–1965*, introduces the unheralded educators who planted the seeds of social reform and progressivism in the soil and soul of American Jewish education. It highlights eleven eminent women who either informed the educational philosophies of the twentieth century's most influential Jewish pedagogues, Samson Benderly (1876–1944) and Mordecai Kaplan (1881–1983), or put them into practice. The women profiled are Ethel Feineman and Grace Weiner, Jessie Sampter, Rebecca Aaronson Brickner, Libbie L. Braverman, Mamie Gamoran, Sadie Rose Weilerstein, Anna G. Sherman, Temima Gezari, Tzipora Jochsberger, and Sylvia C. Ettenberg. They not only recast Jewish education in the progressive, experiential model of John Dewey (1859–1952) and his followers but also implemented a pedagogy based on the primacy of Hebrew language and culture.[1]

Like much feminist scholarship, this book is intended, in part, to fill in the gaps in a history written by men about the achievements of men (the chronicle of captains and kings) and "recover . . . past history and forgotten heroines" (hooks, 2000, xi). Scholars of Jewish education are familiar with the contributions of the Benderly boys, as Benderly's male disciples came to be known, but much less is known about the women who were disciples of Benderly and Kaplan. By illuminating the contributions of these women, this book offers a fuller analysis of American Jewish education. One simply cannot understand the development of the field without a close look at the aspirations, careers, and accomplishments of the women who taught in Jewish schools, wrote books that lined the shelves of Jewish classrooms and homes, created learning experiences for other Jewish women, and experimented with new forms of informal Jewish education in youth groups and camps. To paraphrase Larry Cuban (1992), the eminent historian of American education, if the Jewish community had an itch, it was these women who did the scratching (216).

This volume documents the role these women played in implementing the Jewish communal agendas of instruction and enculturation from 1920 to 1965. As Kaufman (2006) has noted, "In the new world, the feminization of Jewish education would go hand in hand with the Americanization of the Jew" (897). Influenced by the tenets of progressivism and a love of Hebrew

1

and Zionism, these women believed that the United States afforded an ideal environment for Jewish life to flourish. Jewish education could produce an American equivalent of the fabled golden age of Iberian Jewry, one in which Jews would be full participants in American society while still firmly rooted to Jewish culture, customs, and religious practice. The American Jewish synthesis they forged was built on a love of the Hebrew language and literature, and Zionism. To fully appreciate their efforts, it is important to understand the efforts of the generation that preceded them.

In his history of Hebraism in America, Mintz (1993) discussed the efforts of a cultural elite to revive Hebrew in the period just before World War I with the founding of the journal *Hatoren* (*The Mast*) in 1913 and the Histadrut Ivrit (Hebrew Union) in 1916. While *Hatoren* promoted Hebrew literature, the Histadrut tried to foster Hebrew culture and Hebrew nationalism (i.e., Zionism) through lectures, meetings, and eventually, a newspaper. Mintz observes, "It is undeniable that if Hebraism has made any impact on the American Jewish scene it is essentially through its influence on education. The story of how a small band of committed Hebraists 'kidnapped' the Talmud Torah [communally funded supplementary schools] movement and retained control of it for several decades needs to be told" (64).

The Women Who Reconstructed American Jewish Education tells this story. These women and others like them, teachers and authors, were the "kidnappers." It was they who kept Hebrew and Hebrew nationalism alive through education, not only in the Talmud Torah and in the first decades of the suburban synagogue schools, but also in children's literature, camps and youth groups, adult Jewish education for women, and cultural arts programs for all ages.

Contextualizing the Endeavor: American Jewish Education before the Women Who Reconstructed It

In assessing the contributions of Maimonides to the theory and practice of medicine of his time, Sherwin Nuland (2005) used a yardstick that is applicable to other professions as well. What was the state of the profession at the time and how was it affected by the contributions of the person or persons under study? Did the professional add to theory and practice? Did he or she leave a legacy that newcomers to the profession could look to as a model of theory and practice? (154–55).

The history of Jews in the United States is the story of a love affair. The women whose portraits appear in this volume shared this romance and the concomitant belief that America was good for the Jews. From the earliest beginnings of Jewish settlement (1654), America offered the promise of religious freedom and full cultural integration. Each subsequent century brought to American shores Jewish immigrants who were responding to economic insecurity and religious persecution. Although some rabbis may have railed against emigrating to the *treife medina* (the unkosher nation) or *ama reika* (the empty nation), the process of Jewish assimilation into modernity and the weakening hold of traditional religion had begun long before the immigrants reached the shores of the *goldene medina* (the nation of gold) (Sarna, 2004, 154ff).

Making a home in America meant being enculturated into American society: learning English, accepting civic obligations, and understanding American mores and values. It also meant making a Jewish home by learning Hebrew and passing on Jewish folkways, religious practices, and values. These immigrants had to become Americans while ensuring that they and their descendants would remain Jews. Fitting into American society demanded new institutions and new educational models; the communal solutions to these challenges were profoundly influenced by the educational philosophy and institutions of their American neighbors.

The Puritans who founded Harvard College in 1636 believed that secular education and religion were inextricable. Both were accessible through the use of God-given rationality; each was an avenue to the pursuit of truth. No educated gentleman, particularly one destined for the ministry, could be considered literate without knowledge of Hebrew and Holy Writ. Eighteenth-century Sephardic Jews shared a similar view of the intertwining of general and religious education. The board of trustees of Shearith Israel (the Spanish and Portuguese Congregation), the first congregation in the United States, referred to education as "the first thing which ought to be pursued in life, in order to constitute us rational" (Marcus, 1996, 43).

Like their Protestant neighbors, Jews founded schools that included religious and secular instruction, precursors of today's Jewish day schools. Their goals were character education as well as cultural literacy. When the trustees of Congregation Shearith Israel sought a schoolmaster in the mid-1700s, the job description laid out their priorities. Congregational leaders expected the teacher to serve as a moral exemplar who was "single, modest, and sober" (Marcus, 1996, 41) and, of course, male. The instructor would be able "to teach our children ye Hebrew language; English and Spanish he ought to know, but he will not suit unless he understands Hebrew and English at least" (Marcus, 41). In 1762 they hired Mr. Abraham I. Abrahams to teach Hebrew, English, Spanish, writing, and ciphering (Marcus, 42). In 1804 the trustees reaffirmed the rationale for religious education: "In order to make your children virtuous, you must rear them in the strict principles of our holy religion and teach them Hebrew the key to understanding prayer" (Marcus, 43). These schools were charged with turning out good American citizens and knowledgeable members of the Jewish community; they were open to all Jewish children regardless of their parents' ability to pay tuition.

One of the leading figures of nineteenth-century American Jewish history was Rebecca Gratz (1781–1869). The daughter of a successful merchant who immigrated to Philadelphia in 1754 from Silesia, Gratz established the first known Jewish Sunday school in the United States in 1838 (Ashton, 1997). In the era of the Second Great Awakening, some Christian women, friends of Gratz, took a leading role in educational and eleemosynary activities. Other Philadelphians responded to the religious revival by targeting Jews for conversion. These efforts prompted Gratz to establish a school, similar to those established by her Protestant friends, but designed to teach Jewish children the tenets of their faith. Open to all Jewish children, her school, unlike the full-time Shearith Israel model, met only on Sundays. Gratz's institution also differed from the Shearith Israel school by leaving secular studies to private tutors for those who could afford it. Rosa Mordecai, who taught for her great-aunt Rebecca Gratz, recalled that the school was a virtues-driven institution, prizing those qualities that would make children better Americans, not just better Jews. "She was extremely particular [about instilling] neatness and cleanliness. A soiled dress, crooked collar, or sticky hands never escaped her penetrating glance and the reproof or remedy was instantaneous" (cited in Marcus, 1996, 153). The curriculum emphasized piety. Gratz would begin school with a prayer: "Come ye children, hearken unto me, and I will teach you the fear of the Lord." She followed with a Bible reading in English, a Hebrew "hymn," and passing the collection plate for "the poor of Jerusalem." The children had no distinctively Jewish textbooks; instead they used Pike's *Catechism and Scripture Lessons* published by the Christian American Sunday School Union. As Mordecai recalled, "Many a long summer's day have I spent, pasting pieces of paper over answers unsuitable for Jewish children, and many were the fruitless efforts of those children to read through, over, or under the hidden lines" (Marcus, 154). Knowing little or no Hebrew, Gratz could not teach Jewish texts in their original language. Other than the collection of *tzedakah* (charity; literally, doing justice) for their coreligionists in Palestine, the curriculum was a replica of that of the Protestant Sunday schools in the city.

As Reform Judaism, an import from German communities, took root in the United States, Gratz's model for Jewish education was duplicated in places like Charleston, Savannah, and Baltimore. Following in the footsteps of German reformers like Abraham Geiger (1810–74) and Samuel Holdheim (1806–60), American Reform rabbis believed they could create an indigenous American Judaism by dispensing with Jewish differences, excising those nationalistic elements that made Jews unassimilable. By emphasizing the rationality of Jewish religion, conducting prayer and preaching in the vernacular, and adding more decorum and aesthetics to synagogue practices, they imposed a Protestant aesthetic on Jewish worship. Eisen (1983) noted that Judaism became "a religion and not a national identity, a set of beliefs destined to converge with those of enlightened gentiles" (21). A one-day-a-week school taught by well-meaning women with only a modicum of Hebrew who emphasized ethical, not ethnic, behavior suited Reform rabbis' purposes very well.

If there were those who suggested that the key to Jewish success in America was the reformation of Judaism, others opted for a more traditionalist approach, calling for the reformation of Jewish education, thereby ensuring Jewish particularity and Jewish survival. One of these spokespersons was Isaac Leeser (1806–68), the most prolific writer of his day on Jewish issues. Born in Westphalia, Leeser proposed an educational alternative to the model instituted by his fellow Philadelphian Rebecca Gratz. He opted for bringing back the day school model of the Sephardic period. In 1835 he proposed establishing a school that would feature Hebrew instruction with both Sephardic and Ashkenazic (German) pronunciation; instruction in Jewish religion using texts he translated from the German; and lessons in English grammar, geography, history, arithmetic, and writing. Leeser also offered his services to "such Christians as might be willing to send their children to such an institution" (Marcus, 150). He was also willing to add Latin, Greek, German, French, Spanish, Italian, natural history, natural philosophy, drawing, and singing to the curriculum (Marcus, 150).

Suspicious of the newly established "common school," which offered free public education with a dollop of Protestant values, Leeser noted: "As Jews we are to observe many little ceremonies, [and] are to acquire many details of religious duties, which none other but a Jew can impart" (cited in Marcus, 151). He maintained that Jewish religious education had to be more than ethical monotheism and required a special context and a committed teacher to maintain its integrity.

In 1843 Leeser addressed his concern about the Protestant nature of the common school in the pages of the *Occident*, the newspaper he edited: "We are in great error if we suppose that Christian teachers do not endeavor to influence actively the sentiments of Jewish pupils" (cited in Graff, 2003, 71). He was wary of Bible reading in the common schools, seeing it as an attempt to proselytize (Handlin, 1982, 8). Leeser looked to a more intensive Jewish education to reinvigorate a pale American Judaism and rejected the efforts of educational reformers to eliminate those differences that separated Jews from their gentile neighbors. He believed that Jewish education must concern itself with the teaching of moral values, not only skills and knowledge, and considered Hebrew language and literature as a cure for Jewish indifference. "In place of empty benches in the house of worship, in place of public profanation of all our religion holds sacred: there will be an increase of righteousness and religious knowledge; the synagogues will be crowded with worshippers who delight to call on God in their own — dear — national tongue, to them not a dead language; and the reproach of lukewarmness will not be any more uttered against us" (Marcus, 151). As his biographer noted,

"By offering adequate instruction to American Jews, adults as well as children, [Leeser] hoped to simultaneously Americanize Judaism and 'Judaize' American Jews" (Sussman, 1995, 81). This would become a leitmotif in the history of American Jewish education for more than a century.

Even the dean of American Reform rabbis, Isaac Mayer Wise, initially took issue with the Jewish Sunday school movement shortly after he arrived from Germany in 1847. He noted that in America "religious instruction for children is imparted each Sabbath or Sunday by good-hearted young women. What fruits these few hours can bring forth hardly necessitates further description" (cited in Graff, 2008, 27). By 1870 Wise had changed his mind; the overwhelming appeal of the common school put Jewish day schools out of business. "It is our settled opinion here that the education of the young is the business of the State, and the religious instruction, to which we add the Hebrew, is the duty of the religious bodies. Neither ought to interfere with the other. The secular branches belong to the public schools, religion in the Sabbath schools, respectively" (cited in Graff, 2008, 36). Wise's underlying assumption was that Jews thrive when church and state are separate, and what was good for the American people, i.e., serious religious instruction, was good for the Jews. More than twenty Jewish day schools had been established in the 1840s and 1850s; by the early 1870s all of them had closed (Graff, 2003, 70).

Wise's view, not Leeser's, carried the day. The more than 2 million Jews who came to the United States between 1881 and 1924 were smitten by American schools and the promise of universal free public education unimaginable in the Russian Empire, Romania, and Austria-Hungary. The ubiquitous McGuffey Readers drove the curriculum of the common school. The American Book Company, successors to the series' first publishers, estimated that more than 1.2 million copies of the readers were sold between 1836 and 1920 (Mosier, 1965, 168). The series taught children not only reading and American history, but also American values. The authors, a motley group of liberal and conservative reformers united by Christian or Unitarian piety, included William Holmes McGuffey and his brother Alexander, abolitionists like Catherine Lyman and Henry Ward Beecher, and temperance advocates like Lucius M. Sargent and Lydia G. Sigourney. They used heroes as representations of "rugged individualism, the dignity of labor, the basic virtues of thrift, honesty, and charity" (Minnich, 1936, vi). Heroes also served as exemplars of the kind of patriotism the authors were eager to instill in the immigrants streaming to U.S. cities.

In describing contemporary American Jewry, Sylvia Barack Fishman (2000) noted the prevalence of "coalescence," the assumption by many Jews that Jewish and American values are one and the same. This is not a new phenomenon; it explains why Jews were reluctant to embrace the day school movement, unlike Catholics who balked at readings from the King James version of the Bible and had established a system of parochial schools before the Civil War. The values messages of the common school were not wholly incompatible with a Jewish worldview. Hard work, supporting the needy, temperance, respect for one's elders, and reverence for education — these were values that could be found in pietistic Jewish literature (*mussar*) as well as in *Poor Richard's Almanac*.

By the time the women profiled here appeared on the scene, the common, or public, school reigned supreme. For many Jewish immigrants, education had become their religion. It was their passport to full participation in the wonders of America. Civic duty taught in public schools was more compelling than religious duty. American heroes whose stories filled the pages of the McGuffey readers were far more stirring than heroes from Jewish history. Mary Antin (1881–1949), recently arrived from Plotzk, Russia, rhapsodized over George Washington in her 1912 autobiography, *The Promised Land*: "Never had I prayed, never had I chanted the songs of David, never had I called upon the Most Holy, in such utter reverence and worship as I repeated the simple sentences of my child's story of the patriot. I gazed with adoration at the portraits of George and Martha Washington, till I could see them with my eyes shut" (223).

The Uptown Jews of New York, well-established German Jews who belonged to Reform synagogues, undertook the Americanization of the eastern European newcomers in the early twentieth century. They understood that Jewish day schools were not an option, being more appropriate for the Old World and the ghetto. Jewish education in the United States would have to be retrofitted around public schools.

> The isolation of our children in parochial school, though undoubtedly effective from a purely Jewish point of view, might injuriously affect our political and social status in this country, and since the giving of religious instruction at the Public Schools would contradict the basic American principle of eliminating religion from our state institutions, it follows that the present system of teaching our children in Hebrew Schools after Public School hours is the most desirable under existing circumstances. (Winter, 1966, 212)

These leaders also knew that the Reform Sunday school model was alien to the immigrants who tended to come from more traditional religious backgrounds. The *Kehillah* (community) of New York (1908–22), led by Rabbi Judah Magnes of Temple Emanu-El, the most prestigious Reform congregation, had been established to bring the spirit of progressive urban reform to the problems in the Jewish community. Magnes called for a survey of Jewish education and in 1909 entrusted Rabbi Mordecai Kaplan with the task. Kaplan had just become the head of the Teachers Institute at the Jewish Theological Seminary, an institution founded to respond to the problem of "children of immigrants . . . abandoning the synagogues of their fathers and rejecting the Jewish homes of their mothers" (Kaufman, 1997, 568). Kaplan's report, coauthored with Bernard Cronson, a fellow Jew who was also a public school principal, revealed the sorry state of Jewish education: deplorable physical conditions, low enrollment, and ill-prepared teachers. Their findings documented the worst fears of the *Kehillah*. Newly arrived eastern European Jews, unschooled in the tenets of a religious tradition would end up either filling the pews of the city's churches or filling the city's jails. If Jews continued to cling to their Old World ways, they would never become Americanized.

In a letter to Jacob Schiff, one of the financial supporters of the *Kehillah*, Magnes called for a communal educational response to the problems of the new immigrants. "It alone could assure the transmission of the group's moral values to the young. How can we expect young men and women growing up in crowded sections and working in unfavorable conditions to be pure and clean and honorable, if they are allowed to drift from the anchorage which the religion of their fathers might have given them?" (Goren, 1970, 87). The community needed a Bureau of Jewish Education to professionalize and supervise a communally funded system of schools that, unlike the older Talmud Torahs, would be of the highest quality and open to all Jewish children, not only the poor. These Jewish schools would "supplement" the public school by providing a religious and moral orientation that would help Jewish youngsters to grow into "American men and women who prove not a menace to the Republic, but a blessing to it" (Goren, 87). The Benderly-Kaplan era had begun.

The Dynamic Duo: Benderly and Kaplan

The names of Benderly and Kaplan are inextricably linked to the idea of education as a means of addressing the social problems that beset the American Jewish community at the beginning of the twentieth century. Samson Benderly (1876–1944), born in Safed, Palestine, was a physician who stumbled upon the passion of his life, Jewish education, during his medical residency in Baltimore. The committee overseeing Benderly's residency upbraided him for spending his afternoons at the communal school he had founded, rather than in the hospital. When faced with choosing between ophthalmology and Jewish education, Benderly chose the latter (Winter, 1966).

Magnes considered Benderly the ideal person to head up the first central agency for Jewish education in the United States, the Bureau of Jewish Education of New York. An advocate of cultural or spiritual Zionism, Benderly believed that political Zionism was shortsighted. Having a land of one's own was not enough to reinvigorate worldwide Jewry; the *yishuv* (settlement) in *Eretz Yisrael*, as well as diaspora Jews, desperately needed a cultural transfusion. Hebrew could unlock the Jewish canon and serve as the glue to connect Jews all over the world. Benderly was inspired by Ahad Ha'am (1856–1927), who posited: "Hebrew has been our language ever since we came into existence; and Hebrew alone is linked to us inseparably and eternally as part of our being. We are therefore justified in concluding that Hebrew has been, is, and will always be, our national language; that our national literature throughout all time, is the literature written in Hebrew" (cited in Simon, 1936, 284).

The *Kehillah* leaders and Benderly shared a commitment to meliorism that combined Hebrew language and culture, Zionism, and Americanism. Unlike the elitist Hebraists of *Hatoren*, who saw American culture as meretricious and vulgar (Mintz, 1993), Magnes, Benderly, and Kaplan believed that American values and Jewish values were harmonious. They imagined an American Jewish synthesis fueled by Hebrew language and culture. In his letter dated March 9, 1910, accepting the leadership of the Bureau of Jewish Education, Benderly laid out the goal for American Jewish education in the second decade of the century:

> Never before in Jewish history has so large a Jewish community as we form in this country had both the opportunity and the responsibility of proving that the essentials of Judaism, so far from being in contradiction to the cardinal elements of modern civilization, are complementary to them, the two sides being mutually indispensable to each other. Constituting an integral part of the Republic, we are under [an] obligation to demonstrate that the principles for which Israel fought and bled over two thousand years are perfectly compatible with and essential to the fundamental principles upon which the American nation is building a wonderful structure of human liberty and happiness. Our obligation is twofold: On the one hand, we must Americanize, in the higher sense, every Jew in this country, infusing into him the spirit of self-reliance, fair play, and social cooperation; and on the other hand, we must build up the structure of Jewish life, so as not only to enable ourselves to hold our own, Jewishly speaking, but also to become an indispensable element in the progress of the country. (cited in Winter, 1966, 201–2)

The *Kehillah* leaders understood that for Jews to make a home in America they had to become enculturated into American society, that is, to speak English and to acquire American mores, values, and sense of civic duties, while learning enough about Judaism to ensure what would became known to a later generation as "Jewish continuity." This was not a Hebraism for the elite, but for the masses.

Benderly became a nonstop education machine, cranking out programs to touch all facets of the Jewish community: Talmud Torahs, camps, Jewish high schools, classes for preschoolers through adults, family education, professional development for teachers and principals, classroom materials, and curricula.[2] The *Kehillah* dreamed big. In its charter of 1914, it set forth its goals for the amelioration of the social, moral, and economic conditions besetting the immigrant population. The Bureau of Jewish Education was designed to

> stimulate and encourage the instruction of the Jews residing in the city of New York in the tenets of their religion and in the history, language, literature, institutions and traditions of their people; to conduct, support and maintain schools and classes for that purpose; to publish and distribute text-books, maps, charts, and illustrations to facilitate such instruction; to conduct lectures and classes in civics and other kindred subjects; to establish an educational bureau to further the foregoing purposes; to conduct religious service and support, maintain, and establish temporary as well as permanent synagogues; [and] to adjust differences among Jewish residents or organizations in said city. (Marcus, 1996, 334)

Benderly brought his progressive pedagogy to the model schools he established for the *Kehillah* (including a number for girls). Harry Friedenwald, a former student of Benderly in Baltimore, describes teaching Hebrew "the natural way" (*hashitah hativit*) or *Ivrit b'Ivrit* (Hebrew via Hebrew), through a child-centered, experiential pedagogy that reflected Dewey's pedagogic ideals: "In our schools, Hebrew, which some called a dead language, comes to life under the magic of speech, for all instruction excepting history is in Hebrew. The exercises in physical culture and the games and songs are conducted in Hebrew only. This method has the advantage of making a profound and indelible impression" (cited in Winter, 1966, 42).

An energetic and imaginative thinker, Benderly expanded Jewish education beyond the schoolhouse. He created the field of informal or experiential Jewish education, founding the first Jewish camp, Achvah, in 1927, and involving young people in after-school programs and Sunday clubs. Mamie Gamoran and Temima Gezari were products of these clubs. But Benderly was a butterfly, flitting from one project to another. His *Outline of Jewish Knowledge* (1929), coauthored with Israel Goldberg, is a testament to his grandiose vision and to his distractibility, as the subtitle suggests: "Being a History of the Jewish People and an Anthology of Jewish Literature from the Earliest Times to the Present: Including a Brief Account of the History and Civilization of the Nations with Whom the Jews Have Come into Contact, and an Exposition of the Present-day Status and Problems of the Jewries of the World in Twelve Volumes with Maps and Illustrations." Goldberg and Benderly completed three volumes, bringing their readers no further than to the fall of the second temple (70 C.E.).

Miriam Heller Stern (2004) has observed that even if Benderly's "dream did not quite come true," he and the Benderly boys identified the issues that continue to trouble American Jewish education: professionalization, recruitment and retention of teachers, community funding of education, and balancing the teaching of skills with the affective goal of making the learner want to be a part of the Jewish people's past, present, and future.

Benderly's legacy is mixed, but there is no question about the far-reaching impact of his friend Mordecai Kaplan (1881–1983). As Ari Ackerman (2008) remarked, "Perhaps more than any modern Jewish thinker, [Kaplan] was deeply involved in Jewish education" (201). Kaplan's thinking affected all of the denominations of American Judaism. He received ordination from the Jewish Theological Seminary (JTS) in 1902 and was a longtime member of its faculty and head of the Teachers Institute from 1909 to 1944. He began his rabbinical career as the rabbi of a prestigious Orthodox synagogue, Kehillath Jeshurun, and helped to establish the Young Israel movement. He was asked by Stephen Wise to head up a new rabbinical school, the Jewish Institute of Religion, and founded a truly American approach to Judaism. Reconstructionism taught that Judaism was more than just a religion; thus Jewish education must transmit more than ritual practices and knowledge of classical texts. It should address the entire corpus of Jewish culture, including the arts, Jewish languages, and folkways, and should promote an attachment to the land of Israel. In the United States, which encouraged cultural pluralism (a term coined by Kaplan's friend Horace Kallen), a Jew could live simultaneously in two civilizations, as a Jew and an American.

As Kaufman (1997) noted, the Teachers Institute became Kaplan's educational laboratory. To help Benderly realize his dream of professionalizing Jewish education, he created a special course at the Teachers Institute for graduates of City College who were working toward doctorates at Columbia Teachers College. These students would become professors of education at the Teachers Institute and other Jewish teacher training colleges and bureau or central agency directors in cities across the United States. Isaac B. Berkson, one of the Benderly boys, wrote the first dissertation on Jewish education for Teachers College in 1916, on the adjustment of the curriculum of Jewish schools to the conditions of American life.

Kaplan would have preferred that the Benderly boys be drawn from the ranks of the JTS rabbinical students, but Benderly was suspicious of rabbis and synagogues. Benderly's religion *was* education, and his agenda was communal and nationalistic, rather than synagogue-based. Even though Kaplan ([1934] 1967) conceptualized Judaism as a civilization, he believed that ritual practice and religious texts were central to Jewish culture. As early as 1914, Kaplan voiced his concerns about Benderly and the Benderly boys in his diary:

In my heart of hearts I feel there is something wrong with the spirit that animates them in their work. . . . I always missed something in Achad Haam's conception of Judaism. It is wanting in appreciation of the indefinable religious longings and aspirations. It is this spirit that has taken possession of the men and I have found them strange, unresponsive to the deeper appeals of Judaism, so that I have often wished that these men were drawn into the Seminary, where while the religious spirit is lacking, it is at least not pooh-poohed, as is the case in nationalistic circles. (cited in Scult, 2001, 76–77)

While Kaplan consistently downplayed the anxiety of Solomon Schechter, the president of JTS, about the charismatic secularist who was "Benderlyizing the community" (cited in Scult, 1997, 84), he privately railed against his friend's myopia. In an October 4, 1914, diary entry he wrote:

Only by giving Jewish culture a distinctively religious significance in the true modern sense of the term is there any hope of Jewish education being built up in this country. This means that only [by] maintaining the synagogue and vitalizing it by means of the Hebraic movement can the Jews hope to survive here as a distinct group. Only those, therefore, who will give a religious interpretation to Jewish culture will be entrusted with the care and supervision of Jewish education. (cited in Scult, 2001, 77)

But disagreement with Benderly's philosophy never diminished Kaplan's affection for his friend. In one of the most touching musings in his diary, Kaplan noted:

Thank God there is at least Benderly. In spite of all that I may have said in the pages of this Journal in disparagement of him, I still love and admire him. The few hours that he spent with me at my house yesterday afternoon were balm to my soul. To see a man who can go through all that he does and still hold his head and retain his faith in the worthwhileness of the cause to which he has given his life is a rebuke to my wavering vacillating weak spirit. But I revive under such rebuke. (cited in Scult, 2001, 490)

While there is some debate as to how much Benderly actually Benderlyzed the community, there is no question that Kaplan Kaplanized it. Ackerman (2008) maintained it was Kaplan who was responsible for bringing into the field many of the people who would become "the central pillars of America Jewish education" (201). Kaplan not only influenced the Benderly boys, but as dean of the Teachers Institute, he also educated most of the women profiled in this book. And it was they who taught in the Talmud Torahs, the communally funded, professionally staffed Hebrew schools that replaced the deplorable schoolrooms exposed by the *Kehillah* report. These Talmud Torahs became "the normative institution for Jewish education in the United States for the first four decades of the twentieth century" (Elazar, 1993, 132). Even as the

Talmud Torahs gave way to congregational or synagogue schools, the fusion of American Jewish values, fueled by Hebrew language and culture remained the pedagogy of choice.

The Women Who Reconstructed American Jewish Education

This book begins in the heady era in American Jewish education when Benderly and Kaplan began their partnership and explores the optimistic period between the two World Wars when the American Jewish synthesis was popularized. It ends in the 1960s and 1970s when Jewish education, rather than being hailed as the solution to what ailed American Jewry, was seen as the malady. The book begins with a portrait of two San Francisco settlement house directors, Ethel Feineman and Grace Weiner, exemplars of the Progressive Era's urban educational reform that captivated Benderly and Kaplan. The settlement house ideology, blending public health and education, not only inspired the first children's room in the New York public library (Lepore, 2008), but also the child-size drinking fountains and playgrounds in Benderly's model schools (Winter, 1966).

Like the New York activists Julia Richman (1855–1912) in education and Lillian Wald (1867–1940) in public health, Ethel Feineman and Grace Weiner turned Jewish immigrants into Jewish Americans through an experiential pedagogy that would come to be known as informal Jewish education. As late as 1935, long after the heyday of the settlement house movement, Israel Chipkin, one of the first Benderly boys, would express its view of Americanization and Jewish education.

> Jewish education is, therefore, the wholesome process or corrective influence, which seeks the enrichment of the personality of the individual Jew and calls forth the social responsibilities and spiritual manifestations of Jewish group life, so that both individual and group may be integrated harmoniously into the American environment by contributing creatively to its social patterns and cultural values. From this point of view, Jewish education is also a process of Americanization and an expression of American democracy. (Chipkin, 1935, 29)

Feineman and Weiner exemplify one strand of social progressivism that tried to Americanize Jews. Jessie Sampter, who laid the educational foundations of Hadassah, exemplifies a second strand, one that tried to Judaize Americans. An ally of Henrietta Szold and a close friend of Kaplan and Magnes, Sampter was a thoroughly assimilated Jew who sought to build Jewish identity, community, and peoplehood. Cremin (1964) noted that progressive reformers during the first quarter of the twentieth century encouraged ethnic minorities to nurture "their own unique traditions at the same time as they contributed to the broader mainstream of American life" (69). Like

Kaplan's friend and mentor Horace Kallen, Sampter taught that Jews could live comfortably in two cultures, that ethnic languages and celebrations do not diminish one's American identity but in fact enhance it. In linking Hebraism, Zionism, and education, Sampter helped to create a cadre of students for Benderly and Kaplan.

All the women in this volume, with the exception of the two San Franciscan outliers, are part of a complex web linking them to Benderly, Kaplan, and each other. Rebecca Aaronson Brickner is the only true Benderly disciple among these women. In addition to studying and working with Benderly, she married a Benderly boy, Barnett Brickner. It was she who hired Nathan Brilliant, who in turn hired Libbie L. Braverman as a teaching and writing partner. Mamie Goldsmith Gamoran also married a Benderly boy, Emanuel Gamoran, who directed Jewish education for the Reform movement. Temima Gezari, who created the field of Jewish art education, attended a Benderly model school as a girl and illustrated Mamie Gamoran's book *Hillel's Happy Holidays*.

Kaplan's influence, through the Teachers Institute, was even more pronounced than Benderly's. Sadie Rose Weilerstein, married to a Conservative rabbi who considered Kaplan his mentor, shared the Kaplanian view of religious ritual as well as the universal nature of Jewish ethical concerns. Anna G. Sherman, a dedicated Hebraist and language teacher, became a member of Kaplan's Reconstructionist synagogue, the Society for the Advancement of Judaism (SAJ). Tzipora Jochsberger, founder of the Hebrew Arts School, composed music for the SAJ chorus, and Temima Gezari decorated its walls. Brickner, Sherman, Gezari, and Sylvia Ettenberg, the founder of Camp Ramah, were graduates of the Teachers Institute; Mamie Gamoran received a certificate from its Extension School. Kaplan hired Sherman, Gezari, and Ettenberg to teach in the Teachers Institute or its allied schools.

The Teachers Institute

The role of the Teachers Institute is crucial to this narrative. From its very beginnings, the Teachers Institute had a feminine character; the first class consisted of twenty-two women and twelve men (Kaufman, 1997, 578). As Kaufman (1997) observed, "Despite his reputation for egalitarianism, Kaplan believed that the woman's sphere would always be subordinate to the world of men" (583–84). Both Benderly and Kaplan aspired to professionalize Jewish education, but neither ever questioned the necessity of a two-tiered, gender-based profession. Men would become the educational thinkers, administrators, and leaders, Jewish equivalents of Teachers College professors, superintendents of schools, and boards of education; professionalizing women meant making graduates of Jewish teacher training colleges look more like alumnae of American normal schools (Ingall, 1995).

What Kaplan created at the Teachers Institute was the embodiment of the Hebraist, nationalist culture that inspired Benderly and American Zionists like Szold and Sampter. Students were required to take courses in the use of art, music, and dance in Jewish schools and camps. Unlike in the male rabbinical school, classes were taught in Hebrew and brought together Jews, mostly women, from across the Jewish spectrum. The courses in education taught by the Benderly boys were often less than compelling, but the student community with extracurricular activities in theater, publishing, and musical performance inspired generations of students. During Kaplan's long tenure as dean of the Teachers Institute (1909–46) and that of his disciple Moshe Davis (1946–56), the Teachers Institute became a laboratory for Reconstructionism. Believing that more than just a religion, Judaism was a progressively evolving civilization including the arts, Jewish languages, and a strong attachment to the land of Israel, he created an arena for the Hebrew-Zionist pedagogy that would shape American Jewish education for decades. Kaplan turned the Teachers Institute into his laboratory for Reconstructionism, and its graduates brought Kaplan's ideology to the world outside 3080 Broadway.

Commonalities

In addition to the Teachers Institute, other factors link together the life histories of these remarkable women. With few exceptions, they had to rely on influential and supportive men to help them realize their goals. Several were married to Benderly boys; some formed professional relationships with male colleagues; others had husbands who supported their work. Rabbis Brickner and Weilerstein saw their wives' activities as extensions of their rabbinate (Schwartz, 2006). All the women, even the social workers Feineman and Weiner, viewed education as central to their mission. Some began to teach as very young women; they were viewed by others, and often viewed themselves, as "born teachers." Many were introduced to Jewish education by their parents, either at home or in special schools. Brickner and Gezari were products of Benderly model schools where they were introduced to his innovative pedagogy as young girls. Sherman and Ettenberg were first taught by their fathers, who introduced them to classical texts, Hebrew literature and language, as they might have done with their sons. (Ettenberg had no brothers; Sherman's brother was indifferent to Jewish education, making Anna the intellectual partner for her *maskil* [enlightened one] father.) Weilerstein's role model was her mother, an active member of Hadassah in its early years. (The role of Hadassah in the lives of so many of these women is a topic that bears further exploration.)

Unsurprisingly, these women gravitated to careers in Jewish education. They loved Jewish learning, whether they had encountered it as youngsters or in young adulthood. They were passionate about the power of Jewish education to shape their personal and professional lives; they hoped to transform their students as they had been transformed. As educators, they often re-created what they had loved as children: programs in the arts, co-curricular activities to extend the reach of the school, holiday celebrations, and Zionist activity. Outreach to other Jewish women, whether through women's clubs, JTS extension classes, Hadassah, or synagogue sisterhoods is a recurring theme in these women's lives. Their interest in Hebrew language, the arts, informal Jewish education, creating curricula, and teaching adults professionalized the field and shaped its direction. The personal was the professional.

Were these women feminists? Not in the conventional sense of the word. They had no political agenda, nor did they make common cause with other women around issues of discrimination. In only two narratives does the issue of equal pay for equal work appear. But if feminist means being strong and independent, then they were feminists. Their stories are full of examples of how tough they were. Sampter made aliyah and adopted, as a single mother, a Yemenite child. In 1947 Ettenberg flew from New York to Chicago in a tiny airplane to sell her vision of Camp Ramah. Brickner, Braverman, Gezari, Jochsberger, and Ettenberg created teacher training schools, new arenas of Jewish study, schools, and camps. They were not the conventional homebodies of their day idealized in post–World War II suburban America. Sherman's daughter remembers her mother's "special" Shabbat chicken (boiled first for soup, recycled for the next course, baked with ketchup). Weilerstein's daughter recalls that her mother, the daughter of a renowned *balabusteh* (homemaker), had a favorite flavor, "burnt." Braverman hired a maid to free her from domestic chores. They saw Jewish education, not homemaking, as their calling. Although many of their beneficiaries were women, these women were accidental feminists at best. Blending the utopian with the pragmatic, they were passionate about the renewal of the Jewish people, not gender equity.

The Legacy

The anniversary of the centennial of the founding of the Teachers Institute is an appropriate time to study these women who "kidnapped" Jewish education and the ideologies that fueled their utopian dreams. The male disciples of Benderly ended up in administrative positions or in the higher echelons of academia. The women, more often than not products of Kaplan's Teachers Institute, were the ones who implemented the Jewish educational responses to the social and cultural challenges facing the American Jewish community for the first half of the twentieth century.

These women hoped to change Jewish life in America. They were intoxicated by what the philosopher of education Henry Giroux called "pedagogy and the politics of hope" (Giroux, 1997). Although their agenda was markedly different from that of the radical Giroux, they were exemplars of the "transformative intellectuals" Giroux called for. While the settlement house workers reflected a pragmatic strand of progressivism, hoping to turn Jews into Americans, those who followed them were more utopian; they hoped to turn Americans into Jews. But regardless of whether they wanted to Americanize Jews or Judaize Americans, these pioneering women were committed to the progressive ideal of transforming the community through education.

Cremin (1964) observed that, "[f]rom the beginning, progressivism cast the teacher in an almost impossible role: he [*sic*] was to be an artist of consummate skill, properly knowledgeable in his field, meticulously trained in the science of pedagogy, and thoroughly imbued with a burning zeal for social improvement" (168). The growth of teacher training institutions headed up by Benderly's male disciples reflected not only the goals of American Hebraists, but also progressive educators' concern for professionalism. During the first quarter of the twentieth century, Teachers College laid the foundation for teacher education: general culture, special scholarship, professional knowledge, and technical skill (Cremin, 1964, 173). The concern for professionalism at Teachers College, Stanford, and the University of Chicago eventually took on a positivist character with its emphasis on standardization, quantification, and scientism, diverging from Dewey's strand of progressive ideology, which focused on curriculum and teaching. His emphasis on experiential, student-centered, and communitarian education is reflected in the careers of these women.

In Benderly's attempt to professionalize Jewish education, he followed the scientific school of progressive education, choosing male doctoral students at Teachers College to become his disciples. The women profiled in this book, the autodidacts and alumnae of the Teachers Institute and city colleges without the advanced degrees of the Benderly boys, were excluded from administrative roles in Jewish educational institutions across the United States. As practitioners, these women brought the message of the American Jewish synthesis, Hebraism, and Zionism *directly* to students in Hadassah seminars, synagogue sisterhoods, schools, and camps, as well as in the books they wrote for homes and classrooms.

In the early twenty-first century educational researchers began questioning the role of teachers as leaders in school reform (Lieberman and Miller, 2004; Hess, 2007; Gigante and Firestone, 2008, to name but a few). Danielson (2007) observed that teachers' tenure in schools is often considerably longer than that of administrators. Teachers "hold the institutional memory; they are the custodians of school culture" (14–15). In the case of the Benderly-Kaplan agenda, the Benderly boys as administrators were less likely to succeed as change-agents in the reformation of Jewish education than their female counterparts, the teachers Kaplan produced. Miriam Heller Stern (2004) came to a similar conclusion: these women enacted Jewish educational reform, while the men wrote about it.

The "Benderly Girls"—the female counterparts of the "Boys" whose gender set them on a straight path to teaching instead of pursuing doctorates like some of their male peers—did not document their ideas and experiences in writing the way the young men did. Their story—what is was like to teach in the model schools and Talmud Torahs, what it was like to put a fresh female face to Jewish learning and how immigrants and their children responded to progressive Jewish education—would probably tell us more about how much change really occurred than the impression given by the Boys' dissertations. (25)

While the Benderly boys, like their colleagues in general education who received doctorates from the University of Chicago or Teachers College, were trying to standardize curricula and hours, to register children in the Jewish schools and camps, and to recruit students of Jewish education into Hebrew teacher training colleges, the women were "kidnapping" classrooms, camps, libraries, and Jewish homes. With BHLs (bachelor of Hebrew letters) or the rare MEd as their terminal degrees, they taught and wrote. They, not the men with their EdDs and PhDs, became the custodians of the culture of Jewish education, a culture born of Hebraism, Zionism, and Deweyan ideals.

What was the legacy of these women? Mintz (1993) has suggested that they ultimately sold American Jews on Zionism.

These Hebrew educators forcefully imprinted their vision upon several generations of students. This was an education centered around the twin Hebraist pillars of *Eretz Yisrael* and the Hebrew language and on a cultural nationalist interpretation of the Bible, Jewish history, and the festivals of the Jewish year. The masses of American Jews did not become Zionists until well after World War II; when the eventual "Zionization" of American Jewry did take place, it was fueled in part by the latent Hebrew ideals they had acquired as children in Hebrew school. (Mintz, 1993, 17–18)

So what happened to these women's pedagogic reforms? Why is Jewish education still such a hotly contested topic? And when did the synagogue school become the "school everybody loves to hate"? Much of the answer lies in the demography of the mid-twentieth century. After World War II, Jews, like other Americans, fled to the suburbs. Wertheimer (1999) noted that in 1962, six hundred thousand Jewish children, 90 percent of those getting a Jewish education, were enrolled in congregational (synagogue) schools (9).[3] Ironically, the suburban synagogue ultimately proved to be an inhospitable environment in which to plant the intensive Hebraist-nationalist pedagogy taught at the Teachers Institute in the 1920s to 1950s. First, Benderly and Kaplan had created the Talmud Torah for urban children living in double- or triple-deckers, who could walk to the neighborhood public schools and their centrally located Talmud Torah. Benderly, who died in 1944, could never have imagined Jews living in ranch houses with two-car garages on half-acre lots, nor suburban synagogues led by rabbis who insisted on the pitter-patter of little feet in *their* buildings, not in communal institutions. Second, after World War II, there was less need to teach the compatibility of Judaism and Americanism. It was a given. Judaism had become thought of as one of the major religions in the United States, symbolized by the 1955 publication of *Protestant, Catholic, Jew* (Herberg, 1955). Third, Jewish distinctiveness began to erode as Jews became more assimilated. The Rebecca Gratz Sunday school model was a more comfortable fit for suburban Jewry. The Talmud Torah required a child to attend three, possibly even five, days a week. It was the American way to attend religious school on Sundays, whether that school met in a church or a synagogue. Sklare (1967) observed that the test for Jewish ritual for post–World War II Jewry was whether it fit with the religious culture of the Christian community (58); the synagogue had become the Jewish "church." Bar and bat mitzvah became the Jewish equivalent of baptism and confirmation; preparation for this ritual coupled with reduced hours of instruction demolished the rich curriculum of teaching Hebrew, the Bible, Jewish history, and the arts. A leading Hebraist educator bemoaned the synagogue as a bar mitzvah factory with "black-tie and jacket synagogue services [and] rabbi-as-high-priest-and-Protestant-minister" (Picker, 1976). Krasner (2005) noted that the Benderly boys (and the Kaplan "girls" as well) were at odds with the bar-bat mitzvah agenda of the suburban synagogue (177). Their kind of Hebraist nationalism was out of sync with the bland, rootlessness of the period, famously described by Herberg as "cut-flower culture."

Speaking at the General Assembly of the Jewish Federations in 1965, the prescient Abraham Joshua Heschel called on philanthropists and fundraisers to change their priorities.

> A generation ago, the requirement was to integrate the immigrants into American society. Today the problem is not how to adjust our people to the manners and habits of society, but how to keep them from vanishing into the abyss of drabness and vulgarity, how to resist being committed to the nationwide prisons of triviality, how to cultivate the Jewish art of sensing the glory through acts of daily celebration. Integration has been achieved; it is Jewish integrity we must strive for. We have succeeded in receptivity; we must prepare for the test of creativity. (Heschel, 1996, 21)

Heschel's critique of American Jewish life was implicitly a critique of an educational system that had broken down. Jewish education had become vapid and infantile. By 1976 a new group of Jewish reformers calling themselves the Coalition for Alternatives in Jewish Education met in Providence, Rhode Island. After Sputnik was launched by the Soviet Union in 1957, becoming the first man-made satellite to orbit the earth, American public education was also under attack (Bruner, 1960; Kozol, 1967). The public school around which Benderly and Kaplan had built their educational enterprise had lost its appeal for new generations of Jews. The growth of Jewish day schools in the 1960s and 1970s had siphoned off many parents who were interested in intensive Jewish education for their children. As Beinart (1999) observed, Jews were so at home in America, they could now send their children to the Jewish day schools that Benderly had once claimed to be an artifact of the Old World.

The history of Hebraist-nationalist pedagogy paralleled the waxing and waning of Dewey's progressive pedagogy. The national breast-beating after Sputnik that blamed Dewey and his followers for America's fall from grace drove progressive education underground. The Benderly-Kaplan agenda, nourished by the spirit of the Progressive Era and wedded to the American public school, had become an educational artifact. With progressive education and the public school under siege, so too was the kind of Jewish education these women embodied.

The American Jewish community is once again turning to Jewish education to deal with questions of meaning and Jewish cultural literacy. Heschel's question to the General Assembly, "Jewish education for what?" is one for which these women had answers fifty to a hundred years ago. In response to Nuland's final question regarding impact on a profession, what elements of their legacy might be used as a model of contemporary theory and practice in the face of new questions confronting the American Jewish community? One striking element is the boldness of their vision. Like the best progressive educators, they were capable of "utopian thinking about education" (Tyack and Cuban, 1997). They were not incrementalists; they were visionaries who provided big answers to the big curricular question posed by Hebert Spencer, "What knowledge is of most worth?"

In their blending of the curricular and the co-curricular, breaking down the walls between classrooms and clubs, school and camp, between canon and culture, these women made a case for Jewish *education*, not merely Jewish *schooling*. In their embrace of progressive education's learning by doing, they became the pioneers of experiential education in the teaching of Hebrew language and literature, in the arts, youth programming, and in camping.

Today's exciting, edgy programs can be found in the arenas these women staked out decades ago: in informal education, in the arts, in the use of technology to create new learning materials and curricula, and in adult education (still overwhelmingly the province of women). The experiential learning that nurtured these women, and that many then replicated during their professional careers, can now be found in early childhood education (Hebrew language learning), camping, trips to Israel, service learning, and *batei midrash* (houses of study) for the arts.

Once again the supplementary school is receiving attention from the community's policy-makers and implementers (Wertheimer, 2009). As Jewish day school education becomes increasingly expensive, there may be a renewed interest in the communally funded Talmud Torah with its intensive curriculum of Hebrew language and culture proposed by Benderly and Kaplan.

In discussing the waning of progressive education, Cremin (1964) presciently noted, "Perhaps it only awaited the reformulation and resuscitation that would ultimately derive from a larger resurgence of reform in American life and thought" (353). He was right; progressive pedagogy—now called learning by discovery, authentic learning, or constructivist education—is back. So is a commitment to Jewish education by contemporary Jewish communal leaders, like those of the *Kehillah* a century ago. While there is no longer a need to teach the American Jewish synthesis or to "Zionize" American Jewry, there is still a need to educate for Jewish identity and meaning. To do so requires vision and "transformative intellectuals" to enact that vision. We must not forget the debt we owe to these women who understood the power of Jewish education wedded to progressive pedagogy to challenge, renew, and illuminate American Jewish life.

NOTES

1. Dewey is considered the father of progressive education in the United States. Although the term "progressive education" has come to include a panoply of approaches, from discovery learning to vocational education, it appeals to the learners through active experiences and the arts in the hope of fostering involvement in society and reflecting the world outside the schoolroom.

2. This creativity exudes a manic energy. In his diary, Kaplan discusses his friend's bouts with depression. One can't help but wonder if Benderly suffered from a bipolar disorder.

3. In 2008 there were approximately 230,000 children enrolled in supplementary schools (Wertheimer, 2008, 3).

REFERENCES

Ackerman, A. 2008. Individualism, nationalism, and universalism: The educational ideals of Mordecai M. Kaplan's philosophy of Jewish education. *Journal of Jewish Education* 74, no. 2: 201–26.

Antin, M. 1912. *The Promised Land*. Boston: Houghton Mifflin.

Ashton, D. 1997. *Rebecca Gratz: Women and Judaism in Antebellum America*. Detroit: Wayne State University Press.

Beinart, P. 1999. The rise of Jewish schools. *Atlantic Monthly*, October, 21–22.

Bruner, J. 1960. *The Process of Education*. New York: Vintage Books.

Chipkin, I. S. 1935. Twenty-five years of Jewish education in the United States. *American Jewish Year Book*, 26–116.

Cremin, L. A. 1964. *The Transformation of the School: Progressivism in American Education, 1876-1957*. New York: Vintage Books.

Cuban, L. 1992. Curriculum stability and change. In *Handbook of Research on Curricu-*

lum: A Project of the American Educational Research Association, ed. W. Jackson, 216–47. New York: Macmillan.

Danielson, C. 2007. The many faces of leadership. *Educational Leadership* 65, no. 1: 14–19.

Eisen, A. M. 1983. *The Chosen People in America: A Study in Jewish Religious Ideology*. Bloomington: Indiana University Press.

Elazar, D. J. 1993. The national-cultural movement in Hebrew education in the Mississippi Valley. In *Hebrew in America: Perspectives and prospects*, ed. A. Mintz 129–54. Detroit: Wayne State University Press.

Fishman, S. B. 2000. *Jewish Life and American Culture*. Albany, SUNY Press.

Gigante, N. A., and Firestone, W. A. 2008. Administrative support and teacher leadership. *Journal of Educational Administration* 46, no. 2: 302–31.

Giroux, H. A. 1997. *Pedagogy and the Politics of Hope: Theory, Culture, and Schooling, a Critical Reader*. Boulder, Colo.: Westview Press.

Goldberg, I, and Benderly, S. 1929. *Outline of Jewish Knowledge*. New York: Bureau of Jewish Education.

Goren, A. A. 1970. *Jews and the Quest for Community: The Kehillah Experiment*. New York: Columbia University Press.

Graff, G. 2003. Public schooling and Jewish education, 1845–1870. A contemporary perspective. *Journal of Jewish Education* 69, no. 1: 69–76.

———. 2008. *And You Shall Teach Them Diligently: A Concise History of Jewish Education in the United States, 1776–2000*. New York: Jewish Theological Seminary Press.

Handlin, O. 1982. Education and the European immigrant. In *American Education and the European Immigrant, 1840–1940*, ed. B. J. Weiss. Urbana: University of Illinois Press.

Herberg, W. 1955. *Protestant, Catholic, Jew: An Essay in American Religious Sociology*. Garden City, N.Y.: Doubleday.

Heschel, A. J. 1996. *Moral Grandeur and Spiritual Audacity*. Ed. Susannah Heschel. New York: Farrar, Straus, Giroux.

Hess, R. T. 2007. *Follow the Teacher: Making a Difference for School Improvement*. Lanham, Md.: Rowman and Littlefield.

hooks, b. 2000. *Feminist Theory: From Margin to Center*. Cambridge, Mass.: South End Press Classics.

Kallen, H .M. 1964. *Cultural Pluralism and the Critical Issues in Jewish Education*. New York: Farband-Labor Zionist Order.

Kaplan, M. M. [1934] 1967. *Judaism as a Civilization: Toward a Reconstruction of American-Jewish Life*. New York: Schocken Books.

Kaufman, D. 1997. Jewish education as a civilization: A history of the Teachers Institute. In *Tradition Renewed: The Making of an Institution of Jewish Higher Learning*, ed. J. Wertheimer, 567–621. Vol. 1. New York: Jewish Theological Seminary Press.

———. 2006. Women and Jewish education. In *The Encyclopedia of Women and Religion in North America*, ed. R. S. Keller, R. R. Reuther, and M. Cantion, 2:896–906. Bloomington: Indiana University Press.

Kozol, J. 1967. *Death at an Early Age*. Boston: Houghton Mifflin.

Krasner, J. 2005. *Jewish Education* and American Jewish education, Part 1. *Journal of Jewish Education* 71, no. 2: 121–77.

Lepore, J. 2008. The lion and the mouse. *New Yorker*, July 21, 66–73.

Lieberman, A, and Miller, L. 2001. *Teacher Leadership*. San Francisco: Jossey-Bass.

Marcus, J. R., ed. 1996. *The Jew in the American World: A Sourcebook*. Detroit: Wayne State University Press.

Minnich, H. C. 1936. *Old Favorites from the McGuffey Readers*. New York: American Book Company.

Mintz, A. 1993. A sanctuary in the wilderness: The beginnings of the Hebrew movement in America in *Hatoren*. In *Hebrew in America: Perspectives and Prospects*, ed. A. Mintz, 29–67. Detroit: Wayne State University Press.

Mosier, R. D. 1965. *Making the American Mind: Social and Moral Ideas in the McGuffey Readers*. New York: Russell and Russell.

Nuland, S. 2005. *Maimonides*. New York: Schocken.

Picker, C., ed. 1976. *He Kindled a Light: A Philosophy of Jewish Education: From the Speeches and Writings of Shraga Arian*. New York: United Synagogue Commission on Jewish Education.

Sarna, J. D. 2004. *American Judaism: A History*. New Haven: Yale University Press.

Schwartz, S. R. 2006. *The Rabbi's Wife: The Rebbetzin in American Jewish Life*. New York: New York University Press.

Scult, M., ed. 2001. *Communings of the Spirit: The Journals of Mordecai M. Kaplan*. Vol. 1, *1913–34*. Detroit: Wayne State University Press and the Reconstructionist Press.

Simon, L., trans. 1936. *Ten Essays on Zionism and Judaism by Achad Ha-Am*. New York: Arno Press.

Sklare, M., & Sklare, J. G. 1967. Jewish Identity on the Suburban Frontier: A Study of Group Survival in the Open Society. New York: Basic Books.

Stern, M. H. 2004. "A dream not quite come true:" Reassessing the Benderly era in Jewish education. *Journal of Jewish Education* 70, no. 3: 16–26.

Sussman, L. 1995. *Isaac Leeser and the Making of American Judaism*. Detroit: Wayne State University Press.

Tyack, D., and Cuban, L. 1997. *Tinkering toward Utopia: A Century of Public School Reform*. Cambridge, Mass.: Harvard University Press.

Wertheimer, J. 1999. Jewish education in the United States. In *American Jewish Year Book*, 3–115. Bloomsburg, Pa.: Haddon Craftsmen.

———. 2008. *A Census of Jewish Supplementary Schools in the United States, 2006–2007*. New York: AVI CHAI Foundation.

———. 2009. *Schools That Work: What We Can Learn from Good Jewish Supplementary Schools*. New York: AVI CHAI Foundation.

Winter, N. H. 1966. *Jewish Education in a Pluralist Society: Samson Benderly and Jewish Education in the United States*. New York: New York University Press.

1 : Redefining Jewish Womanhood through Informal Education
Ethel Feineman and Grace Weiner

1894–1924

*Jewish girls at the Emanu-El Sisterhood do their patriotic duty by
volunteering for the Red Cross war effort, circa 1917. Resident Head
Worker Ethel Feineman is in the top row, second from the right.*
Courtesy of Judah L. Magnes Museum, Berkeley, California

"It doesn't matter what kind of house we live in, but what kind of dreams," Ethel Feineman, resident head worker of the Emanu-El Sisterhood, declared to her board of directors in 1919. As the directors of San Francisco's Jewish settlement houses in the wake of turn-of-the-century eastern European migration, Ethel Feineman and her colleague Grace Weiner saw themselves not only as social workers and educators but also as dream weavers. By mentoring working girls and presiding over a neighborhood center modeled as a home away from home, Feineman believed they were "embroidering a social fabric" that strengthened the existing community and enabled young women to fulfill their dreams and contribute to the future community. Feineman was one of the first full-time paid social workers on the West Coast. She, Weiner, and others like them led the then emergent approach to educating young Jews informally through social work.[1]

The story of the Jewish female philanthropists who created Jewish settlement houses and the professional social workers who directed them is a little-known but important chapter in the history of women who shaped American Jewish education. During the tumultuous era of immigration at the turn of the century, these Jewish women developed a new model of what today would be called "informal Jewish education": a program of informal activities and formal instruction designed to instill a certain kind of American Jewish identity in its young participants. In an era when "education" in the United States had become synonymous with "school" and school leadership was largely the domain of men, these women carved out their own leadership niche in the areas of "personal service" and social work, feminizing the profession. Although their initiatives were outside the boundaries of formal education, the educational power of their initiatives is worthy of study and analysis, as they designed programs to shape the habits, beliefs, and aspirations of young female Jewish immigrants through intense mentoring relationships and transformative socializing activities. Their innovations were an important precursor to the field of informal education that has assumed such an essential place in the landscape of contemporary Jewish education.

When urban America struggled to absorb millions of immigrants at the turn of the twentieth century, social reformers created new institutions to address the newcomers' educational and social needs. One of the most famous of these activists was the iconic Jane Addams, who founded one of the first American settlement houses, Chicago's Hull House, in 1889. Her colleague Lillian Wald, a Jewish leader in the field, was the central figure in the nonsectarian settlement house movement in the Jewish ghetto of New York's Lower East Side. Neighborhood centers of this type were created to educate and provide relief to the shiploads of newcomers arriving daily on American shores from eastern and southern Europe. By the early 1900s, over four hundred settlement houses, both religious and nonsectarian, had been established across the country.[2] Jewish communities were quick to found their own settlement houses to provide distinctly Jewish services to Jewish immigrants, to counter the efforts of Christian missionary homes and to Americanize their coreligionists on their own terms.

Notably, it was often Jewish women who created these programs, as volunteers and as social service professionals, establishing their own sphere of Jewish communal work. Charged by the pioneering spirit of San Francisco, the trend of the Christian Social Gospel, and the opportunity to spearhead social reform, San Francisco's Jewish female elite founded settlement houses in two Jewish immigrant neighborhoods, testing a new model of education in the rapidly changing Jewish community.[3] Ethel Feineman and Grace Weiner stand out as examples of women whose leadership set a new standard for the social work professional as educator, mentor, and surrogate mother. At the Emanu-El Sisterhood for Personal Service and the Esther Hellman Settlement House, Feineman and Weiner led by example, guiding adolescents through their struggles to define their identities as young Jewish women in America.

To discuss the settlement house in an educational context demands a definition of education that is broader than the parameters of "school" and that focuses on the educational power of transformative mentoring relationships. A useful conception of education to frame this story can be borrowed from Ellen Lagemann's *A Generation of Women*, a study of the most educative moments in the lives of Progressive female reformers. Lagemann defines education as "a process of interaction by which individual potential (instincts, propensities, talents) is activated, shaped or channeled and a change (an observable or consciously felt difference) thereby produced in the self."[4] This definition emphasizes life experience, as opposed to just formal schooling, and highlights the interactions with other people that mold one's sense of self. This definition seems appropriate, in this case, particularly since Lagemann's study focuses on mentors and contemporaries of Feineman and Weiner, such as Lillian Wald. This chapter analyzes the educational influence these women had on the next generation.

The mentoring relationships that defined the educational experience of the settlement house developed in the unique context of the settlement home, as opposed to the more formal institutional structure of school. As urban schools expanded to accommodate the influx of immigrants, female settlement house founders endeavored to design a more intimate home away from home to support immigrant education in a stable, safe environment. While public schools in this period prepared young people for citizenship, the San Francisco Jewish settlement house trained young immigrants, with specific attention to girls and young women, for "a new kind of preparedness": not just education for citizenship, but also for motherhood, domestic life, and social mobility.[5] The settlement house was an alternative educational form, a "model home" used as a vehicle for learning about life, relationships, and community in an intimate setting fostered by strong female role models. The Jewish settlement house during the immigration period of the late nineteenth century through the early 1920s provides a historical case study of a multigenerational, informal approach to education that promoted an explicit set of values in an experiential learning environment.

The program of activities and classes focused on engendering certain values and behaviors rather than teaching academic subjects; thus the settlement house experience reinforced an amalgamation of middle-class and Jewish cultural values associated with the home, which the founders considered the cornerstone of Jewish life and community stability. The founders broadly conceived the curriculum to consist of practical instruction (e.g., sewing, cooking, English), along with Bible classes, social clubs, lectures, recreational events, and Jewish holiday and wedding celebrations. Although the Emanu-El Sisterhood only defined a portion of its activities as "educational," in reality the whole culture of the settlement house—the environment created by the elite volunteers and progressive social workers who served as role models, and the values that they taught—was the real heart of the settlement house educational experience. Practical classes like millinery or nutrition were infused with moral lessons on proper manners and middle-class refinement. Likewise, social events were not merely recreational but were designed to foster community, family, and a commitment to service. Public celebrations of Jewish holidays and weekly Sabbath programs reinforced the Jewish character of the home, creating a comfortable space for young immigrant women to connect their heritage with their new American way of life as they plotted their course along the twisting paths of tradition and modernity.

Despite the warm image presented in Sisterhood reports of the happy hearth, a closer reading of available documents reveals that this "model home" was also contested terrain, the nexus for negotiation between women and girls of divergent classes and cultures who differed in their religious beliefs, goals, value systems, and ideas about womanhood and the concept of home. Studies of settlement houses have typically highlighted the "social control" settlement house workers exercised over immigrants, arguing that these social reformers pushed their own agenda and thereby limited immigrant opportunity rather than broadening their possibilities for the future. But as historian Peggy Pascoe has pointed out, the danger of interpreting settlement education as a form of elite social control focuses too narrowly on class differences, obscuring the bonds between women and the shared cultural values that transcend class, cultural, and religious differences. Focusing on social control also creates a false dichotomy of powerful and powerless, veiling the agency of the immigrant clients. Indeed, the National Council of Jewish

Women's approach to immigrant aid, which was often carried out by "friendly visitors" (i.e., elite volunteers), was based on the common bond of motherhood that volunteers and immigrants shared; they viewed motherhood as the source of hope and stability for the future. The interaction between women was central to the educational program of the Jewish settlement, where volunteers articulated a particular set of women's values that were negotiated in the real circumstances of immigrant women's and girls' lives. In an era of changing gender roles, the settlement was home to a complex intermingling of Victorian middle-class virtues of womanhood, traditional Jewish values, feminist aspirations, and fresh expectations for female independence and economic self-reliance.[6]

While it is true that the Jewish settlement house founders approached the young immigrants with a certain degree of benevolent condescension, and the professional workers did strive to impose structure on the girls' lives, this is only part of the story. First, as middle-class professionals, Feineman and Weiner were able to soften the tone of the founders' refinement agenda, demonstrating to them how to relate to the poor more respectfully, and thereby helping to narrow the social class rift that characterized the early years of the institution. Second, there is evidence that the adolescent girls in many respects embraced the message of their settlement house role models, particularly that of the head workers, but they also found ways to push back and assert their own authority over their destinies. Settlement house culture was shaped not only by the teachers but also by the hundreds of eastern European immigrants who passed through the settlement houses over the years, bringing with them their own set of experiences, values, and expectations. The interactive, personalized educational setting of sewing classes, club meetings, holiday celebrations, and home visits created an atmosphere where Jewish immigrants of different classes and different religious and cultural backgrounds could negotiate what it meant to be a Jewish woman in America. Far from the East Coast epicenter of the evolving American Jewish culture, the settlement house in San Francisco was a meeting place and educational environment where Jewish women and girls elevated themselves and each other economically, socially, and spiritually, and whether consciously or not, began to shape the future of their community.

This ongoing process of give and take spawned important educative moments at the settlement house. The elite founders appreciated the importance of role modeling and viewed personal contact with higher-class, "refined" mentors as the cornerstone of the settlement house education. Feineman and Weiner took this role modeling to a new level of personal engagement and parental love, which combined caring and strict discipline. This chapter analyzes how Feineman and Weiner fostered the special relationships, learning environment, and "tough love" pedagogy that characterized the settlement house experience as an educational model.[7]

The Jewish settlement house in San Francisco, "a home in its highest sense," as Feineman described it, was meant to be a model home for its immigrant family, not only teaching domestic skills but also emphasizing healthy family relationships and home life, cooperation, and mutual concern. By teaching for home life, settlement house workers and volunteers delivered a gendered educational agenda. Initially, the goal for these immigrant girls was economic self-sufficiency, with the hope that ultimately they would stop working, get married, and preside over a socially uplifted home. Moreover, the founders and leaders of the settlement house took for granted that only girls needed specific training for family living; when neighborhood boys started tagging along with their sisters to the Sisterhood, the women created a boys' club, with activities like scouting, carpentry, and elementary mechanics. In the early years, the Sisterhood provided activities for both girls and boys, but by 1910 the leadership began to shift their focus toward "working girls," leading them to establish a residence club where young women could have a secure and supervised living environment. While the Esther Hellman Settlement House always provided services for boys and girls, the clubs were gender-segregated by gender-appropriate interests. I focus here on the girls' experience because of the wealth of source material by female participants in settlement house life, including letters from immigrant girls to the head worker and the head worker's own annual reports. The available oral histories from regular attendees of the co-ed Hellman House are from women who highlight the distinctive "mother-daughter" relationship that emerged between themselves and the settlement house head worker. In a case of historical irony, the girls' voices from these settlement houses are more readily accessible in the archival material than those of the boys.

Mothers and Daughters at the Settlement House: The Early Years

When the elite German Jewish women of San Francisco's Reform Temple Emanu-El founded the Emanu-El Sisterhood for Personal Service in 1894, their stated purpose was "elevating the moral standard of the people, improving the conditions of their homes, teaching them self-reliance and self-respect, promoting their moral and mental education, and developing technical skill."[8] The "people" they referred to in their mission statement were the approximately seven thousand Jewish immigrants who had recently made their way from eastern Europe to San Francisco, which was already home to thirty-five thousand Jews, mostly of German descent.[9] Initially the Sisterhood provided a range of relief and training programs for male and female immigrants of all ages. Then they began to channel more of their energies into two groups of people within the immigrant population: mothers and working girls. Sisterhood members viewed motherhood as the primary source of refinement and stability for the home, and they saw themselves as ideal role models uniquely qualified to teach immigrant women and girls to uplift themselves and their community.

The San Francisco women proclaimed that they were "launching an entirely new movement." They were in fact part of a movement of more than a dozen congregations (mostly Reform and in New York) that established Sisterhoods for Personal Service in the late 1880s and 1890s. Several factors motivated the women and their rabbis who founded these organizations. First, these efforts were in keeping with the popular notion of charity as the proper domain of women, a sphere where women could express themselves and assume leadership roles. Second, the Sisterhood created an opportunity for women to express their religiosity in a public forum otherwise unavailable in congregational life. Third, they were inspired by the Christian social gospel movement that had thrust Christian women into public charity work, merging their religious duty with the duties society advocated for women. Finally, the influx of immigrants into urban centers and the rapid expansion of secular and Christian Americanization and missionary efforts motivated Jews to take care of their own. These women took that responsibility squarely on their own shoulders.[10]

Unlike previous notions of charity that focused on monetary donations, the concept of personal service involved volunteering one's time and actually interacting with the needy. For the first two decades, Sisterhood women and their daughters did most of the work themselves, running the clubs, teaching the classes, and organizing activities. The settlement house was continuously abuzz, with hundreds of people availing themselves of its services and programs on a regular basis and hundreds more attending occasional special events. The house itself was tastefully decorated and always well appointed with fresh flowers and plants. Founding members would arrive in chauffeured limousines to visit and to lead club activities. From afternoon through evening, immigrant children, adolescents, and mothers would filter in from the neighborhood or from their places of employment for a variety of educational and social programs. A visitor to the house might have heard the clicking needles and chatter of girls sewing, the clatter of pots and pans as young women learned about American cooking, the steady tapping of typewriter keys in a stenography class, the voice of a physician lecturing the Mothers' Club on maintaining a proper diet, or the ethical teachings of a children's Bible class or story hour. If it was around the time of a Jewish holiday, there would have been elaborate decorations, and women and girls would have been busily preparing a festive celebration or pageant.

The Sisterhood women, along with the members of the National Council of Jewish Women (NCJW) who built San Bruno's Esther Hellman Settlement House, were among San Francisco's elite. Their families, mostly of German origin, had arrived during and immediately after the gold rush and had quickly become leaders in all areas of business and industry. San Francisco Jews were founders and patrons of such artistic entities as the San Francisco Symphony, and they were regents of California State University and the University of California. The women dedicated their leisure time to leading cultural and civic organizations and spearheading charity and volunteer social work in San Francisco. The Emanu-El Sisterhood women made their presence known at the settlement house; in their elegant black gowns and fancy veiled hats with plumes, they were Jewish aristocracy.[11]

For these wealthy women, volunteerism reinforced their already high status in the city's social hierarchy. This was especially true in San Francisco, where benevolent work was so commonly viewed as the path up the social ladder for middle-class women that in the late 1800s the city witnessed what one historian has called a "charities explosion."[12] Several scholars have noted that for middle and upper class Jewish women of the late nineteenth and early twentieth centuries, "personal service," or women's charity work, was an escape from domesticity and a way of proving their womanhood.[13] Jewish women of the West were exceptional however, having created roles for themselves in public affairs since their arrival in the region in the mid-nineteenth century.[14] The settlement house in San Francisco provided these women a chance to invest their long-standing tradition of volunteer work with progressive methods, thus bringing their personal service to a new level of activism and efficient management. While their husbands closed stock-market deals, managed banks, traded furs in Alaska, controlled industries, or presided over courtrooms, Sisterhood and council women operated their philanthropic endeavors with the same efficiency demonstrated by their businessmen husbands, in the spirit of the new era of scientific philanthropy.

Whatever the class or club, be it embroidery, cooking, Bible stories, or dance, the Sisterhood leadership believed that their personal contact with the immigrants was essential because of their "refining influence." Presiding over these clubs also served to establish the volunteers as "experts" in the discipline of moral refinement and homemaking. While the volunteers took their authority on this subject for granted, the immigrant mothers who attended the mothers' clubs did not always trust them. In the early years, before the Sisterhood dedicated its efforts to working girls, immigrant mothers were among the settlements' most important, and challenging, constituents. Although there are no records of the mothers' perspectives on the clubs or their motivations for joining, the otherwise positive Sisterhood annual reports subtly betray some of the mothers' feelings. Mothers' Club chair Adelaide M. Rothchild complained that the mothers were uncooperative and that "for two years we had labored with the mothers to gain their confidence and to make them one with us."[15] Perhaps the mothers were more interested in meeting their own pressing needs—such as a bath, sewing supplies, or English lessons—than in becoming part of a friendship circle of homemakers as the founders intended.

Some of the mothers felt patronized by the wealthy volunteers, who associated social class with morality and assumed that immigrants lacked both. One graduate of the Esther Hellman Settlement House recalled how angry her mother was that "the ladies" believed that she learned to say "yes, ma'am" and "no, ma'am" because of their influence. Her mother resented their presumption. "We weren't taught by them. This is the way we really are."[16] However offended her mother might have been, that incident did not stop that student from adoring "the clubhouse," as it was known in the neighborhood, savoring every detail of its environment—its flowers, plants, spacious library, and lovely furnishings—and feeling a sense of belonging when she was there. While immigrant children may have learned to be polite at home, the settlement house taught girls that proper behavior was only the first step toward fulfilling their full potential as women: a world of fresh flowers and beautiful possessions of their own was waiting beyond the immigrant neighborhood and the world of the settlement house.

The educational goals of the settlement house gradually expanded from training for the present to training for the future, as immigrant girls made their own goals known to the Sisterhood leadership. In the early years, attempts to educate young immigrant women for domestic work backfired, as a 1904 annual report admitted, "We regret however that although our pupils are taught housework and our endeavor is to make neat little housekeepers of them, the desire is lacking altogether to take positions as such."[17] Jewish immigrant women were often unwilling to take jobs as domestic servants because they could earn more in other trades and considered the work demeaning.[18] Sisterhood girls viewed their class identity differently than their benefactresses did, favoring skilled work as clerks, stenographers, bookkeepers, salesgirls, telephone operators, or dressmakers. As a result, the Sisterhood altered its approach, emphasizing cooking, housekeeping, and home design as preparation for the immigrants' future homes (although the young women sometimes practiced these skills as "helpers" in the wealthy volunteers' homes). Self-reliance, resourcefulness, and self-respect were core values that the guides hoped to imbue in their students and club members. They would learn the work ethic to maintain gainful employment in the present and imbibe the virtues and skills that would make them good wives and homemakers in the future.

The House Becomes a Home: The Immigrant Daughter Meets the Professional Mother

In 1910 the Sisterhood established a residence at 1057 Steiner Street for "normal girls" to combat the problem of "white slavery"—prostitution among girls in the city who were living on their own. The Sisterhood wanted to provide a safe place where women in their late teens and early twenties (and a few who were older) could live, hone skills that would qualify them for employment and future homemaking, and engage in wholesome social activities. Some were graduates of the local orphan asylum; some had come to America or to the West Coast in search of a new life, leaving their families behind in Europe or in other American cities. With the residence club as its new focal point, Sisterhood used the house as a locus for neighborhood activity and continued to offer classes and clubs to nonresidents until all settlement activities were shifted to the Young Women's Hebrew Association (YWHA) in the early 1920s. The residence became so popular that Sisterhood had to annex space across the street. They also added a summer cottage in Larkspur. Around the same time, the Council of Jewish Women began to establish more programs for children of all ages as well as mothers in San Bruno, sometimes collaborating with Sisterhood on activities.

The period from 1915 to 1918 brought a transition to San Francisco's Jewish settlement house culture. A new role model who was more in touch with the realities of the immigrants' lives was hired to lead the institution: the professional social worker. Like the workers at Hull House and other university settlements, the Sisterhood professional staff actually lived with the working girls at the residence club, the Sisterhood's main project by this time. Although the class hierarchy of the settlement house was still in place, the socioeconomic and cultural gap between the middle-class professionals and the immigrants was not quite as stark as it was between the founders and the immigrants. Furthermore, by this time more of the immigrant clientele were somewhat acculturated, shrinking the cultural divide that had alienated them from the volunteers. The middle-class professional women were somewhat better equipped to relate to the immigrant girls. Moreover, the girls were probably more willing to regard these women as role models as they themselves became more rooted in their new environs with these mother figures at the helm.

Ethel Feineman, the "head worker," as she was titled, was the first full-time professional presence at the Sisterhood's settlement house, marking a shift for the Sisterhood from an all-volunteer organization to an institution run by a paid, trained professional. When the Council of Jewish Women opened the Esther Hellman House, they recruited Sisterhood associate staff member Grace Weiner to direct the neighborhood clubhouse. Born in 1887, Feineman came out West from her hometown of Kansas City, where she had been involved in social work and Jewish education, and had published a history of the Kansas City Jewish community.[19] She had been trained at the University of Chicago, and occasionally traveled east to social work conferences, returning to San Francisco quoting Jane Addams' newest strategies for the scientific management of the neighborhood house and the qualities of life it should promote. Feineman drew heavily on the rhetoric of home and harmony to promote her vision of the settlement house. The 1922 *Who's Who among Women in California* characterized Feineman as "a young woman of efficient executive ability, keen intelligence, and warm sympathies, whose understanding has increased the great social work carried on there as a great upbuilding force for the womanhood of the community."[20] Little is known of Weiner's personal background, but it is clear that she operated with similar standards of professionalism.[21] For educated women like Feineman and Weiner, the settlement house was a place where they could pursue progressive social reform on a professional level and apply the theoretical principles they had learned in college and graduate school to the real social problems of the urban working class and poor. In this capacity, they were able not only to touch the lives of individual young people but also to expand this new model of girls' education.

Feineman and Weiner were single, middle-class, prim and proper Jewish women. Weiner was described by an alumna as "a wonderful-looking woman, very haughty."[22] Feineman exudes a simple elegance in the Sisterhood photographs, always tastefully dressed in a blouse, a skirt, and a single strand of pearls, with her hair neatly pinned up. One alumna described Weiner as a "lady" and supposed that she "came from probably a very lovely home herself." Both women appreciated fine things and took care to decorate the houses tastefully, with plants and fresh flowers. One of the goals was that the girls would learn simple taste in design, and several alumnae commented on having developed an appreciation for such things at the settlement house. The girls looked up to Weiner, in part because she "understood the things that mattered," such as caring for a home properly and maintaining its elegance.[23]

These women were more than role models for the younger immigrants: they were surrogate mothers. During this era, educated middle-class and elite women increasingly postponed marriage to pursue careers in social reform; over half of female college graduates with professions never married.[24] It was not socially acceptable for middle-class women to have children and a job (although many working-class women did it by necessity). Jane Addams, one of the most famous women in this category, described this predicament as "the constant and totally unnecessary conflict between the family claim and the social claim."[25] Heading a settlement house gave women the chance to pursue an independent career and still enjoy the experience of motherhood. Settlement house professionals were able to have a close relationship with the girls and a powerful influence on their lives.

One settlement house alumna described Weiner as "the greatest Jewish mother. She never had any children, but she had about five hundred of them really. She was the greatest example of the nagging Jewish mother." Even though Weiner did not actually live with her charges at the Esther Hellman House, her influence was pervasive among the San Bruno neighborhood children. Many children whose parents were Orthodox immigrants looked to her as a second mother, who was in touch with the American scene and the path to success. She was the American middle-class parent they did not have, pushing them to attend the best public high schools and universities and to aim for loftier goals than the economic security their parents desired. She frowned on girls who were satisfied with merely becoming a salesclerk or going to technical school. "She nudged and pushed and nagged and looked very disapproving," one of her "children" later recalled. The young people who came under her care were "afraid of her disapproval" and "excelled because of her."[26]

Weiner's pedagogical approach to teaching values and responsibility could be described in contemporary terms as tough love. She was loving, yet distant; she cared deeply for her girls but held high standards for discipline. As one alumna later recalled, "She was very firm and very strict, but very loving. . . . Really she was a most wonderful woman. Yet psychologists now would have said that she was much too harsh and strict. She didn't put her arms around you, love you or hug you *ever*. I don't remember ever being fondled or kissed by her." This former student also remembered the fear and awe she felt toward Weiner when she reprimanded her for throwing away a half-eaten apple, saying, "She overawed me, really. She was a frightening person, in a way."[27]

Feineman commanded similar respect from the working girls of the Sisterhood, who regularly penned letters to "Dearest Mother F," apologizing when they feared they had somehow disappointed her and proudly reporting when they had fulfilled her expectations by getting married and keeping a tidy home. The relationship was not always harmonious—some of the girls' letters reveal moments of hostility or disrespect toward Feineman. But these incidents were often followed by letters begging for her forgiveness. One writer declared, "Miss Feineman may not be right always but I do think we should give her the same respect we would our mother. I know I do."[28]

As mother figures, Weiner and Feineman redefined the "nagging Jewish mother" role through their teaching relationships with their charges. The particular way they fashioned themselves as mothers was an important component of their pedagogy. As a single, educated social reformer, the settlement house worker was not the stereotypical Jewish mother of early twentieth-century lore, overfeeding her children and stifling their independence. On the contrary, one of the primary values of the settlement house was self-reliance and personal responsibility; the Sisterhood working girls were expected to cook for themselves and be financially independent. Feineman and Weiner pushed the girls to push themselves toward self-sufficiency and success.

Ultimately, the girls knew how much Feineman and Weiner cared for them. For example, Ida Z. thanked Feineman for her caring send-off from the Sisterhood, so much like that of her own mother, only with more modern sensibility: "How like a real mother you were putting those oranges in my grip—my mother is always afraid I will become faint on the train and slips a few *gefilta* fish sandwiches in my bag—and usually stains my clothes—but her intentions are good—so why worry over a few fishy pieces of clothes."[29] Feineman's having exchanged the odors of ethnic food for the fresh scent of fruit captures the Americanization process guided by the settlement house mother. A modern mother figure—familiarly Jewish, but American-educated and sophisticated—was just what many of these girls were looking for.

Some students maintained their attachment to Feineman even after they moved on. A girl named Hannah wrote, "I can frankly state that your influence has been with me constantly, your wise advice popped up at the psychological moment, and that I have thought of you very often." She signed the letter, "Just one of your girls, Hannah." Some girls became quite emotionally dependent on Mother F, like Ella, who wrote "I miss you so terribly much. . . . I am just plain tired of life. . . . I realize more than ever before that you were my torch, my inspiration, inspiring me to give the best within me to all but now my heart and soul are dark and there is no one to enlighten them. I will never forget the happy days under your care."[30] Feineman's close relationship with her students was the foundation of the home they shared.

Like their peers at settlement houses across the country, Feineman and Weiner had a deep commitment to the personal needs of their immigrant charges. Weiner was known to use her own money to provide financial assistance to someone "in trouble." She was "constructively critical" and many looked to her as a trusted confidant.[31] Girls turned to Feineman for simple advice such as how to choose an apartment as well as to share more serious feelings of depression or despair. For some of the girls, especially those who had no family in the city, Feineman's attention to them as individuals was extremely important for their development. "The intense interest that you show in me is more than any human being can deserve," Sonia wrote.[32]

The settlement house mother was also involved in the personal lives of her daughters as self-appointed *shadkhan* (matchmaker). Ironically, though these surrogate mothers were themselves single women, the settlement culture clearly signaled that marriage was the desideratum. Life cycle events were an integral part of the Sisterhood curriculum. Alumnae often held their weddings at the house, and later would bring their husbands and children to visit "Grandma Feineman." In her 1921 report, Feineman proudly announced the statistics for what she called "the Matrimonial Headquarters"—fifty girls married in six years. She encouraged the girls to entertain at the home and engage in "wholesome" social activities with their male guests such as discussing literature around the fireplace. Each girl's original application card was later marked if the young woman married, and further identified the spouse as "Jew" or "non-Jew," indicating that a girl's spouse's religion was of some interest. An active alumnae association kept the girls coming back to visit, and the Sisterhood leadership credited the association with ensuring the continuity of the Sisterhood message long after a girl got married. As Feineman assured the Federation of Jewish Charities, "Our sons-in-law have been able to provide well for their households and our girls are carrying into their new homes many of Sisterhood's ideals."[33]

The Modern American Jewish Home

The house itself was a lesson in social mobility, and Feineman and Weiner made sure that the young immigrants felt like it was their own. One alumna recalled, "You just felt expansive when you went there. This was your house. It was a lovely house."[34] The library was the centerpiece of the home, as literacy was an indicator of social class. The children borrowed books from the club's library every Friday and enjoyed frequent speakers on literature. The Sisterhood library hosted regular meetings of "the Literarians," a book club that drew participants from the University of California at Berkeley across the bay. The parlor was the site of many a club meeting, as well as being a place where the girls could entertain and have parties. The well-stocked kitchen served as a culinary classroom, a place where girls learned new cooking methods and cooperated to produce daily sustenance and more elaborate Sabbath and holiday meals. Although the kitchen did not strictly adhere to Jewish dietary laws, there was no pork, ham, bacon, or shellfish, in order to make girls from more observant backgrounds comfortable. On a typical day, the girls might make fudge in the afternoon, have a guest for supper who would later conduct a session in palm reading, and then spend some quiet time reading by the fire, all in the comfort and tasteful environment of the Sisterhood home.[35]

One of the Sisterhood's ideals was the creation of a proper home, and the head worker set the example by demonstrating good taste, self-reliance, and personal responsibility. It did not seem to matter that their model "mother" was not *actually* a mother at all, but someone who had substituted marriage for a career. The Sisterhood approach to education was based on the premise that "from the Home radiates all good," a belief that mothers had the ultimate power to influence the character of their husbands and children and uplift them morally. Mothers were the hope for the present and the future; as Feineman explained, "the girl is the future mother of the community and she must be early acquainted with community standards, contacts, and responsibilities."[36]

At the Sisterhood, the thirty-five girls in residence were in charge of maintaining their collective home, cooking, planning social and religious activities, managing their finances, and contributing to a "good works" fund. During World War I they volunteered for the Red Cross, bought Liberty bonds, and organized evenings of entertainment to raise money for war relief. Feineman discouraged girls who held their weddings at the house during wartime from accepting gifts; instead, girls were encouraged to give donations to Jewish war relief and the Red Cross. "We are eager to instill a spirit of self sacrifice and service as well," Feineman reported.[37] The residents orchestrated all these activities through a system of self-government. Being part of "the family" was a central element of Sisterhood life; settlement workers created opportunities for individual self-expression in order to promote "social solidarity" and strengthen the Sisterhood residence community.

One of the ways Sisterhood aimed to engender a sense of love and community at the settlement house was through communal religious observances that brought the volunteers, the staff, and the immigrants in contact with one another. Religious activities provided a more neutral ground for interaction and shared experience than the moral lessons cloaked in vocational instruction. These celebrations were a cornerstone of the settlement house experience and such an integral part of the culture that Feineman claimed that religious observance did not have to be enforced, for it was "enkindled."[38] Every autumn, the Sisterhood constructed a *sukkah*, accompanied by an elaborate pageant for the Feast of Tabernacles. The winter season brought the Hanukkah celebration and bazaar. Every spring at the Sisterhood residence club, the working girls and their invited guests, the professional staff, and several of the founders—including state supreme court judge M. C. Sloss, who led the service—dined together at a Passover *seder*. Holiday pageants throughout the year brought immigrant parents and other community members to the settlement houses to see their children perform, and various clubs made the decorations and costumes. This was a home where Jewish values mingled with middle-class American values, a place that supported the creation of a family-like community.

Sabbath observance, although not strictly traditional, was part of the weekly rhythm of the home. Every week, the Sisterhood girls prepared Friday night dinner and had a "family at home night," which featured the traditional lighting of Sabbath candles and blessings over the wine. Following dinner, Sisterhood became the neighborhood hot spot for more than 150 people. Friday evening entertainment ranged from public lectures to dances with a live jazz band. The Sisterhood dances offered a wholesome alternative to the popular dance halls and clubs that social reformers viewed as a path to moral downfall. For at least one resident though, even the chaperoned Sisterhood dances were too promiscuous, creating an atmosphere too much like a dance hall for her taste. Zara Witkin complained that the intimacy and "dying art of conversation" that had been the keystone of Friday nights at home had been compromised by live musical entertainment. She longed to return to the family feeling that was lost in the new Friday night "dance hall." One can only imagine what sort of dancing took place that led Witkin to remark, "I am not a prude. I was appalled last week at some of the things I saw and heard."[39]

Witkin's criticism notwithstanding, the Sisterhood prided itself as a place for wholesome socializing. Like other settlement houses and working girls' residence clubs across the country, settlement staff favored having this supervised social alternative at home, even if dance partners got closer to each other than some would have liked.[40] Feineman encouraged her girls to invite potential suitors over to chat by the fire. She proudly reported to the board of directors that girls were opting to spend New Year's Eve celebrating at home as opposed to out on the streets or at unsupervised parties. Feineman's model home was a place for "wholesome recreation," and she wanted the girls to feel comfortable and proud inviting guests over to mingle in their parlor and library.[41] By playing hostess, the Sisterhood was able to choose the entertainment, control the quality of the visitors, and preserve the feeling of neighborhood home that was so central to Sisterhood's identity.

Feineman was proud that the resident girls had more opportunities to mingle with other people who came to the events, because "their resources are fewer, their background and traditions more rigid." As she declared in one of her reports, they were "able to assimilate without becoming assimilated."[42] By hosting social events like Friday nights at-homes, Feineman felt they had achieved the right balance of traditional practice and modern social sensibility. They seemed to be fulfilling her vision of the proper balance between the Jewish and American parts of their identities. The Jewish home was the anchor of their lives, but its doors were open to modernity and American social mores.

Although Feineman's annual reports depict a group of working girls all striving toward the vision of the Sisterhood women, the letters she saved from the young women whom she mothered reveal more varied results. The girls did not accept uncritically every guest lecturer who came to the house. They saw through the pretensions of some speakers. Min reported in a letter to Feineman that the girls applauded gleefully when it was announced that the next night's speaker would be the last of the season, since "sometimes we had to sit thru a tiresome lecture or listen to an adumbrating prima donna."[43] Like a real home, the settlement house could nurture specific values, but ultimately, when its daughters reached a certain age, they began to make their own decisions, and there was a limit to how much of their behavior the settlement house mother could control. Some of the girls embraced the settlement house's middle-class promise for the future, going on to furnish the kind of homes that had been modeled for them in their clubs and classes and in the residence. An alumna named Sara wrote to Feineman with great pride that she had appointed her new home with drapes with tassels to match her rug.[44]

There were, however, exceptions to the rule. Libbie Volk proudly wrote to Feineman and the girls about being the only female to work at the Southern Pacific Railroad Company. At remote desert stations in California, Libbie spent her days processing train orders, fixing equipment, and disbursing pay-checks to the Mexican railroad crews. At night she went home to her boxcar and slept outside with the scorpions to escape the heat. The fearless Libbie even sent her former housemates the tail of a rattlesnake that dared to cross her path, a symbol of her self-reliance and her triumph over the desert waste-land. She told of how trainmen often brought melons and tomatoes "to our little Helen Holmes," a reference to the film star who was famous for doing her own stunts in the silent film serials *The Hazards of Helen* (1914–16). Lib-bie was quite content with her working life, and felt she was living out the legacy of women of the American West, an ideal quite different from that of the Western women who sponsored the settlement house. "A man's life is quite right when I have to chop wood to build a fire for cooking with the thermometer at 120°. But it's a life that has no camoflauge [*sic*], so will make of me what our pioneer women were."[45]

Along with her unconventional career, Libbie defied another typical be-havior of the Sisterhood: traditional courtship and marriage. Airing her own lack of interest in the age-old institution, in one of her letters, Libbie teased her former housemates for scrambling to get engaged saying, "Tell Estelle and Lonia that I wish them the very greatest happiness possible, and hope they learn how to make 'gefilte fish' for 'hubby.' S'pose friend Minnie will also try the 'Better or Worse' stunt soon? How many girls at 1057 [Steiner Street] now?"[46] Despite having chosen an unusual, even controversial, path for a young woman, the warm tone of Lizzie's letters reveals a sincere loyalty to "Mother F." She knew Feineman would be proud of her self-reliance and work ethic. At the same time she felt comfortable challenging the Sisterhood's con-ventions of marriage and women's work — conventions that Feineman herself redefined in her own life choices as a single woman and professional social worker.

Every educational program has its Libbie Volks, students who take certain lessons from the institution and remain loyal to their teachers, but still chal-lenge some of its ideals. Libbie learned the importance of self-reliance and hard work. Nonetheless, she rejected the expectation that she should pursue more feminine work and spend her evenings at home chatting with potential suitors rather than working the 4:00 P.M. to 1:00 A.M. shift and then sleeping outside with the scorpions. One can only guess how Feineman responded to Libbie's letters, but her reaction may not have been too negative. Libbie continued to write and her tone suggests a warm relationship; nor does it betray the anxiety of other girls' letters when they feared they might have disappointed Mother F. It is also possible that Feineman played up the image of Sisterhood graduates as happy little homemakers in her annual reports in order to please the board of directors, while in reality she was more sup-portive of the individual paths the residents chose. One thing is certain: Ethel Feineman, surrogate mother, teacher, and role model, played a significant role in these girls' lives, and her influence was at the core of their education at the Emanu-El Sisterhood.

Feineman understood that each girl was a unique person who required individual attention and care. The Sisterhood culture may have promoted certain middle-class values of womanhood, but Feineman fostered a learning environment that allowed the young women to pursue their own goals as long as they learned the essential qualities of responsibility and self-discipline. "Superimposing our standards from the top instead of sensing and starting at the bottom, is a form of paternalism which, thank God, is being rapidly shunted out of Social Service work," she declared in her 1918 annual report.[47]

That is not to say that Feineman was without her own prejudices. In a single sentence, she could refer to the "big, happy, healthy family all living under one roof" at the Sisterhood and then refer to some of the daughters as having "untrained or mistrained minds and characters." Feineman did show a unique sense of concern for the girls and their individual needs though. Her pedagogical approach reflected a shift from the broad benevolence of the founding days to a more personalized love, as she concluded in her first annual report in 1915. "Over and above all, each and every one of them must be loved and trusted, rather than ruled—loved and loved and loved—then, and then only, will all of us arrive at a closer, nobler understanding of one another and lead a happier, more purposeful and more harmonious existence."[48]

Revisionist historians have with good reason been suspicious of the motives of settlement house workers, pointing to settlement house education as a means of social control during a time of perceived social chaos and prejudice against immigrants. Some historians have softened the argument, describing the settlement house dynamic as "social control with a conscience."[49] Valid as these claims may be, the "social control" historical narrative obscures the power of the homelike institution as an educational model and the value of family-like relationships and cooperative activities for giving students a feeling of belonging and identity and promoting community loyalty—something the urban public schools may have been too large and impersonal to achieve. Against the backdrop of the historiography of settlement houses, this examination of the institutional home as educational points to the challenges of empowering students in an environment with an inherent degree of paternalism and within the parameters of an in loco parentis teaching relationship. Indeed, the line between caring and paternalism was sometimes blurry at the settlement house. Feineman's own words exhibit self-contradictions, as she might advocate trusting the girls in one sentence and mistrusting them in the next. Even so, Feineman and Weiner served as powerful female role models for the immigrant girls. They were mother figures to girls who were orphans and to girls who went home to their own mothers every evening. The girls loved them, trusted them, admired them, and feared them.

These female settlement house leaders redefined Jewish motherhood and education. As modern, single, surrogate mothers, they modeled Jewish motherhood in a manner that defied the common caricature of the Jewish mother. As women on the front lines of education and social service, they created their own model of informal education to meet needs that were not being addressed by the schools or the prevailing thinkers in education. The difficulty of their jobs and their ability to manage change, advocate, and compromise should not be underestimated. Feineman and Weiner were high-powered, educated women who established a niche for themselves in a male-dominated professional sphere. Not only were they fighting for a place among men, they reported to a lay leadership consisting of some of the most powerful and elite women in the city. Finally, and perhaps most importantly, they achieved a delicate balance between their own professional goals, the founders' charitable agenda, and the immigrants' personal aspirations. Their desire to care and nurture was tempered by the perceived need to establish order in a Jewish community unsettled and irrevocably changed by the arrival of newcomers. Feineman and Weiner were tough, yet loving, allowing the girls some freedom to discover their own way while these two women themselves forged their own path in American society and Jewish institutional life.

By creating a public home, settlement house workers began to break down the barriers between public education and the privacy of home that had been (and continue to be) so rigid in American education, pioneering a new model of education. The settlement house is a model for how an institution that is designed with the intimacy of a home is conducive to the constant personal interactions and individual attention that are educationally meaningful for both students and teachers. Their textbooks were the variety of lived experiences the immigrants and their teachers brought to the household. In the settlement house kitchen, library, and parlor, teachers and students worked together, cooked together, learned together, and celebrated together. The settlement was subject to the same tensions and shifting power hierarchies of a real home: the members of this "family" loved each other, but they also challenged each other and at times even defied each other. Immigrants felt some ownership of the settlement house and therefore felt comfortable making their own choices and pushing their teachers to address their own prejudices. In this public home, the values and attitudes of Jewish women of different social classes converged and clashed; as they learned about each other they also learned something about themselves. In an era when women of different classes individually and collectively negotiated difference and equality, motherhood and labor, traditions and modern sensibilities, the Jewish settlement house provided an intimate and pluralistic setting for that debate to take shape.

NOTES

This chapter focuses on the work of San Francisco's Emanu-El Sisterhood during the Progressive Era in education and social work and the era of Jewish immigration ending in 1924. After this period, the Sisterhood transferred its Americanization club work to the YWHA and focused on providing housing for working girls, Jewish and non-Jewish alike, through the 1960s.

1. Ethel R. Feineman, "Annual Report of the Head Worker," in *Ninth Annual Report of the Federation of Jewish Charities, 1918* (San Francisco, 1919), 100.

2. Ruth Hutchinson Crocker, *Social Work and Social Order: The Settlement Movement in Two Industrial Cities, 1889–1930* (Urbana: University of Illinois Press, 1992).

3. Female members of San Francisco's Temple Emanu-El founded the Emanu-El Sisterhood for Personal Service in the Fillmore-McAllister district in 1894. Members of the Council of Jewish Women established settlement activities in the San Bruno neighborhood at least as early as 1910 (when their requests to collaborate with the Sisterhood appear in Sisterhood board minutes), but they did not officially name the Esther Hellman Settlement House until 1918.

4. Ellen Condliffe Lagemann, *A Generation of Women: Education in the Lives of Progressive Reformers* (Cambridge, Mass.: Harvard University Press, 1979), 6.

5. Ethel R. Feineman, "Annual Report of Head Worker," in *Eighth Annual Report of the Federation of Jewish Charities, 1917* (San Francisco: 1918), 85.

6. Peggy Pascoe, *Relations of Rescue: The Search for Female Moral Authority in the American West, 1874–1939* (New York: Oxford University Press, 1990), xix–xxii; Faith Rogow, *Gone to Another Meeting: The National Council of Jewish Women, 1893–1993* (Tuscaloosa: University of Alabama Press, 1995), 134–36.

7. On the social control agenda of settlement houses, see Eileen Boris, "The Settlement Movement Revisited: Social Control with a Conscience," *Reviews in American History* 20 (June 1992); Crocker, *Social Work and Social Order*; Allen Freeman Davis, *Spearheads for Reform: The Social Settlements and the Progressive Movement, 1890–1914* (New Brunswick, N.J.: Rutgers University Press, 1984); Rivka Shpak Lissak, *Pluralism and Progressives: Hull House and the New Immigrants, 1890–1919* (Chicago: University of Chicago Press, 1989). For a more balanced view of Jewish girls' experiences in alternative educational institutions like settlement houses, including the empowerment of girls and the bridging of social classes, see Melissa R. Klapper, *Jewish Girls Coming of Age in America, 1860–1920* (New York: New York University Press, 2005).

8. "Emanu-El Sisterhood Constitution and By-laws," Emanu-El Residence Records, 1/1.

9. Fred Rosenbaum, *Visions of Reform: Congregation Emanu-El and the Jews of San Francisco, 1849–1999* (Berkeley: Judah L. Magnes Museum, 2000).

10. "Activities Survey," Emanu-El Residence Records 20/6, 1922; Felicia Herman, "From Priestess to Hostess: Sisterhoods of Personal Service in New York City, 1887–1936," in *Women and American Judaism: Historical Perspectives*, ed. Pamela S. Nadell and Jonathan Sarna (Hanover, N.H.: Brandeis University Press, 2001).

11. Rose Perlmutter Rinder, *Music, Prayer, and Religious Leadership: Temple Emanu-El, 1913–1969* (Berkeley: Regional Oral History Office, Bancroft Library, University of California, Berkeley, and the Judah L. Magnes Memorial Museum, 1971); Rosenbaum, *Visions of Reform*.

12. Pascoe, *Relations of Rescue*.

13. For the history of Jewish women's charity and personal service work, including settlement house activities, see Herman, "From Priestess to Hostess"; Seth Korelitz, "A Magnificent Piece of Work: The Americanization Work of the National Council of Jewish Women," *American Jewish History* 83, no. 2 (1995); Faith Rogow, *Gone to Another Meeting*; Nancy B. Sinkoff, "Educating for 'Proper' Jewish Womanhood: A Case Study in Domesticity and Vocational Training, 1897–1926," *American Jewish History* 77 (June 1988); Beth Wenger, "Jewish Women and Voluntarism: Beyond the Myth of Enablers," *American Jewish History* 79 (Autumn 1989).

14. William Toll, "From Domestic Judaism to Public Ritual," in *Women and American Judaism: Historical Perspectives*, ed. Pamela S. Nadell and Jonathan Sarna (Waltham, Mass.: Brandeis University Press, 2001).

15. Adelaide M. Rothchild, "Report of the Mothers' Club," in *Third Annual Report of the Emanu-El Sisterhood for Personal Service*, 1896–97, Emanu-El Residence Records, 2/3, 20.

16. Jean Braverman LaPove, *San Francisco Jews of Eastern European Origin, 1880–1940* (A Community Oral History Project of the American Jewish Congress and Judah L. Magnes Memorial Museum, 1979), 6.

17. "Tenth Annual Report of the Emanu-El Sisterhood for Personal Service," 1904, Emanu-El Residence Records, 2/3, 17.

18. Elizabeth Ewen, *Immigrant Women in the Land of Dollars: Life and Culture on the Lower East Side, 1890–1925* (New York: Monthly Review Press, 1985).

19. Ethel R. Feineman, "A History of the Jews of Kansas City," *Reform Advocate* (March 28, 1908).

20. "Emanu-El Sisterhood," in *Who's Who among the Women of California, 1922*, http://www.calarchives4u.com/women/whotxt/189-213.htm.

21. Grace Weiner is vividly portrayed as a professional in oral histories and Sisterhood records, but I have been unable to recover personal or biographical data about her. Many San Francisco birth records were destroyed in the 1906 fire; it is also possible that, like Feineman, she was a transplant from another city.

22. Viviane Dudune Solomon, *San Francisco Jews of Eastern European Origin, 1880–1940* (A Community Oral History Project of the American Jewish Congress and Judah L. Magnes Memorial Museum, 1977), 22.

23. LaPove, *San Francisco Jews of Eastern European Origin, 1880–1940*, 24.

24. Karen Manners Smith, "New Paths to Power, 1890–1920," in *No Small Courage: A History of Women in the United States*, ed. Nancy F. Cott (New York: Oxford University Press, 2000).

25. Jane Addams, *Jane Addams on Education*, Classics in Education, no. 51, ed. Ellen Condliffe Lagemann (New York: Teachers College Press, 1985), 67.

26. Solomon, *San Francisco Jews of Eastern European Origin*.

27. LaPove, *San Francisco Jews of Eastern European Origin*, 24.

28. Unsigned letter to Ethel Feineman, n.d., Emanu-El Residence Records, 2/14.

29. Ida Z. to Ethel Feineman, n.d., Emanu-El Residence Records, 2/12.

30. Ella to Ethel Feineman, n.d., Emanu-El Residence Records, 2/14.

31. Sinkoff, "Educating for 'Proper' Jewish Womanhood"; LaPove, *San Francisco Jews of Eastern European Origin*, 24.

32. Sonia to Ethel Feineman, April 20, 1922, Emanu-El Residence Records, 2/14.

33. Ethel R. Feineman, "Emanu-El Sisterhood Annual Report of the Head Worker," in *Twelfth Annual Report of the Federation of Jewish Charities, 1921* (San Francisco: 1922), 84.

34. LaPove, *San Francisco Jews of Eastern European Origin*, 24.

35. Min to Ethel Feineman, n.d., Emanu-El Residence Records, 2/14.

36. Ethel R. Feineman, "June, July, August 1919," Emanu-El Residence Records, 18/1.

37. Ethel R. Feineman, "October and November 1918," Emanu-El Residence Records, 18/1.

38. "Activities Survey," Emanu-El Residence Records 20/6, 1922.

39. Zara Witkin to Ethel Feineman, December 4, 1921, Emanu-El Residence Records, 2/12.

40. At New York's Clara de Hirsch Home for Working Girls, the resident director suggested instituting a class in social dancing in order to set standards of conduct for their Sunday evening dance nights. Sinkoff, "Educating for 'Proper' Jewish Womanhood," 589.

41. Ethel R. Feineman, "Emanu-El Sisterhood Annual Report of the Head Worker," in *Twelfth Annual Report of the Federation of Jewish Charities, 1921* (San Francisco: 1922), 86.

42. Ethel R. Feineman, "Emanu-El Sisterhood Annual Report of the Headworker," in *Ninth Annual Report of the Federation of Jewish Charities, 1918* (San Francisco: 1919), 95.

43. Min to Ethel Feineman, n.d, Emanu-El Residence Records, 2/14.

44. Sara to Ethel Feineman, August 2, 1921, Emanu-El Residence Records, 2/13.

45. Libbie Volk to Ethel Feineman, April 1, 1918, Emanu-El Residence Records, 2/12; Libbie Volk to Ethel Feineman, June 5, 1918, July 22, 1918, Emanu-El Residence Records, 2/13.

46. Libbie Volk to Ethel Feineman, June 5, 1918, Emanu-El Residence Records, 2/13.

47. Ethel R. Feineman, "Emanu-El Sisterhood Annual Report of the Headworker," in *Ninth Annual Report of the Federation of Jewish Charities, 1918* (San Francisco: 1919), 98.

48. Ethel R. Feineman, "Head Worker and Resident Worker's Report," in *Sixth Annual Report of the Federation of Jewish Charities, 1915* (San Francisco, 1916), 106.

49. Eileen Boris, "The Settlement Movement Revisited: Social Control with a Conscience," *Reviews in American History* 20 (June 1992).

2 : Jessie Sampter and the Hadassah School of Zionism

1883–1938

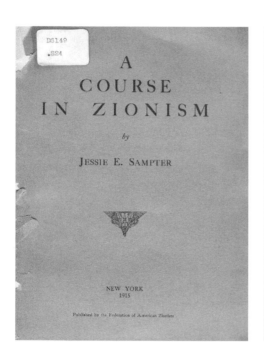

A
COURSE
IN ZIONISM

by

JESSIE E. SAMPTER

NEW YORK
1915

Published by the Federation of American Zionists

The cover and table of contents of
Jessie Sampter's A Course in Zionism.
Courtesy of the American Jewish Historical Society,
New York, N.Y., and Newton Centre, Mass.

Jessie Sampter, a young protégée of Hadassah founder Henrietta Szold, was responsible for creating the educational infrastructure that introduced Zionism to thousands of American women. She single-handedly spearheaded Hadassah's earliest educational efforts when she became the director and chairman of Hadassah's Cultural Committee in February 1914. Sampter quickly established the Hadassah School of Zionism in order to encourage study and train Zionist leaders and educators.[1] In addition, she compiled and edited *A Course in Zionism*, a collection of essays, maps, and data highlighting Zionist history from the Bible through Herzl, including contemporary Zionist politics and Palestinian settlement. Sampter grounded her School of Zionism with the belief that "knowledge is the only safe foundation for ideals, and everywhere there is a demand for knowledge and methods of imparting knowledge."[2] Her educational work on behalf of Hadassah sought to anchor the Zionist movement in America to facts and data, thorough knowledge of Zionist history and intelligent leadership. Hadassah leaders believed that an informed membership steeped in serious Zionist education would provide the foundation for a successful, thriving Zionist organization.

The preamble to Hadassah's first constitution, adopted at its founding convention in Rochester, New York, in June 1914, stated, "The purpose of this Association is to promote Jewish institutions and enterprises in Palestine, and to foster Zionist ideals in America."[3] To that end, in 1913, Hadassah dispatched two nurses to Palestine to establish a public health and welfare station in Jerusalem for maternity care and the treatment of trachoma. In 1918, Hadassah organized a mission to Palestine of forty-five physicians and nurses under the auspices of the American Zionist Medical Unit. On the American scene, Hadassah established the Hadassah School of Zionism in 1914 to educate American Zionist women and train them as "efficient club-leaders, propagandists, and organizers."[4] From the outset, Hadassah founders equated their mission in Palestine with their educational program in America. Szold viewed "the aim of fostering Zionist ideals in its members as an integral and inseparable part of (Hadassah's) program."[5] At the third annual Hadassah convention in 1916, delegates endorsed a resolution to encourage members to educate themselves about Zionism:

> Whereas, experience has shown that Zionist societies can be sustained, and can work intelligently for the advance of the movement, only if the underlying principles of Zionism are thoroughly understood by the members, and the scope of Zionist institutions and the bearing of Zionist achievements are thoroughly familiar to the members, therefore

Be it Resolved, that every Chapter of Hadassah be urged earnestly to organize a Zionist reading circle or a Zionist study circle, and that such circle or circles keep in touch with the Hadassah School of Zionism for guidance or cooperation.[6]

Hadassah's emphasis on education mirrored other Zionist organizations' goals. Both the Zionist Organization of America (ZOA) and Pioneer Women aimed to educate American Jews and included statements about education in their constitutions. However, they both fell short in supplying American Jewry with serious Zionist study programs. The Federation of American Zionists (FAZ, forerunner of the ZOA) sponsored an essay contest in 1900 to encourage young American Jews to learn about Zionist history; one year later, the organization began publishing a monthly magazine, the *Maccabaean*, in order to publicize and strengthen its Zionist message.[7] The *Maccabaean* offered news on Zionist congresses and conventions, publicized visits of prominent European Zionists to the United States, published articles that explained Zionist principles, and offered news on the development of the *yishuv* (settlement in Palestine). In addition, the magazine published articles by scholars and popular writers on Jewish history, art, philosophy, fiction, and poetry. Book reviews and guidelines for study circles also found their way into the journal. However, "the scholarly and educational emphasis dulled over time, and the later volumes dealt primarily with contemporary developments in the Zionist world and information on the *yishuv*."[8]

The reason for the decrease in scholarly and educational materials lies in the fact that the *Maccabaean*'s main purpose remained propagandistic. The *Maccabaean* regularly appealed for new members and exhorted members to distribute their copies of the periodical to friends and potential Zionist converts. The magazine also advised, "When you see a Jew who is not a Zionist, hand him a Zionist pamphlet. If you haven't one with you, hand him an argument."[9] With propaganda its main purpose, the *Maccabaean* fell short in its educational goals.

In its 1918 constitution, the ZOA called for "strengthening and fostering of Jewish national sentiment and consciousness" as a means "to establish a publicly recognized and legally secured home for the Jewish people in Palestine."[10] Despite this rhetoric and their attempts at educating the public, the FAZ and later the ZOA failed to live up to their educational commitments.[11] Lackluster attempts at education for American Jewish youth stood out as the most glaring disappointment of the FAZ during its first twenty years. "They failed to impart to Jewish youth the enthusiasm of the European *chalutz* [pioneer] movement or the idealism of aliyah. Zionists preached the need of a Jewishly educated community, but they provided neither schools nor specific guidelines of their own."[12] Szold privately berated the lack of educational emphasis at the Federation of American Zionists. In a 1917 letter to Jessie Sampter, she complained that only three women and one man showed up for a FAZ Executive Committee Meeting convened to discuss the "educational question." She lashed out at FAZ officers who "occasionally have the audacity to criticize Hadassah" for neglecting Zionist education, but who couldn't be bothered to show up for a meeting about education.[13]

While Pioneer Women shared Hadassah's ambitions to widely educate American Jewish women, its educational program neglected to mention Zionism or nationalism. Instead, Pioneer Women called for "systematic cultural and propaganda work to educate the American Jewish woman to undertake a more conscious role as coworker in the establishment of a better and more just society in America and throughout the world."[14] Pioneer Women's educational efforts encompassed a broad range of goals with no mention of specific Zionist work. While educational work earned an honored place in both the institutional goals of the ZOA and Pioneer Women, only Hadassah placed Zionist educational programs front and center as a goal.

Hadassah's educational program proved integral to its mission and purpose. Hadassah leaders firmly believed that in order to build an organization of women committed to Zionism, they had to train a cadre of educated volunteers to spread Zionist education and ideals throughout the United States. The result of these efforts, a well-informed, educated membership, would not only strengthen the organization but also serve to dispel accusations that Hadassah stood as a simple charity with no Zionist credentials or commitment. Hadassah leader Eva Leon, in a speech on the importance of education and Hadassah's School of Zionism, warned Hadassah chapters against "degenerating into mere collection agencies" and spoke out against detractors who dubbed Hadassah members as "lachrymose, whining sisters of a brotherhood that stands for staunch manhood and dignified self-assertion, and looks upon charity as a necessary evil." Resolutions passed at Hadassah's 1917 convention urged chapters to take up the study of Hebrew, utilize Hadassah's library, and establish at least one study circle. Three out of six resolutions adopted at the convention focused on education.[15] In that same year, Szold confessed to Sampter, "I am more than ever convinced that yours is our most important work. A nation cannot be made by instinctive, vague, misty feeling, however fine the instinct may be. . . . We must bring emotion out of its obscurity into the clarification of thought. Else Zionism will remain forever an 'ideal.'"[16]

Sampter, of course, agreed with Szold. She realized she faced an uphill battle in trying to persuade others that although studying lacked the panache of an emotional appeal to "rally the troops," education stood as the foundation of the Zionist movement. Sampter asked Hadassah members, "Are we willing not to stand upon platforms and shout to a crowd, but to sit together in a little room and study maps and figures? It is intensive work without glory. For both teachers and pupils it means digging trenches, digging in the dark, digging for light."[17]

Sampter's veneration of learning and knowledge, along with her penchant for flowery prose, characterized her personality from a young age. Born on March 12, 1883, the second daughter to Rudolph and Virginia Sampter, Jessie grew up in New York, in a mansion on Fifth Avenue, surrounded by freethinkers. Rudolph, a well-known lawyer and avid reader, held liberal beliefs about education and religion. He became a disciple of the agnostic orator Robert Ingersoll and befriended Felix Adler, the founder of the Ethical Culture Association. A self-proclaimed atheist, Rudolph introduced his family to ethical culture, but not to Judaism. Jessie grew up in a highly assimilated household where Easter and Christmas replaced Passover and Hanukkah. While education assumed an integral role in the Sampter household, Jessie never attended a formal school (except one year at Horace Mann) because she was weak and often ill. A childhood bout with polio left her crippled in 1895, the same year her father suddenly died at age forty-five. To console herself, Jessie turned to poetry. She published her first poem in 1897 and won many poetry prizes from *St. Nicholas* magazine.[18]

Sampter befriended fellow writers Mary Antin and Josephine Lazarus, older sister of Emma, and joined the Poetry Society. Perhaps looking for a father figure, she developed a close relationship with the president of the society, Merle St. Croix Wright, who introduced Jessie to the Unitarian Church where he served as minister. Sampter, always searching for open discussions and truth, joined the church in 1909.[19] Dissatisfied with the Ethical Culture movement her father had embraced, Sampter sampled Reform and Orthodox Judaism and found them both lacking. She turned instead to Unitarianism because she favored the church's embrace of individual choice and decision over dogma.[20]

Sampter sought a group or religion that spoke to her desire for truth, individual choice, and the improvement of humanity. To that end, she formed a small study group of Jewish teenagers that met once a week in the apartment she shared with her mother. The group, which called itself the Seekers Club, discussed and debated philosophical and theological questions. Sampter founded the club in order to explore two difficulties: "the lack of unity, of a common purpose, in the deeds of the community of men, and the problem of moral and religious education for children." While Sampter and her sister served as tutors to younger cousins on family trips, the Seekers Club served as her debut outside the family as an informal educator. The experience would prove important for her Zionist work. Guiding her students to take ownership of their education and contribute to their "syllabus," Sampter collected essays from her students and published them in 1910 under the title *The Seekers*. The book reflected the Progressive Era's preoccupation with science over faith and research over blind adherence to religion.[21] Sampter later replicated this interactive teaching method in the Hadassah School of Zionism. Like other Progressive educators of the early twentieth century, she believed that students needed to "live" and experience their education, not simply absorb what the teacher taught. The Progressive Era's commitment to reason and facts rather than belief and myth would guide Sampter's teaching and writing throughout her life.

Sampter's encounter with the Unitarian Church, which coincided with her convening the Seekers Club, proved short-lived; she turned to Zionism and finally found a spiritual home. Ironically, Wright pointed the way when he quoted Hyman Segal's *The Book of Pain and Struggle* in one of his sermons. Sampter read the book, which sparked her interest in Zionism, including the passage, "In pain and struggle I sought thee, that thou bring faith to mankind. Go therefore in haste: For the land languishes without its own people and man without his ancient faith."[22] Wright introduced Sampter to the author at a meeting of the Poetry Society, and Segal in turn introduced her to Szold. Szold would serve as Sampter's mentor in Judaism and Zionism.

While Sampter at first rejected Zionism as a narrow philosophy and failed to understand how the acquisition of Palestine could solve the "Jewish problem,"[23] she quickly embraced Zionist ideology as understood and espoused by Szold and other progressive American Jewish thinkers. Zionism to Szold, Sampter, Louis Brandeis, Horace Kallen, Josephine and Emma Lazarus, and other American Jews encompassed a wide range of goals and objectives. Not simply a movement aimed at self-rule for the Jewish people in their own land, Zionism stood for progressivism, equal rights, democracy, and the spiritual elevation of Judaism and all of humanity. For many American Zionists, the movement not only aimed at settling Jews in their ancient homeland, but also served as a catalyst to further the progressive march of mankind toward equality, justice, and freedom.

American Zionists gravitated to Zionism in an effort to fuse their American and Jewish identities. Unlike the movement in Europe, Zionism in America shaped its philosophy and idealism based on American needs and circumstances. American Zionist leaders faced a Jewish community striving for acculturation and acceptance; therefore they accommodated "their movement and message to the realities of the American and American Jewish scenes. The product they created was an *Americanized* Zionism, a movement that was as much American as it was Zionist." Many American Zionist leaders in the first quarter of the twentieth century arrived at their notions of Zionism through the lens of the Progressive Movement. Brandeis, for one, believed "a Jewish Palestine would be the social laboratory in which Zionists experimented with new forms of economic and political democracy."[24] Josephine Lazarus, in articles for the *Maccabaean* in 1904 and 1905, presaged Brandeis when she wrote that Zionism would create a "spiritual democracy." She believed that "like Americanism, [Zionism] is a sifting of the nations of the globe, among all of whom our people are to be found, and the recasting of them into a new mold . . . with more exalted and more fearless ideals of freedom, and a more assured conviction of the inherent dignity of the race and the individual."[25]

The elevation of the individual and the contributions of a specific people are a recurring theme for American Zionist leaders. Rather than accede to the drive toward assimilation popularized in Israel Zangwill's play *The Melting Pot*, American Zionist leaders posited a different route for new Jewish immigrants to America. In his groundbreaking essay for the *Nation* in 1915 "Democracy versus the Melting Pot," Horace Kallen asserted that "America continually revitalized itself not by forcing everyone to emulate an Anglo-Saxon norm, but by allowing each person to draw on the comforts of his ethnic group, while respecting the tenets of a democratic politics." Kallen coined the term "cultural pluralism" to describe the "evolving relationship between American democracy and ethnic identity."[26] Sampter, too, believed in "a diversity of cultures and languages" as indispensable in a free and animated society. She claimed that individuals contributed "to the richness of the world by enabling their unique national characters to flourish."[27] In *Nationalism and Universal Brotherhood*, a Hadassah booklet published in 1914, Sampter exclaimed, "By all means let us exchange cultures. But then we must have cultures to exchange."[28] Both Kallen and Sampter used "cultural pluralism" to articulate their Zionist views.[29] Kallen arrived at his Zionism "not as a fulfillment of prophecy," but rather "through his philosophic commitment to American pluralism."[30]

Zionist leaders used this notion of pluralism to defend their movement against accusations of dual loyalty. They explained that the contributions of each individual culture and nation in America enhanced the American ideal of equality and freedom; therefore loyalty to Zionism deepened one's loyalty to America. As Sampter explained in 1916, "With our ideal of nationalism, there can be no conflict between different nationalisms within a state. The patriotism of the Irish Home Rulers in America has never been doubted. As for my Americanism, whatever deepens my humanity deepens my Americanism, and my Zionism deepens my humanity."[31]

Zionist leaders took this idea one step further and insisted that Zionist values and American values were one and the same. "The strongest weapon of those who defended the compatibility of Zionism with Americanism was the claim that the essence of Zionism was democracy."[32] Writers for the *Maccabaean* peppered their articles with phrases such as, "Zionism stands for democracy of the Jewish people" and "Zionism has everything in common with the needs of a democracy."[33]

Through her friendship with Josephine Lazarus, conversations with Szold, weekly study sessions at the home of Mordecai Kaplan, and exposure to other progressive American Jewish thinkers, Sampter's Zionism evolved from a parochial vision of territorial acquisition to a universal vision of equality, democracy, social welfare, pacifism, and cooperation between all peoples.

Sampter articulated her vision of the powerful, positive effects Zionism would bestow onto mankind:

> In working for our right, we are working for the right of all oppressed peoples. That is the task of the Jew—to make the world see the individuality and responsibility of nations, to teach them that the national unit is something more and different that the sum of the individuals who compose the nation. Shall we not give to the world in the future national law and national righteousness, as we have given to the world in the past individual righteousness? This is the ideal which underlies the labors and hopes of every Zionist.[34]

Szold, Sampter, and other Hadassah leaders embedded the idea of a universal Zionism into their organization and their ideals informed subsequent generations of Hadassah members. Twenty years after Sampter's death and more than ten years after the death of Szold, one Hadassah leader explained Hadassah's Zionism in language reminiscent of both leaders:

> For us in Hadassah, in addition to helping Israel fulfill its destiny as a democratic nation, Zionism means creative Judaism in the [United States], adherence to and practice of democratic principles, and [an] endeavor to meet the greatest challenge of our times: the challenge to develop alongside with the miraculous advance of science, the art of being truly human. This means advocacy of justice, freedom, equality and peace for all mankind.[35]

When Sampter found a spiritual home in the Zionism of Szold and Hadassah, she found a "unity . . . a common purpose, in the deeds of the community of men," and she began to tackle "the problem of moral and religious education for children."[36]

In 1913, as Sampter learned about Zionism and became active in Hadassah, she changed the direction of the Seekers Club, introducing Zionist ideology to the group.[37] This group of six girls continued to explore Zionist themes with Sampter every Saturday for a year and formed the nucleus of the Hadassah School of Zionism. The girls, according to Sampter, sought "more intensive training," and so she initiated the School of Zionism, on a small scale, in 1914. In addition to her desire to give her young protégées a more rigorous training in Zionist ideology and history, Sampter also sought to improve the Jewish and Zionist education offered to American Jews at Young Judaea clubs. In an article introducing her ideas for the School of Zionism, Sampter recalled that a Zionist leader speaking to a group of Jewish girls was appalled to discover that when shown a picture of Rachel's tomb, the girls could not identify Rachel's husband; however, they could all sing *Hatikvah*.[38] Sampter also bemoaned the fact that when Young Judaeans graduated from Young Judaea, they also graduated from Zionism. Sampter attributed this loss to the ineptitude of the club leaders. "We as club leaders are . . . untrained in three things — in the underlying principles of Zionism, in the principles of psychology and leadership, and in the most effective use of speech." While a Hebrew song and a few stories hold the interest of young children, once they reach fourteen, according to Sampter, they are "keenly critical, keenly intellectual and even philosophic. An emotional appeal is not enough. A song is not enough. If Zionism is to hold its own and become a dominant interest to these young people, it must be presented by natural leaders with training and intellectual grasp."[39] Sampter started the School of Zionism, not to educate the Jewish public but to instruct future Zionist educators. The school catered to "a small group of Zionists training themselves to do Zionist work."[40]

The Hadassah School of Zionism, with an enrollment of thirty women, began to offer classes in October 1914 at the Young Women's Hebrew Association on 110th Street near Fifth Avenue.[41] The women's ages ranged from seventeen to over twenty-five, and they included those who had barely attended high school as well as college graduates. Students were businesswomen and teachers, college students, and "women of leisure."[42] The school offered three classes that met on three different evenings from 8:00 to 9:45. In line with Sampter's educational goals for the School of Zionism, classes focused not only on the history of Zionism and its contemporary manifestations, but also on how to impart this knowledge to others, children and adults alike. Classes concentrated on educational methods, the art of public speaking, and of course, Zionism, taught by Sampter herself.

Club Leadership, taught by a psychologist, encompassed discussions on child psychology and how to teach Zionism to "immature minds." Public Speaking, taught by a trained Zionist leader, "was truly a worker's class, where somewhat severe, but just and impersonal criticism put a strain upon the character and perseverance of the students."[43] Sampter believed that only well-trained, experienced public speakers could effectively teach Zionism to the public. Therefore, she expected her students to "be willing to work, to serve, to discipline themselves."[44] Those who found the work too difficult eventually dropped out of the school; Sampter believed this "falling off" was to be expected, because "such an intensive course of study must prove a weeding process. It is hoped that even those who dropped out gained something." Despite her tough rhetoric, but in line with her inclusive teaching philosophy, Sampter eventually bowed to pressure from her students and in 1916 offered a new course on propaganda, organization, and public speaking, that was organized and led by the students.[45]

In keeping with Sampter's refusal to allow passion, faith, or emotion to stand in for "reason, facts, and figures," she insisted that the School of Zionism present its students with precise data to prove its case about Zionism.[46] Sampter argued that she faced an "exceptional task" as "Zionism has . . . never yet been systematically taught."[47] No Zionist textbooks existed from which she could teach. As a result, Sampter, along with her students and teachers, produced one during the first year of the school, *A Course in Zionism* contains geographic information, including a map of Palestine; population statistics; a synopsis of Zionist political parties; a view of Jewish education in Palestine; quotations from Leo Pinsker's *Auto-Emancipation*; a timeline of the life of Theodore Herzl; and history lessons in Judaism and Zionism dating from biblical times to the present. Each chapter in the book represents a topic on the course syllabus and includes a bibliography and extensive suggestions for discussion.[48] Just as Sampter included and integrated her students' input and voices in *The Seekers*, so too, *A Course in Zionism* was a genuine collaboration. She incorporated suggestions, ideas, and changes put forth by her students as well as many "experts."[49] She not only believed in the Progressive Era's insistence on rational, scientific-based education, but also embraced its child-centered classroom philosophy. John Dewey and other Progressive educators claimed that classroom lessons must accommodate children's natural impulses to conversation, questioning, construction, and expression.[50] Sampter employed this philosophy whether teaching young teens, young adults, or women older than she. She actively sought the participation of her students in compiling a textbook for the School of Zionism and refrained from publishing the book until her ideas and methods were fine-tuned in the classroom. Sampter did not believe in tests, as the aim of the course was not memorization, but intellectual development. Instead of formal examinations, she suggested papers and inclusive questions.[51] Sampter's School of Zionism reflected Dewey's vision of "schooling committed to cooperative effort on the one hand and scientific methods on the other."[52]

Despite Sampter's embrace of rational education, free from emotion, the poet in her could not refrain from inserting some sentiment in her introduction to *A Course in Zionism*. The book's purpose was to serve as the textbook for the School of Zionism and as a basis of study for less intensive groups, but she hoped the facts would serve to "drive away the fears, doubts and delusions of the nightmare of exile." Furthermore, she asserted, "We are a sick people. Our national will has been atrophied by age-long inertia. But here and there certain organs are coming back to life and action. We must exercise and strengthen them with work."[53] By "work," Sampter meant serious study and education. She embraced the doctrine of progressive writer Lester Ward Creed who "conceived of education as the foremost activity of mankind, the 'great panacea' for all social ills."[54] For Sampter, Zionist education would serve as the "great panacea" for American Jewry's paltry knowledge of and indifference toward Judaism, Jewish nationhood, and Zionism. To that end, *A Course in Zionism* concludes with a chapter titled "Zionism as an Ideal of Life," in which Sampter drifted away from statistics and hard facts. The last chapter expounds on personal ideals and character traits such as loyalty and group morality. "Loyalty is the basic human virtue," she wrote. "A Jew therefore fails in morality unless he is loyal to his people. Loyalties do not conflict. Each loyalty enriches." The chapter also includes a section on the "romance and poetry of Jewish nationalism."[55] Although Sampter attempted a purely rational Zionist education in *A Course in Zionism*, the book also contained some Zionist indoctrination based on emotional and historical longings.

Sampter continued this blend of fact and flowery prose in her assessment of the School of Zionism in 1915 and 1916. She referred to the School of Zionism as Hadassah's "educational experiment station" and likened her educational plans to a prophecy just as "an architect's plan is prophetic of the building."[56] Sampter's combination of prose and passion echoes in her goals for the school. "We mean to do no less than transform American Zionism, to make definite and articulate the ideal that has often been too vague and effervescent. We want to encourage no Zionist dilettantism. Zionism is a passion and vision of life. To study Zionism is to study Jewish life and history from the right end, from the present."[57]

Sampter's summary of the school's first two years included honest evaluation and some frank critiques. She admitted that the school had shortcomings, including the fact that only a few Hadassah chapters established schools in their areas and that the courses proved too intense for many students. While not retreating from her vision, Sampter scaled back her ambitions for the school. By 1916, with few Hadassah chapters and outside groups participating in the correspondence school, Sampter reformulated her goals. Instead of an elite program for future Zionist educators and leaders, she described the purpose of the school as providing Zionist education for "all those Jews who seek this Jewish knowledge." Backing away from her insistence on "no dilettantism," Sampter introduced flexibility into the program. Students who felt the courses or materials were too demanding could set up reading circles and discuss the materials rather than submit to rigorous classes. In this way, affiliation with the School of Zionism became "pliable in the extreme." Sampter defended this change by claiming that at least the school was able to supply Zionist materials to affiliate groups while connecting these groups to Hadassah. She hoped to further the Zionist education of the affiliates by providing one paid Zionist teacher, a graduate of the School of Zionism, for each major city and dreamed of the school's future alumnae as "our standing army, or, at least, our reserve force." Sampter conceded, however, that these graduates were too few and admitted that "our sense of obligation and discipline is pitifully weak."[58]

Sampter's assessment hit the mark. From the outset, Hadassah claimed that its education programs in America were equally as important as its programs in Palestine. In practice, Hadassah's American educational endeavors activities lagged behind. The American Zionist Medical Unit, renamed the Hadassah Medical Organization (HMO) in 1920, operated out of the Meyer de Rothschild Hospital in Jerusalem and expanded from 90 beds in 1918 to 190 beds in 1935. The HMO also opened and operated clinics, hospitals, and infant welfare stations in Tel-Aviv, Haifa, Tiberias, and Safed from 1918 through the early 1920s.[59] In addition to its medical activities in Palestine, Hadassah initiated a number of programs to enrich and sustain the youth population of the country. Hadassah launched a school luncheon program in 1923 for children in Palestine, and in 1928 the organization took over and expanded the activities of the playground in Jerusalem's Old City under Hadassah's playground program. By 1933, Hadassah's medical and nonmedical services and programs benefited the entire population of Palestine, Arabs and Jews alike.

Hadassah's successes in Palestine consumed the organization's finances and resources to the detriment of its educational and civic goals in America. Although Szold admired and promoted Sampter's *A Course in Zionism* and claimed that her brother-in-law called it the "Zionist's Bible," she bemoaned the fact that by 1918 only three hundred had been sold.[60] In 1919, Hadassah closed its Hadassah School of Zionism, after just five years of operation.[61] In the 1920s Hadassah offered little in the way of substantive educational programming. However, in the 1930s, the leadership renewed their efforts on the education front. The 1932 report of the education committee stated, "Our members have come to realize that Hadassah's second aim — 'the fostering of Zionist Ideals in America' — is of equal importance with the maintenance of a health program in Palestine."[62] One year later, education chairman Minnie W. Halpern announced the formation of the Education Committee; its mission was "keeping our members aware of the changing world of Jewish affairs and alive to the problems of Jewish life."[63] Hadassah members passed a resolution at the 1935 convention pledging to "rededicate ourselves with fresh vigor and a new strength to the sacred task of revitalizing our educational work."[64] However, as a 1936 education survey of Hadassah chapters revealed, the problems faced by Sampter in 1916 still plagued the organization twenty years later. Hadassah chapters complained about a lack of trained leaders for study courses, inadequate local libraries, and problems in securing dynamic speakers.[65] To remedy this situation the education committee earmarked additional funds for the coming year to expand the education program.[66] At Hadassah's 1944 convention, delegates agreed that the future of the organization and Zionism itself depended on Zionist education. Sampter would have applauded the classes offered through Hadassah's education department in 1944, which included Toward a Jewish Commonwealth; Jewish Survival in the World Today; Zionism, A Brief Survey; Palestine Land of Promise; and The American Jew.[67]

As Hadassah's goals and programs in the United States expanded and changed throughout the twentieth century, so too did its educational programs. Although the topics of its classes, books, and lectures changed, Hadassah's commitment to education remained steady, and its publication of books, pamphlets, and study guides continues today. The 1940s saw the introduction of educational materials not only to enlighten members regarding problems facing Jews and Zionist, but also "to practice social idealism" to ensure that the "proper political climate" existed for Zionism to flourish in the United States and internationally.[68] The education program sought "to equip the individual for intelligent participation in safeguarding the principles and practices of democracy, these being basic to Jewish survival."[69] In keeping with these themes, Hadassah study guides and publications of the 1990s reflect Hadassah's commitment to Zionist and Jewish education as well as social justice and feminism. Titles include *Jewish Women Living the Challenge: A Hadassah Compendium*; *Moonbeams: A Hadassah Rosh Hodesh Guide*; *Pray Tell: A Hadassah Guide to Jewish Prayer*; *Judaism and Ecology*; and *The Talmud and You*. Hadassah study guides and other publications encourage discussion, exhibit diverse thinking, and promote the formation of varied opinions. This educational model and Hadassah's commitment to quality education reflect Sampter's vision and philosophy. In 1998, Hadassah launched a program reminiscent of Sampter's School of Zionism, the Hadassah Leadership Academy, which offered classes in Jewish women's history, Zionism and Israel, community leadership, and social advocacy.

Although the Hadassah School of Zionism closed in 1919, Sampter continued to initiate and supervise various educational projects, and to write poetry. She revised *A Course in Zionism* in 1920 and in 1933, wrote *The Book of the Nations* and a book of poetry titled *The Emek (The Valley)*. In 1919, she traveled to Palestine as a reporter for the ZOA and a short time later decided to move there permanently. Unable to endure what she saw as injustice and inequality toward Yemenite girls and women, Sampter set up classes for Yemenite girls in Jerusalem and Rehovot and helped organize a Yemenite kindergarten. She also helped organize the Deaf and Dumb School, Boy and Girl Scout groups, and parents' groups. Sampter aided Jewish minorities in Palestine; she sought to help Arabs as well. In an article titled "Jewish Ideal of Nationalism," Sampter stressed that Jews must "make the Arabs realize that our economic interests are identical with theirs and our political and cultural aims complementary to theirs."[70] Although she never married, Sampter adopted a Yemenite girl, Tamar, and eventually set up residence at Kibbutz Givat Brenner where she and Tamar lived with Jessie's companion Leah Berlin. Sampter built a convalescent home for the community in Givat Brenner and died there in 1938. Hadassah convened a memorial service to honor Sampter, planted a garden in Palestine in her memory and devoted money to the convalescent home she built.[71]

Throughout her life, Sampter displayed an unwavering commitment to teaching and learning, equality, and social justice. Whether arguing for Jewish rights, Yemenite women's rights, or Arab rights, Sampter's passion and action caught people's attention. Sampter's first and most enduring crusade,

WOLF

however, was aimed at expanding minds. Early on, she showed a special affinity for educating young people who were eager to question and explore. As Hadassah leader Tamar de Sola Pool observed, "My first recollection of Jessie Sampter is of two brilliant eyes illuminated as from within. . . . She was teaching a group of college students the fundamentals of Zionism. . . . There was fire in her words and depth in her thought."[72] Sampter did not shy away from controversial or unpopular questions and issues, whether in her writings or in the classroom. At a time when Hadassah and other Zionist organizations were fighting an uphill battle to convince American Jews to believe in and support Zionism, Sampter's School of Zionism and *A Course in Zionism* proved groundbreaking. From the Seekers Club to the Hadassah School of Zionism, to the Yemenite kindergarten, Sampter's educational vision and foresight influenced not only those who learned directly with and from her, but also entire generations of Zionist women. Hadassah's vast educational department stands as a testament to Jessie Sampter. In her tribute to Sampter, former student Margaret Doniger summarized Sampter's life with a blend of poetry and factual accuracy that Sampter would have appreciated: "In a prosaic world, she dared to think and strive for that which to most others seemed vague, remote and abstract — basic spiritual truths. To her, truth alone was reality. Today . . . her life seems a rare example of courage, of keen spiritual awareness and fulfillment."[73] Perhaps the most moving and appropriate tribute to Sampter came from Henrietta Szold. When Jessie died, Szold's longtime friends saw her weep for the first time. Szold wrote, "One of my teachers has gone from me."[74]

NOTES

1. Rose G. Jacobs, "Beginnings of Hadassah," in *Early History of Zionism in America*, ed. Isidore S. Meyer (New York: American Jewish Historical Society 1958), 237.

2. Jessie E. Sampter, "The Hadassah School of Zionism," *Maccabaean*, August 1916, 14.

3. "Report of Proceedings of First Hadassah Convention," June 29–30, 1914, Hadassah Archives, New York, RG3/Hadassah Annual Conventions Series/Box 1/Folder 1.

4. *Hadassah Bulletin*, August 1915, 2; Jessie E. Sampter, *A Course in Zionism* (New York: Federation of American Zionists, 1915).

5. "Report of Proceedings of 21st Annual Hadassah Convention," Nov. 28–Dec. 1, 1935, HA Rg3/Hadassah Annual Convention Series/Box 8/Folder 1.

6. "Report of Proceedings of Third Annual Hadassah Convention," July 3–4, 1916, HA Rg3/Hadassah Annual Conventions Series/Box 1/Folder 3.

7. "Report of Third Annual FAZ Convention," June 10–11, 1900; *Cultivating an Awareness*, vol. 1 of *American Zionism: A Documentary History*, ed. Aaron S. Klieman (New York: Garland Publishing, 1990), 351; "ZOA." *New Encyclopedia of Zionism and Israel*, ed. Geoffrey Wigoder, vol. 2 (Teaneck, N.Y.: Fairleigh Dickinson University Press, 1994), 1461.

8. *Maccabaean*, December 1901, 134, quoted in Naomi W. Cohen, *The Americanization of Zionism, 1897–1948* (Waltham, Mass.: Brandeis University Press, 2003), 16.

9. Cohen, 25.

10. "Constitution of the ZOA," adopted by the 21st Annual Zionist Convention in Pittsburgh, Pa., June 1918; *From Many, One*, vol. 3 of *American Zionism: A Documentary History*, ed. Aaron S. Klieman (New York: Garland Publishing, 1990), 9–10.

11. See Mira Katzburg-Yungman, "The Impact of Gender on the Leading American Zionist Organizations," in *Gender, Place, and Memory in the Modern Jewish Experience*, ed. Judith Tydor Baumel and Tova Cohen (Portland, Ore.: Vallentine Mitchell, 2003), 165–86; Melvin I. Orofsky, "A Cause in Search of Itself; American Zionism after the State" *American Jewish History* 69, no. 1 (Sept. 1979): 79–91.

12. Cohen, 38.

13. Henrietta Szold to Jessie Sampter, Oct. 29, 1917, Henrietta Szold Papers, Central Zionist Archives, Jerusalem, cited in Carol Bosworth Kutscher, "The Early Years of Hadassah: 1912–1921" (PhD diss., Brandeis University, 1976), 174.

14. Mark A. Raider, *The Emergence of American Zionism* (New York: New York University Press, 1998), 56.

15. "Report of Proceedings of Fourth Annual Hadassah Convention," June 25–27, 1917, HA Rg3/Hadassah Annual Conventions Series/Box 1/Folder 4.

16. Henrietta Szold to Jessie Sampter, March 27, 1917, HA Rg13/Henrietta Szold Series: Correspondence Subseries: Associates and Friends/Box 30/Folder 1.

17. Sampter, "The Hadassah School of Zionism," *Hadassah Bulletin*, August 1915, 6.

18. "Biography—Jessie Sampter, 1933," HA Rg4/Origins of Hadassah Series/Box 2A/Folder 26A; Tamar de Sola Pool, "Brand Plucked from the Fire," April 15, 1937, Press Release from Jewish Publication Society of America, HA Rg4/Origins of Hadassah Series/Box 2A/Folder 26A; Margaret Doniger, "Remembering Jessie Sampter," *Hadassah Newsletter*, Jan. 1939, 86–87; Bertha Badt-Strauss, *White Fire: The Life and Works of Jessie Sampter* (New York: Reconstructionist Press, 1956).

19. "Biography—Jessie Sampter, 1933"; "Hadassah to Honor Memory of Jessie Sampter January Fifth," December 31, 1938, Press Release HA Rg4/Origins of Hadassah Series/Box 2A/Folder 26A.

20. Badt-Strauss, 30.

21. Ibid., 25–26.

22. Ibid., 26.

23. The "Jewish problem" for Sampter included not only the age-old problem of antisemitism and displacement, but also the spiritual bankruptcy of the Jewish people. As Jewish communities assimilated into secular culture, they lost their spirit and their own culture. Sampter believed that Zionism would heal both the physical and spiritual dislocation of the Jewish people.

24. Badt-Strauss, 34.

25. Cohen, 1, 7, 25.

26. William Toll, "Horace Kallen: Pluralism and American Jewish Identity," *American Jewish Yearbook* 85, no. 1 (March 1997): 58.

27. Susan Blanshay, "Jessie Sampter: A Pioneer Feminist in American Zionism" (PhD diss. McGill University, 1995), 91.

28. Jesse E. Sampter, *Nationalism and Brotherhood* (New York: Hadassah, 1914), 5, quoted in Blanshay, 91.

29. Both Kallen and Sampter frequently attended Mordecai Kaplan's weekly study sessions held in his home. It is unclear whether Sampter arrived at her ideas independently of Kallen, in conjunction with him, or because of him. See Blanshay, 30.

30. Toll, 68.

31. Jessie E. Sampter, "Zionism and Ethical Culture," *Maccabaean*, January 1916, 15.

32. Cohen, 25.

33. *Maccabaean*, April–June 1904, 185–87, 291, quoted in Cohen, 25.

34. Ibid.

35. "October 21, 1958, Press Release," HA Rg3/Hadassah Annual Convention Series/ Box 19/Folder 10.

36. Badt-Strauss, 25.

37. Doniger, 86–87.

38. Sampter, "The Graduates of Young Judaea," *Maccabaean*, July 1914, 7–8.

39. Ibid., 7.

40. Sampter, *A Course in Zionism*, 5.

41. Sampter, "The Graduates of Young Judaea," 9; Sampter, "The Hadassah School of Zionism," Bulletin, 2.

42. Sampter, "The Hadassah School of Zionism," *Hadassah Bulletin*, August 1915, 2.

43. Ibid.

44. Sampter, "The Graduates of Young Judaea," 9.

45. Sampter, "The Hadassah School of Zionism," *Maccabaean*, Aug. 1916, 14–15.

46. Sampter, *A Course in Zionism*, 5.

47. Sampter, "The Hadassah School of Zionism," *Hadassah Bulletin*, Aug. 1915, 3.

48. Sampter, *A Course in Zionism*.

49. The experts included Henrietta Szold, president of Hadassah; Hyman Segal, editor of the *Maccabaean*; Mordecai M. Kaplan, professor at the Jewish Theological Seminary of America; H. M. Kallen, social historian; Louis Lipsky, Zionist leader; Lotta Levensohn, Hadassah leader; Eva Leon, Hadassah leader.

50. Lawrence A. Cremin, *The Transformation of the School: Progressivism in American Education, 1876–1957* (New York: Alfred A. Knopf, 1961), 118.

51. Sampter, *A Course in Zionism*.

52. Cremin, 136.

53. Sampter, *A Course in Zionism*, 7.

54. Cremin, 97.

55. Sampter, *A Course in Zionism*, 88.

56. Sampter, "The Hadassah School of Zionism," *Hadassah Bulletin*, August 1915, 1.

57. Sampter, "The Hadassah School of Zionism," *Maccabaean*, August 1916, 24.

58. Ibid., 16.

59. Donald Herbert Miller, "A History of Hadassah, 1912–1935" (PhD diss. New York University, 1968), 250–58, 291–92.

60. Henrietta Szold to Jessie Sampter, April 18, 1918, HA Rg13/ Henrietta Szold Series: Correspondence Subseries: Associates and Friends/Box 30/Folder 1.

61. "Report of Proceedings of 24th Hadassah Convention." HA Rg3/Hadassah Annual Convention Series/Box 9/Folder 5.

62. "1931–1932 Hadassah Annual Report," HA Rg3/Hadassah Annual Conventions Series/Box 6/Folder 8.

63. *Hadassah Headlines*, October 1933, ser. 11, no. 1, 7.

64. "Report of Proceedings of 21st Annual Hadassah Convention," Nov. 28–Dec. 1, 1935, HA RG3/Hadassah Annual Conventions Series/Box 8/Folder 1.

65. *Hadassah Year Book 1936*, HA RG3/Hadassah Annual Conventions Series/Box 8/Folder 2.

66. "Report of Proceedings of 21st Annual Hadassah Convention," Nov. 28–Dec. 1, 1935, HA RG3/Hadassah Annual Conventions Series/Box 8/Folder 3.

67. "Report of Proceedings of 30th Annual Hadassah Convention," Nov. 13–16, 1944, HA RG3/Hadassah Annual Conventions Series/Box 12/Folder 3.

68. "Report of Proceedings of 32nd Annual Hadassah Convention," Nov. 10–14, 1946, HA RG3/Hadassah Annual Conventions Series/Box 13/Folder 3.

69. "Report of Proceedings of 25th Annual Hadassah Convention," Oct. 24–29, 1939, HA RG3/Hadassah Annual Conventions Series/Box 10/Folder 2.

70. David Geffen, "Pioneer Zionist Remembered on Centennial of Her Birth," *Jewish Week and American Examiner*, August 19, 1983, 16.

71. "Biography—Jessie Sampter, 1933"; "Hadassah to Honor Memory of Jessie Sampter January Fifth"; Geffen, 16.

72. De Sola Pool.

73. Doniger, 86.

74. Henrietta Szold to Mrs. Wackenheim, December 10, 1938, CZA, cited in Joyce Antler, "Zion in Our Hearts: Henrietta Szold and the American Jewish Women's Movement" in *American Jewish Women's History: A Reader*, ed. Pamela S. Nadell (New York: New York University Press, 2003), 140.

3 : Rebecca Aaronson Brickner

Benderly Boy?

1894–1988

Rebecca Aaronson Brickner, circa 1960.
Courtesy of the Jacob Rader Marcus Center
of the American Jewish Archives

I n her biographical notes, Rebecca Aaronson Brickner described herself as a "teacher, educator, lecturer and organizer" and as "the first professional woman in Jewish education."[1] This self-presentation derived from a long association with and devotion to the field of Jewish education, which began in childhood both at home and through her early association with the Jewish educational pioneer, Samson Benderly. Throughout her life, Brickner took great pride in her manifold efforts to promote the fledgling field of American Jewish education. If she was the first professional woman in Jewish education, does she merit inclusion as a full member in the group known as the Benderly boys?

Born on February 22, 1894, in Baltimore, Maryland, Rebecca Aaronson was one of thirteen children. She remembered her parents being strong supporters of Jewish education who opened their home on Sabbath afternoons to Jewish educators and community leaders. Rebecca attended a German English school during the day. But thanks to the persuasiveness of her grandfather, Rebecca also attended the newly formed Sabbath school led by the young Jewish educator Samson Benderly. Rebecca's mother wanted all her children — daughters as well as sons — to have the benefit of a formal Jewish education, but she planned to employ a private teacher to do so. She objected to Benderly's new school because she feared it was "'one of those missionary schools' that were springing up all over the city." But when Rebecca's grandfather vouched for Benderly's reputation, her mother relented partially, allowing her daughters but not her sons to attend the school. In doing so, Rebecca's mother gave her daughter the opportunity not only to gain an intensive Jewish education but also to discover her life's passion.[2]

Studying Bible, prayers, and literature in Hebrew, Rebecca also learned about Palestine and Zionism. She later recalled the transformative nature of this education, explaining that she was "re-born," becoming "athirst and eager for the culture of my people. I drank it in like a thirsty flower in the desert. . . . Judaism . . . became part of my life. . . . My mother thought I was 'verkisheft,' enchanted." By the age of thirteen, Rebecca, like some of the other talented students, began teaching in the school. Desperate for teachers, Benderly understood that only by employing his own students could the school perpetuate itself. He actively encouraged young women to enter the field of Jewish education. As the *Jewish Comment* noted of his early experiments: "He wisely chose Jewish girls . . . who are able intelligently to grasp his ideas. He has succeeded in imbuing them with some of his abundant enthusiasm, and they are now pursuing advanced studies." Adapting stories from European Hebrew magazines or conjuring up new ones from her imagination, Rebecca gained expertise developing a graded Hebrew reading curriculum.[3]

When, in 1910, Benderly took the position in New York City as director of the first Bureau of Jewish Education in the United States, Rebecca Aaronson moved to New York to serve as his secretary. Continuing the work they had begun in Baltimore, she worked with Benderly on Hebrew curricular materials. That she saw herself as Benderly's professional (albeit junior) partner is evident in the way she described their efforts to create educational materials. As Brickner explained, equipped with what she believed to be the first Hebrew typewriter in the world, "*We* began to publish our own text-books."[4]

A member of the initial group of Benderly's New York trainees, Aaronson studied at Columbia University with John Dewey and at the Jewish Theological Seminary's Teachers Institute with Mordecai M. Kaplan and Israel Friedlaender. She met with young women throughout the boroughs of New York City, trying to interest them in pursuing careers in Jewish education. She then organized a preparatory school through the Teachers Institute to train these women, teaching them Bible, Jewish history, and modern Hebrew literature. During this period, she also introduced the study of Hebrew language into the Sunday school of New York City's Temple Emanu-El. A member of the Jewish Teachers' Association, Aaronson surely saw herself as a professional Jewish educator by that time.[5]

Expanding her reach still farther, she also began teaching adults. Judah Magnes, then president of New York's Kehillah, who first learned of Aaronson during a visit to Benderly's school, asked her to teach Hebrew language to the clubwomen of the Daughters of Zion. Her involvement with this study circle placed her among the nucleus of women who established Hadassah in 1912.[6]

Rebecca's future husband, Barnett Brickner, was also a disciple of Benderly. A speaker, a teacher, and one of the founders of what became the Zionist youth organization Young Judaea, Barnett, too, studied at both Columbia University and the Teachers Institute of the Jewish Theological Seminary. With last names close together in the alphabet, Rebecca Aaronson and Barnett Brickner met when seated next to each other in class. Barnett was director of extension education for the Bureau of Jewish Education (1910–15). Drawn to each other by their commitment to Jewish education and Zionism, the Brickners were married by Israel Friedlaender in 1919, the year of Barnett Brickner's ordination from Hebrew Union College.[7]

After their marriage, both Brickners continued their studies in Cincinnati —he for a PHD at the University of Cincinnati, she at Hebrew Union College. She later recalled that she knew more Hebrew than most of her classmates and helped them with their Hebrew language skills. There is no indication that Brickner hoped to earn ordination by studying at Hebrew Union College as Martha Neumark did a few years later. Rather, Brickner simply took full advantage of the opportunity to expand her knowledge, a habit she retained throughout her life.[8]

In 1920, the Brickners moved to Toronto, where Barnett became rabbi of Holy Blossom Temple and Rebecca worked with the Temple's Sunday school. She hired and trained the teachers, work she was well qualified to do. She also assumed more typical duties of a rabbi's wife, such as entertaining guests and forming a Sisterhood.[9] Brickner chafed at what she felt were the more frivolous aspects of her role as a rabbi's wife, and she shared her frustrations with her mentor, Benderly. He empathized but counseled patience: "I can readily understand why you are longing to be among your own people instead of constantly chaperoning the ladies of the Sisterhood. You are still very young and your day may come yet."[10]

In 1925, the Brickners moved to Cleveland, where Barnett served as rabbi of the Euclid Avenue Temple (later called the Fairmount Temple) until his death in 1958. Here the Brickners' partnership continued. As their son Balfour later remarked to the congregation: "For thirty years you really had two rabbis. . . . You only paid one; and two rabbis served this congregation alternately for many, many years."[11] With hired help to assist her, Rebecca Brickner focused primarily on her rabbi's wife duties. She conducted holiday workshops and contributed explanatory sections on the Sabbath and holidays to the temple cookbook.[12] She entertained congregants, having guests for dinner on Sunday after the main service of the week and hosting an annual reception for the entire congregation on Rosh Hashanah. Brickner also took on pastoral duties, paying hospital visits and condolence calls and keeping in touch with congregants by phone and mail.[13]

But Brickner also involved herself with educational matters. She prepared the graduating students for confirmation and delivered numerous invocations, talks, lessons, and speeches to the Sisterhood on a wide variety of topics.[14] When Barnett was traveling abroad in 1927, Rebecca hired a new educational director, Nathan Brilliant, and several teachers for the religious school. Supplying Brilliant with "the curriculum and all the school stuff for his perusal during the summer," she assured her husband that everything would "be running smoothly by the time you get back."[15] Barnett knew how capable his wife was in this area, and he happily depended on her to take charge. As he wrote, "I am relying on you to see that Brilliant gets started . . . and also that the Bulletin comes out."[16]

Within a year of her arrival in Cleveland, Brickner began to work in the larger Jewish community to promote Jewish education. She lectured frequently on Jewish history, Zionism, and Judaism to Hadassah, United Jewish Appeal, Pioneer Women, the Parent Teacher's Association, and ORT (Organization for Rehabilitation through Training) groups. When Stephen Wise wanted to establish a Cleveland branch of the Women's Division of the American Jewish Congress, he asked Brickner to organize it, and given her long-standing commitment to Zionism, she accepted. Brickner's reputation spread, and she was invited to address Sisterhoods and other women's groups in distant cities. She also attended biennial conventions of the National Federation of Temple Sisterhoods, where she advocated expanding Sisterhood's role in religious education.[17]

Dearest to her heart was the creation of a college of Jewish studies that would provide advanced Jewish learning in Cleveland and train teachers for area schools. In 1952, Brickner served as first acting chairman of the Cleveland Institute of Jewish Studies, precursor to the Cleveland College of Jewish Studies (now Siegal College of Jewish Studies), which came into existence in 1963.[18]

In 1932, Brickner traveled to Palestine with her children, Joy and Balfour, from March to August. She was practicing what she preached, providing an individualized, child-centered, experiential, Hebrew language, and Zionist education for her own children. Yet Brickner also had high personal aspirations for this trip, and she took full advantage of her time there. Brickner and her children toured the country together, and Brickner recalled how inspired she was from the landscapes, beaches, historic sites, agricultural accomplishments, and medical advances. After arranging her children's schooling, she hired a private tutor to improve her own Hebrew language skills, and together she and the tutor studied Jewish lore and modern Hebrew essays. Taking classes at Hebrew University for fifteen hours a week, Brickner relished being back in an academic environment. It made her feel as though she "were living those Friedlaender days over again." Living among other American Jewish Zionist educators, Brickner reconnected with old friends from her Benderly days, including Isaac Berkson and Bertha Schoolman.[19]

Through contacts from Joseph Klausner, one of her professors, Brickner participated in discussions and lectures, including several with the renowned Hebrew poet Hayim Nahman Bialik. Teachers and scholars who met Brickner expressed great pleasure at her excellent Hebrew. She cherished their praise, repeating it to her husband. For example, Brickner reported that her Hebrew teacher told her: "I am the most talented student that has ever come to him Michutz La-Aretz [from outside Palestine] and he will hate to give me up." And: "Everybody is simply astounded at my knowledge of Jewish culture and Hebrew. They can't understand how it could have been done in America. Even Dr. Klausner marvels at me." She admitted, "It was thrilling to find yourself finally acknowledged. When the students saw me taking down my notes [in Hebrew] with accuracy and speed, they didn't believe their eyes." Klausner continued to sing Brickner's praises a decade later. When Barnett traveled to Palestine in 1943–44, he visited Klausner and reported to his wife: "Well, was he glad to see me! . . . He regards you as one of the best pupils he had ever had."[20]

Satisfied that Joy and Balfour had learned Hebrew during those months in Palestine, Brickner achieved the ostensible goal of her trip. But she also blossomed both by advancing her knowledge and by rekindling her connections to the professional Jewish educators she had worked with years earlier in New York. In contrast to Cleveland, Palestine gave her the thrilling feeling of being "at home." She felt herself "rejuvenated every day. Much fresher in spirit and lighter in body and keener of whatever mind I have." Surely, Brickner's exhilaration stemmed in large measure from being in the Jewish homeland for the first time, but she also attributed her newfound vitality to the many opportunities she discovered for personal growth. As she explained, "Of course I feel that this trip has already done so much for me. It has opened up new vistas for me and lifted me out of the rut I was falling into."[21]

Understandably, Brickner worried about how she would manage when she returned home. "I don't know how I shall be able to [go] on without this fresh stream of *Mekor Mayim Chayim* [source of living waters] when I get back. It will be hard." Her solution involved imagining ways to channel her new knowledge and energy into educating others about Palestine and raising needed funds for it. "Needless to say I come home dejected, but with a firm resolve to do more and more for Hadassah." Brickner incorporated her new learning and passion into her courses, invocations, and sermons and redoubled her efforts to enhance the Jewishness of the congregation's women.[22]

Brickner was widowed in 1958 when her husband died after a car accident during a trip to Spain. She remained in Cleveland for more than two decades. She continued to guide the Fairmount Temple Sisterhood and grew increasingly accomplished as a speaker. In talks on a variety of topics, she further educated her audience, including Hebrew quotes from biblical and rabbinic sources as well as popular citations from American literature and government.[23]

Brickner also branched out to support other causes, devoting herself especially to the World Union for Progressive Judaism, the international organization dedicated to promoting liberal Judaism outside the United States and Canada. She joined their governing body in the 1960s and began raising substantial funds.[24]

In 1969, Brickner was the recipient of several honors to mark her seventy-fifth birthday. The Cleveland College of Jewish Studies created a scholarship fund in recognition of her pivotal role in establishing the school some twenty-five years earlier. The Bureau of Jewish Education bestowed upon her the Friedland Award, an honor that Brickner's decades-old mentor Mordecai Kaplan saw as the crowning achievement of her lifelong commitment to Jewish education. But Brickner was never one to rest on her laurels even at the mature age of seventy-five. She announced plans to organize a women's association for the college, a task that she accomplished within a year. She then served as its honorary president.[25]

In 1971, Brickner became the first recipient of an honorary doctorate in

Hebrew letters from the Cleveland College of Jewish Studies, another acknowledgment of her important role in establishing that institution.[26] Brickner evidenced demonstrable pride in the triumphs of the College:

We have been successful. We in this city have just succeeded in establishing a Hebrew High School, & our plan to keep on teaching during the summer in the camps, & via tours to Israel, [has] been a boon with good results. As for qualified teachers—you have the answer today. Teacher training schools were organized which today are developing into colleges for Higher Jewish learning, as this college has developed. There are today 11 such accredited colleges in the U.S. Our College, though barely 20 yrs old has this year become accredited by the State of Ohio & can boast 400 students.[27]

Ever the student, Brickner was not content with just an honorary degree. The following spring, she earned a master's of Hebrew literature from the college. She took extensive notes for her comprehensive examinations, almost all in Hebrew. Her thesis, submitted in the spring of 1972 and written entirely in Hebrew, is titled "Prophecy, Ethics, and Messianism in the Teachings of Professor Joseph Klausner."[28]

Alfred Gottschalk, president of Hebrew Union College–Jewish Institute of Religion, marked Brickner's eightieth birthday with a special citation. Celebrating her pioneering role in Jewish education, the citation proclaimed Brickner's accomplishments as being "in the forefront of those who have helped indoctrinate a whole generation of Jews with the ideals, the hopes, and the aspirations of our people and our faith."[29]

Given her lifelong efforts on behalf of Jewish education, can we conclude that Rebecca Brickner merited the appellation "Benderly boy?" In his 1975 memoirs, Alexander Dushkin lists the Benderly trainees other than himself in a footnote. He enumerates the men and then after an "also," he lists the women. Rebecca Brickner is first among them. Apparently Dushkin understood them all to be Benderly trainees, though gender conventions inclined him to see the men as primary. Jonathan Krasner argues that the gender distinction is more substantive. Krasner acknowledges that Brickner and other women, including Libbie Suchoff Berkson, Hanajlka Langer, Dvora Lapson, and Leah Klapper, were among the elite circle of students whom Benderly personally trained for leadership positions. But, in his view, the fact that they either took on supporting roles or left the field entirely to raise families disqualifies them from being full-fledged Benderly boys. "Since professional leadership roles were reserved for men," in Krasner's view, only men truly merit being called "Benderly boys."[30]

Despite viewing herself as a Benderly protégée, Brickner would have agreed with Krasner to some extent. In the issue of *Jewish Education* dedicated to Benderly's memory, seventeen "friends, colleagues and disciples" wrote tributes to Benderly.[31] Brickner was one of two women to contribute to the issue (the other was Dvora Lapson), but she was the only one whose name appeared without a title after it. Similarly, in Brickner's article, she listed the "group of men" that Benderly selected to interest them in the profession of Jewish education. Noting that others, including one woman, Mrs. I. B. Berkson, later joined the initial group, she does not include herself among either group.[32] Similarly, in response to receiving the Friedland Award, Brickner recounted the beginnings of the field of Jewish education by remarking that her husband "was invited to join a group of College Men who were thinking seriously of making Jewish Education their career." Again, she does not mention her own role. In each instance, either humility or gender conventions prevented her from including her name among the "boys."[33]

Brickner's reticence is echoed in her response to the possibility of ordination. Though she had studied with rabbinic students at Hebrew Union College and taken on many rabbinic roles over the years, she did not initially aspire to the rabbinate. Given the conventions of the era, she could not imagine the rabbinate as a career for herself. However, in later years, after second-wave feminism had made its mark, Brickner realized that she would have wanted just that. Because of this, she saw the 1974 Gottschalk tribute as being "in lieu of Ordination," explaining that in her day, women were not ordained. By 1983, when asked whether she would have been a rabbi had it been possible, Brickner admitted: "I could have conceived of that for myself."[34]

Studying the life and career of Anna G. Sherman (1897?–1980), Carol K. Ingall poses the same question of whether Sherman was a "Benderly girl." Though Sherman taught Hebrew language at the various extension schools of the Jewish Theological Seminary for almost nearly forty years, Ingall concludes that Sherman did not merit the appellation. According to Ingall, a true female Benderly disciple had to have been selected to study and work directly with Benderly, married a Benderly boy, been devoted to the education of children, and earned an advanced degree. According to these criteria, Sherman fell short. But Brickner met all four criteria to varying degrees. Chosen by Benderly even before he chose the boys, and married to Barnett, Rebecca easily met the first two criteria. Though concerned with Jewish education at every level, Brickner worked especially to promote religious education for children both in her own congregation and throughout the Reform movement. Finally, Brickner earned her MHL degree, though she did not do so until much later in life, and she never earned a doctorate as many of the male disciples did. Despite this, on balance Rebecca Brickner surely functioned as a Benderly girl.[35]

Mel Scult agreed. In his biography of Mordecai M. Kaplan, Scult insists that the Benderly boys included Rebecca Aaronson and notes that "being called 'boys' betrays the sexism of the period." In her reassessment of the

Benderly legacy, Miriam Heller Stern uses the term "Benderly girls," to describe "female counterparts of the Benderly boys whose gender set them on a straight path to teaching instead of pursuing doctorates like some of their male peers." Since teaching was as essential to realizing Benderly's vision as academic leadership, the women who disseminated Benderly's vision surely merit being counted as disciples as much as the men.[36]

Though gender constraints meant that Rebecca rarely took on paid leadership positions in her own right and didn't describe herself as a Benderly "boy," she continued to see herself as a professional Jewish educator. In the same 1969 address in which she discusses her husband as a Benderly disciple, she spoke authoritatively about the field. She recalled, "I felt that the emphasis in American Jewish life should have been in the classroom & not in the pulpit. Without a well-informed & educated congregation, the Synagogue could never fulfill itself. . . . Only by educating the Adults as well as the Children, could we ever tackle the Sea of Ignorance & Indifference that was costing us our spiritual life-blood in America." Similarly, addressing the board of trustees of the United Religious Schools in Cleveland 1972 on "motivating the Jewish student: past present and future trends," she described Jewish education as her "life-work as a professional over these many decades."[37]

Rebecca not only married a Benderly boy who shared her vision for Jewish education, but also worked unceasingly on her own to promote Jewish education throughout her life. Her husband channeled his efforts primarily through the congregational rabbinate; Rebecca furthered the cause of Jewish education in the congregation and beyond. Whether introducing Hebrew language into the New York City's Temple Emanuel school, training teachers for the Teacher's Institute, running the Hebrew School in Toronto, teaching Sisterhood women in Cleveland, or working to establish the Cleveland College of Jewish Studies, Brickner had a lifelong impact on Jewish education in the United States, albeit in a gender-circumscribed manner. Though exercising power like a "girl," she very much belonged to the maverick group of Jewish educators known as the Benderly boys.

In a 1983 interview, Brickner explained that the only choices for women in her era were writing or teaching. "You accepted what was given, you didn't think about it."[38] Surely, Brickner did more than accept what was given. Within the gender limitations of her era, she had a profound impact on American Jewish education in Cleveland and beyond. To look only at prestigious leadership positions or paid work is to miss the contributions that women have made to furthering Benderly's vision and promoting Jewish education. I hope that, in time, as the rich contributions of women like Rebecca Brickner come to light, scholars will reconceptualize the history of American Jewish education, taking into account the central role played by women in each and every aspect of the field.

1. There are several drafts of this biography. Two can be found in 8/7, Barnett R. and Rebecca A. Brickner papers, American Jewish Archives (AJA), Cincinnati, Ohio.

2. Interview with Rebecca Ena Aaronson Brickner, 23–24 Feb. 1983, American Jewish Committee Oral History Collection, New York Public Library; notes for "B'nai B'rith Great Books Series" talk, undated, 7/1, Brickner Papers; Samuel M. Silver, *Portrait of a Rabbi: An Affectionate Memoir on the Life of Barnett R. Brickner* (Cleveland: Barnett R. Brickner Memorial Foundation, 1959), 13; and Rebecca A. Brickner, "As I Remember Dr. Benderly," *Jewish Education* 20, no. 3 (Summer 1949): 53.

3. Brickner, "As I Remember," 55–56. *Jewish Comment* quoted in Isaac M. Fein, *The Making of an American Jewish Community: The History of Baltimore Jewry from 1773 to 1920* (Philadelphia: Jewish Publication, Society, 1971), 189.

4. Emphasis mine. Brickner claimed that the typewriter had been made especially for Benderly by the Remington Co. Brickner, "As I Remember," 57.

5. Interview with Brickner; notes for "B'nai B'rith Great Books Series" talk, undated, 7/1; and "Biography — Rebecca A. Brickner," 8/7, Brickner papers; *The Jewish Communal Register of New York City, 1917–18* (New York: Kehillah of New York City, 1918), 459; Jacob Kohn to Herman Rubenovitz, 18 Feb. 1914, in Herman H. Rubenovitz and Mignon L. Rubenovitz, *The Waking Heart* (Cambridge, MA: Nathaniel Dame), 1967, 135–36; Mel Scult, *Judaism Faces the Twentieth Century: A Biography of Mordecai M. Kaplan* (Detroit: Wayne State University Press, 1993), 392n56; and David Kaufman, "Jewish Education as a Civilization," in *Tradition Renewed: A History of The Jewish Theological Seminary of America*, ed. Jack Wertheimer (New York: Jewish Theological Seminary of America, 1997), 1:584–85.

6. Rose G. Jacobs, "Beginnings of Hadassah," *Early History of Zionism in America*, ed. Isidore S. Meyer (New York: American Jewish Historical Society, 1958), 242; and Bernard A. Rosenblatt, "The Beginning of Hadassah." *American Zionist* (Jan. 1960): 6.

7. Silver, *Portrait*, 13.

8. Interestingly, Brickner's name does not appear on any student roster of the period though Martha Neumark's name does. Boxes B-14 and D-12, Hebrew Union College papers, AJA; and Pamela S. Nadell, *Women Who Would be Rabbis: A History of Women's Ordination 1889–1985* (Boston: Beacon Press, 1998), 62–72.

9. Interview with Brickner; Invitation to Ladies Meeting, 10/3, Brickner papers; and Silver, *Portrait*, 26.

10. Samson Benderly to Rebecca Brickner, 14 September, 1923, 6/2, Brickner papers. He wrote the letter to "Tobacco," his nickname for Rebecca. The two remained in close touch throughout their lives. Brickner, "As I Remember," 58.

11. Balfour Brickner, Remarks, "Rebecca Brickner: Luncheon in Honor of her Seventy-fifth Birthday," Fairmount Temple, 28 January 1969, tape recording, AJA.

12. *The Fairmount Cookbook*, ed. Irene Rousuck (Cleveland: Fairmount Temple Sisterhood, 1957). Brickner described how to observe the holidays and included relevant blessings. She also contributed many recipes for traditional holiday foods, including kreplach, sweet and sour cabbage, and matzo balls.

13. Helen-Rose Klausner to Rebecca Brickner, 13 Feb. 1964, 8/8, Brickner papers; Brickner, Remarks, "Rebecca Brickner: Luncheon."

14. "Mrs. Brickner Tells of Her Faith in Girls of Today," *Cleveland News*, 25 April, 1926, in 9/3; and 7/1-6, Brickner papers.

15. Rebecca Brickner to Barnett Brickner, 15 July 1927, personal files of Balfour Brickner.

16. Barnett Brickner to Rebecca Brickner, 10 August 1927, personal files of Balfour Brickner.

17. Lauren B. Tishkoff, "Jewish Scholar Rebecca Brickner leaving Cleveland," *Cleveland Press*, 25 October 1981; "Biography — Rebecca A. Brickner," 8/7; 7/1-6; 8/5; Stephen S. Wise to Rifkahleben, 27 Apr. 1936, 6/10; and "How Hadassah Was Born," 20 Apr. 1950, 6/8, Brickner papers; Irving I. Katz, *The Beth El Story, with a History of the Jews in Michigan before 1950* (Detroit: Wayne State University Press, 1955), n.p.; and Transcript of Ninth Biennial Assembly (1931), 2/4, *Proceedings of the National Federation of Temple Sisterhoods*, Women of Reform Judaism papers, AJA.

18. The college was established and accredited in 1963. Convocation of the Cleveland College of Jewish Studies Proceedings, 13 Dec. [1971]; and Louis Hurwich, "Origin and Development of Jewish Teacher-training Schools in the United States: A Brief Historical Survey," in *The Education of American Jewish Teachers*, ed. Oscar I. Janowsky (Boston: Beacon Press, 1967), 6.

19. Rebecca Brickner to Barnett Brickner, 17 May 1932, personal files of Brickner.

20. Joseph G. Klausner (1874–1958), literary critic, historian, and Zionist, settled in Palestine in 1919. When Hebrew University was established, he assumed the chair of Hebrew literature. Klausner was especially interested in the transformation of the Hebrew language into a modern spoken tongue.

Rebecca Brickner to Barnett Brickner, 10 and 13 April, 2 and 17 May, 6 June 1932, personal files of Balfour Brickner; and Silver, *Portrait*, 67.

21. Rebecca Brickner to Barnett Brickner, 10 Apr., 2 and 8 May 1932, personal files of Balfour Brickner.

22. Rebecca Brickner to Barnett Brickner, 6 and 28 June 1932, personal files of Balfour Brickner.

23. "Sisterhood — 60th Anniversary," 20 Jan. 1970, 8/1; 8/2; and 8/3, Brickner papers.

24. 6/11; Rebecca Brickner to Friend, 20 Feb. 1968; and "They Adopt a Temple," *Press*, 23 Jan. 1964, in 9/2, Brickner papers.

25. "Bureau of Education Friedland Award to Rebecca Bricker," 1 June 1969, 7/1; "Resolution," 8/9; Mordecai M. Kaplan to Rebecca Brickner, 17 June 1971, 6/1; and Rebecca Brickner to friend, undated, 6/5, Brickner papers.

26. "Convocation of the Cleveland College of Jewish Studies Proceedings," 13 Dec. 1971, personal files of Balfour Brickner.

27. Rebecca Brickner, response, Convocation of the Cleveland College of Jewish Studies, 13 December 1971, 7/1, Brickner papers.

28. "Commencement of the Cleveland College of Jewish Studies Proceedings," 11 June 1972; "Review of the Cleveland College of Jewish Studies," 1972; and "Prophecy, Ethics, and Messianism in the Teachings of Professor Joseph Klausner," (Hebrew) MHL thesis, Cleveland College of Jewish Studies, personal files of Balfour Brickner; 9/5;and "Biography — Rebecca A. Brickner," 8/7, Brickner papers.

29. Cooper, "Honored, Revered"; David E. Powers to Rebecca Brickner, 18 Feb. 1974; and "Tribute to Mrs. Barnett R. (Rebecca) Brickner," 22 February 1974, 8/10, Brickner papers.

30. Alexander M. Dushkin, *Living Bridges: Memoirs of an Educator* (Jerusalem: Keter, 1975), 10n11; and Jonathan Krasner, "*Jewish Education* and American Jewish Education, Part I," *Journal of Jewish Education* 71, no. 2 (May 2005): 122n2.

31. *Jewish Education* 20, no. 3 (Summer 1949).

32. Brickner, "As I Remember," 55.

33. "Biography—Rebecca A. Brickner," 8/7, Brickner papers; personal files of Balfour Brickner; and interview with Brickner.

34. Interview with Brickner.

35. Carol K. Ingall, "Anna G. Sherman: A Benderly Girl?" *Journal of Jewish Education* 70, nos. 1 and 2 (Summer 2004): 32–39.

36. Scult, *Judaism*, 392n55; and Miriam Heller Stern, "A Dream Not Quite Come True: Reassessing the Benderly Legacy," *Journal of Jewish Education* 70 (Fall 2004): 25.

37. Brickner, talk to the Bureau of Education (Cleveland), 1 June 1969, 7/1; Brickner, address to United Jewish Religious Schools, 22 Oct. 1972, 8/2; and Joseph Barrat to Rebecca Brickner, 23 Oct. 1972, 6/10, Brickner papers.

38. Interview with Brickner.

4 : Libbie L. Braverman

A Woman for All Seasons

1900–1990

Libbie L. Braverman, 1979.
Courtesy of the Western Reserve Historical Society

Born to Teach

Libbie L. Braverman, born in Boston on December 20, 1900, came to cherish learning at an early age. She fell in love with it despite having to adjust to many new schools as her parents, Rabbi Morris A. and Pauline (Drucker) Levin, moved the family frequently. The Levins finally settled in Cleveland when Libbie was in high school. The many dislocations did not disrupt her studies or her early and lifelong appreciation for Jewish family life. She loved her maternal grandmother, who ran a Jewish bookstore and made the wine for their Passover celebrations. She admired her maternal grandfather, "the proud scholar who rarely left his books or the House of Worship."[1] Her grandfather and father, Orthodox rabbis who served in congregations and communal settings, inspired her with the value of Jewish learning. She studied at her father's knee and admired him as a scholar and great educator.

Yet Braverman was far from a docile, passive recipient of knowledge. She defiantly reveled in being the only girl in Torah and Hebrew classes at Chicago's Talmud Torah and rejoiced at besting boys for school prizes, foreshadowing, at the dawn of the twentieth century, the militant feminism that was to become a significant part of her persona and led her later to emphasize how remarkable it was for her, a woman, to hold an influential position in a synagogue.[2] She became the first woman board member of the National Council for Jewish Education (1952) and later became its vice president. She was the first woman to lecture for the Jewish Chautauqua Society.[3] Her flamboyant hats, knee-length plastic boots, and regal demeanor said more than "take note of me." Her appearance proclaimed a refusal to succumb to the past, a rejection of gender stereotyping, and a public announcement of her determination to make it as woman in a profession overwhelmingly dominated by men.

Libbie D. Levin married Sigmund Braverman in 1924. Despite her strong feminism, she always preferred the name, Libbie L. Braverman.[4] Libbie and Sig agreed to honor each other's separate careers, unencumbered by children. But Jewish teaching assuredly honors them as "parents."[5] Teacher Libbie was a nurturing mother to students and children of students, teachers and thousands more who learned from teachers she trained. Architect Sigmund was an artisan in whose buildings, adorned with Jewish symbols and Hebrew letters, untold numbers of children and adults studied. Their art- and award-cluttered penthouse apartment in Cleveland Heights, Ohio, in a building Sig designed, became a sanctuary and a meeting place for Jewish intellectuals.

Braverman was very proud of the fact that she became a Hebrew teacher while still in high school, although she later attended Cleveland Normal School and earned a BS at Western Reserve University. Her first job was as Hebrew teacher in a Chicago Talmud Torah; later she taught in a Chicago Reform temple. When the family moved to Cleveland, where her father led the Cleveland Hebrew Schools, Libbie carried a letter of reference to Euclid Avenue Temple (Reform) where Rabbi Barnett Brickner, a Benderly boy, promptly engaged her. Braverman also taught at Cleveland's Congregation B'nai Jeshurun (Conservative). But it was Euclid Avenue Temple (later Anshe Chesed Fairmount Temple) that became her home from her high school years to adulthood. As a youngster, she never mustered the courage to tell her Orthodox father that she walked to the Reform temple every Saturday to teach. She would later claim the she brought Yiddishkeit (Jewish learning and living) to Euclid Avenue Temple, remaining there for thirty-five years of a long career, progressing from teacher to educational director, a position Rabbi Brickner had originally created for Nathan Brilliant in 1927, when eleven hundred pupils crammed the classrooms.[6]

Brilliant's arrival heralded a novel partnership that bolstered Braverman in her ceaseless campaign to share with teachers and pupils her fervent devotion to Hebrew, Zionism, Yiddishkeit, and the arts. She acknowledged the difficulties, noting, "We were often accused of bringing back Orthodoxy (heaven forefend)," but she never forgot her goal: to introduce Zionism to students and their parents through drama, pageantry, music and student activities.[7]

Braverman distinguished between Orthodoxy and tradition. She rejected the Orthodoxy of her father and grandfather that, she believed, erected Keep Off the Grass signs.[8] She championed responsible Reform Judaism based on knowledge and respect for Jewish origins. She carried that message first to students and teachers in her schools, then to the American Reform movement by sharing her ideas and enthusiasm with teachers around the country. Those who knew her work remember her best for her labor in the trenches, although her Jewish educational worldview, influenced by Dewey, Kaplan, Benderly, and Emanuel Gamoran, led her to theorize about goals, means, and educational systems. Braverman was an out-of-the-mold school principal and a teacher of teachers who, in their turn, carried her commitment to Reform Judaism, Zionism, Israel, and Hebrew to the next generations. Her venues were community activities, teacher workshops, articles, and her many books for teachers and children.

Braverman was a grateful pupil who acknowledged standing on the shoulders of predecessors like A. H. Friedland, her inspiration and mentor. Her tribute to Friedland gave full credit to Jewish education's historical context by including a review of Samson Benderly's work and the founding of the Council for Jewish Education.[9] Though not one of the Benderly boys, she was a kindred spirit who personified the innovation, modernity, community, and experimentation Benderly represented. For that very reason, Friedland's Cleveland Bureau of Jewish Education was a logical and grateful beneficiary of her talent, enthusiasm and material support. She chaired annual meetings and celebrations, served on committees, and was an unofficial and welcome adviser to its professional and board leadership until shortly before her death.[10] She received the Bureau's prestigious A. H. Friedland Award in 1975, and an honorary doctorate from the Cleveland College of Jewish Studies (June 6, 1981) for her achievements, financial support, and advocacy. The Cleveland Jewish Community Center named her a Life Trustee in recognition of her contributions to its education program through the arts. She became an honorary member of the UAHC-CCAR Joint Commission on Jewish Education not only for her accomplishments, but also because she so effectively championed Reform Judaism in her community activities and her writing.

Incorrigible Rebel

A stubborn feminist, feeling underpaid and underappreciated because she was a woman, Libbie abruptly resigned from Euclid Avenue Temple in 1952 having served as teacher (1917–32), head of the club and Hebrew departments (1933–39), associate education director and director of extension activities (1940–46), and education director (1946–52). Colleagues and friends, surprised by her resignation, remarked on the event, dividing into two camps typified by these comments: "I was shocked to learn of your separation from the Euclid Avenue Temple . . . a great blow to the cause of Jewish education." "PPS And lots of luck in your new status as a free woman & educator. I hope your husband will be happy to have you around more often. He's a lucky guy & I hope he appreciates it."[11]

Libbie welcomed Nathan Brilliant's influence on her and her future. She credited him with keeping her involved in the temple until she finally retired from her public school teaching to work with him, creating new educational initiatives. Euclid Avenue Temple soon became famous as a laboratory for modern Jewish education, for which she credited Brilliant's deep understanding of the needs of the time.[12] Conscious of her place among her people and the responsibility that entailed, she honed her native abilities to excel at writing, training teachers, enthusing students, experiencing her large world intimately and completely. The Brilliant-Braverman nexus modeled the best that synagogue schools could be.[13] It also enriched the Jewish education literature, particularly and uniquely in the use of performance and Hebrew to teach Jewish life cycle and holidays. Word of their avant-garde work reached Emanuel Gamoran, director of the Reform Commission on Jewish Education, who encouraged them to share their pioneer achievements with a wider audience.[14] They reported their work in three groundbreaking publications that schools across the continent quickly began to utilize.[15] Gamoran lauded the uniqueness of *Supplement* and *Activities*: "The major contribution of these two volumes . . . is to be found not only in the discussion of how to conduct various activities in the Jewish school, but also in the detailed descriptions of the experiments initiated and carried out under the direction of the writers and in the creative work which these experiments stimulated on the part of both teachers and children."[16]

Braverman's departure from Euclid Avenue Temple was neither the blow to Jewish education Friedland called it nor her acceptance of the homemaker role Cohen predicted. She and Sig were confident she could continue in her career because "we had a good maid who would take care of the house and get his meals."[17] She became the educational consultant at Temple Israel, Akron, Ohio, in January 1953, and in 1966, the educational director at Temple Sinai, Stamford, Conn.[18] She remained with the Stamford congregation for only one year, even though its rabbi, Samuel M. Silver, was an old friend and colleague. Troubled by an absence of educational standards in the school, furious at parental resentment over many of her decisions, convinced that she did not receive the support she expected from her rabbi, and cajoled by her Cleveland friends to come home, she returned to Cleveland in 1967. Once there, Braverman joyfully entered on what became a gratifying and highly productive life as lecturer, trainer of teachers, and author. She produced four major works in little over a decade while continuing a flurry of newspaper and journal articles and speaking engagements, as well as organizational activities for Cleveland Hadassah.[19]

For Zion, Everything

With notable exceptions, the founders of American Reform Judaism believed in the ascendance of a messianic era, a united humanity, unobstructed by alienating national demarcation lines. For them, "nation" was chief among the obstacles to messianic fulfillment. Thus they were opposed to Zionism and were reluctant to accept the Jewish state.[20] Braverman was among the minority of Reform leaders who worked selflessly for Palestine and Israel.[21] She considered Palestine essential to the souls of Jews of all ages and recognized early on its cultural importance to the diaspora Jewry. Unapologetically enamored of *Eretz Yisrael*, she early and often spoke about her Palestine adventures and promoted the welfare of its Jews.[22] She campaigned for Israel's rebirth and visited Palestine and Israel frequently, often for a month or longer. She supported its institutions financially and morally, even as she insinuated Zion into her teaching and her writing. Starting in the early 1930s, she turned her energy to local and national Hadassah, which became a forum for lecturing and writing about life and politics in Palestine and, later, Israel. She was a respected Hadassah leader, was present with Henrietta Szold when she founded Youth Aliyah, chaired several committees, and was president of the Central States Region from 1939 to 1940. In December 1937, she celebrated the Cleveland chapter's twenty-fifth anniversary with a pageant about the recent Arab revolts against Palestine's Jews.[23] She was an early supporter of Israel Bonds,[24] and in 1956, the founding chair of its Cleveland women's division.[25] She spoke before many groups throughout the 1930s and beyond about Palestine and, especially, about Youth Aliyah, through which she worked diligently to help children who settled in Palestine.

Braverman's early Zionist activism earned her a delegate's seat at the seventeenth World Zionist Congress in Basle in 1931. She recalled the extraordinary and overwhelming assembly. "It was exciting to see representatives of the Jews of the world gathered together in Switzerland. I saw all the greats of modern Jewish history. . . . Heated discussions dominated the Congress. To please the Arabs, a not unusual activity of the British, His Majesty's government issued a white paper to curb Jewish immigration."[26] She conveyed her observations and reactions to the public.[27] Five years later, when she returned from her 1936 visit, she emphasized Palestine's growing need for assistance to keep alive its prophetic march to statehood.[28]

She was again a delegate when the twenty-first World Zionist Congress met in Geneva in 1939, on the eve of World War II. What happened next reinforced her gratitude for being a Jew in America, in a way she never imagined. Braverman described the plight of the delegates fleeing Geneva, making their ways to Paris, then to Le Havre to board a refugee ship the French refused to release despite President Roosevelt's intervention. After several traumatic days in port and following an urgent U.S. demand, the ship, in total blackout, finally sailed. Its sailing impressed on her how fortunate American Jews were. "We weren't refugees after all—driven from pillar to post. It was good to be an American—to feel that America vouched for us and would do all it could to obtain a safe return of its sons and daughters."[29]

For Braverman, the twenty-first congress telescoped the tragedy of Europe and the distress and misery of European Jewry who sought freedom from lands of bondage and new homes in the Promised Land. The vitality and courage of the Palestine group captivated her. It was the only group, she believed, to express optimism, as they stood ready to defend their rights to the national home and to welcome refugees seeking to return home. Her remarks emphasize American Jewry's obligation to give help and moral support to the defenders of Palestine who "stand ready to give so much!" Her report includes a fervent appeal to support immigration to Palestine, a theme to which she returned often.[30]

In early 1948, Braverman warned her audiences that the real task lay before them because of British "neutrality" and the Arabs' avowed goal to destroy the fledgling Jewish state. Nevertheless, she was firm in her conviction in the indestructible will of the Jewish people to build its homeland despite the tremendous struggle to come. "For at long last," she concluded, "the Jewish people is coming home."[31] Her diaries and miscellaneous musings capture her understanding of the connection between Jews and *Eretz Yisrael*. Two examples are "a people has a soul and the soul of the Jewish people — all that the Jewish people feels and sings and lives by — is in Jerusalem," and "we have soaked up the tides of the incoming refugees like a thirsty sponge."[32] Braverman's words influenced others through the power of her passion and personality. Si (Isaiah) Kenen, director of information for the Israeli Delegation at Lake Success, probably spoke for all her disciples when he wrote. "I do think you should know how deeply I sense my obligations to you both for having done so much in the years I was in Cleveland to make me conscious of both the responsibilities and rewards of being a Jew."[33]

Energized by her devotion to the land, refreshed by visits to familiar haunts, and eager to record changing political and social conditions, Braverman was prepared to take herself to Israel at a moment's notice. At the same time, she recognized that the Jewish future belonged to youth, for whom group tours were essential. Her 1953 teen program apparently sold out.[34] She created the Fairmount Temple NFTY (North American Federation of Temple Youth) Exchange Student Award (Cleveland, 1978) to encourage high school students to participate in the Eisendrath Israel Student Exchange Program (Reform). For adults, her Hadassah activities included organizing and leading tours for the Central States Region, the first on Purim, 1959. Soon after the Six-Day War, she published a two-part report on Israeli families and the war's high human cost.[35] During three months in Israel in 1971, her letters brought readers eloquent, optimistic, and graphic depictions of everyday life. Nine months later, she initiated a series of articles to share her impressions of Soviet immigrant absorption, a Jewish-Arab student dialogue project and vignettes of life at the *kotel* (Western Wall).[36] She contributed a series on life in Israel to the *Cleveland Jewish News* while on an extended visit in 1972. Her ceaseless and intense concern for Israel is evident as late as 1985. Her blistering review of Jimmy Carter's report of the Camp David accords in his book *The Blood of Abraham* included a firm defense of Menachem Begin and Israel.[37]

While Cleveland Hadassah satisfied her self-imposed hometown Zionist obligations, it hardly sufficed to carry her ardent Zionism to the larger audience she sought, so she turned to writing textbooks. For Braverman, Zionism and teaching were inseparable. She insisted on twin teaching objectives: to understand the marvelous development then taking place in Palestine and to appreciate that life in Palestine was a source of inspiration for Jewry throughout the world and enriched and vitalized holidays in the diaspora.[38] From her earliest Cleveland days, she had produced a steady stream of books and publications to connect Jewish children in America with their Israeli family. She emphasized three themes: the need for American children to know about their ties to a biblical homeland; the homeland's cultural and religious importance for diaspora America; the obligation to support the valorous Palestine Jews in their march toward nationhood. The latter appears very early in the pageant *Havlagah* (Self-restraint), in which she extols the heroism of Palestine's Jewish pioneers and represents on the school stage their character traits she so admired.[39]

Her first Palestine trip, a monthlong journey in 1931, produced an assessment of progress in the Zionist colonies, and a series of "twins" stories in several publications.[40] The adventures of the Palestine twins introduced Hebrew terms and Palestine's sites to young, English-speaking readers. One interviewer noted:

> In the summer of 1931 she went to Palestine. When she returned, the children at the Euclid Avenue Temple naturally wanted to know all about her trip. Conscientious teacher that she is, she wanted to give the children more than just a Cook's tour lecture. . . . She proposed to give the children a well-rounded picture of the normal, natural, year-round life of the modern Palestinian Jews. She therefore invented [twins] Temar and David . . . to make real . . . the natural, wholesome lives of our Halutzim and the wonder of the new Jewish Homeland. . . . Chapter by chapter, the story was told by Mrs. Braverman from the assembly platform. . . . Their young American friends could not hear enough. . . . It was only natural, therefore, that the adventures of the twins should be written down. . . . Upon her return from her second trip, Mrs. Braverman went back to her twins . . . and now it is a book.[41]

One reviewer called *Children of the Emek* "pioneering," but warned club leaders and teachers not to use the book as a textbook, rather to allow children to enjoy it as an experience and not as a homework assignment.[42] I am sure Braverman took this as a high compliment. Always the pedagogue, she produced a workbook complete with formal learning activities, illustrated horah dance instructions, puzzles, music, and a foldout map of Israel — everything the teacher required to turn the stories into teaching opportunities.[43] For Braverman, the school assembly was another significant way to maintain contact with pupils through her own storytelling and a medium for student expression in plays and pageants.[44] Because she insisted that performances come out of the classroom experience, she also looked on the assembly as a "mirror of the school."[45]

In *Children of Freedom*, Braverman undertook to tell young readers Israel's saga starting with the ingathering of Holocaust survivors. Morris Epstein thought it lacked continuity, was too preachy, and too filled with facts.[46] It reads that way today as well. In a sense, Braverman suffered the consequence of a fervor that impelled her to assess and to chronicle — especially for American Jewish children — the magnitude of the miracle of Israel's rebirth a mere five years after the event. Perhaps she reached too high too soon with

Children, which she unabashedly called the record of the story enacted by the children of Israel, and demanded that students have a right to know in depth about the modern ingathering and its biblical roots.[47]

The 1967 Six-Day War prompted *The Six-Day Warriors*, coauthored with Samuel Silver in 1969, continuing Libbie's desire to point out the similarities between American and Zionist values. One reviewer observed, "The spirit of Israel shines through the too-few pages of this book. Without propagandizing, the authors make it clear why all Americans can feel a spiritual kinship with the kind of patriots, young and old, who laugh at odds."[48] Braverman was right, of course, about the big picture and the pedagogic value of making explicit the comparisons between Israel's struggle for independence and freedom and America's early history. She wanted to share her passion for the burning Jewish cause of the mid-twentieth century.

The Mother Tongue

Braverman included Hebrew in as many school settings as possible and spared nothing to provide teachers with training sessions and the tools they needed, like carefully selected Hebrew language textbooks, including her own. She believed that a light hand and fun enhanced Hebrew learning, but admonished that games and the like are important only as a means to an end.[49] She early and consistently advocated for an integrated curriculum. Thus, in 1955, shortly before *Teach Me to Pray* appeared, she cautioned that Hebrew in the one-day-a-week school is not a subject in itself but rather part of a broader learning experience that includes topics like customs and ceremonies, holidays and religious worship.[50] An earlier, prescient publication called for Hebrew readiness in kindergarten followed in ensuing grades by increased numbers of Hebrew prayers and songs and greater emphasis on understanding prayerbook Hebrew. Her goal was to enrich the teaching of the holidays, integrate the Hebrew language with customs and ceremonies, train students in fluent and accurate prayer reading, and prepare them for participation in children's services.[51] This much Hebrew teaching was remarkable in the 1940s in a large Reform congregation that was indisposed to Hebrew altogether and to Braverman's commitment to Yiddishkeit.

She vigorously promoted sales of her Hebrew materials, many written with Nathan Brilliant. Large numbers of schools ordered multiple copies of titles like *Devices for Teaching Hebrew*, *Prayer Study Manual and Teacher's Guide*, and *Hebrew Prayers*, the latter a Hebrew-centered curriculum that sold out by September 1952, attesting to the growing need for such material in the Reform movement and Libbie's genius in marketing. Although she valued Hebrew as a living language and a link to the ancestral home and studied in an *ulpan* (immersion program designed to promote fluency) frequently, she did not want to teach Hebrew as a separate subject. Rather, she channeled her Hebrew curriculum through the language of prayer and holiday celebrations to allow for repetition. She understood the centrality of reinforcement through performance, but she also wanted to embed Hebrew study in memorable childhood encounters in order for children to live Jewishly and to grow up with an awareness of the richness of their heritage and the beauty of its holidays.[52]

Knowing well what teachers need, she wrote large numbers of practical, user-friendly pedagogic aids and classroom-based projects about teaching prayer, Jewish holidays and home observances. She included how-to components so teachers could present the novel material easily. In her very early "A Purim Carnival," for example, she articulates her bedrock confidence in risking new approaches for new times. She presents a Purim observance in American schools to mirror the holiday in Palestine when Jews and Arabs would stream into Tel Aviv (in contrast to "the usual anemic form that the celebration of Purim takes in this country"), painstakingly detailing instructions for everything teachers required to fulfill her vision.[53] This may all seem obvious today, but the approach was new with her, a perfect melding of her beloved Palestine and her holiday curriculum, the forerunner of today's Jewish-content Purim celebrations. While many of Braverman's writings were published by her congregations, others appeared in a variety of venues, including holiday publications.[54] Her self-promotion and her unquestioned innovation made an impact on a wide educational community.

Theory and Practice

Braverman's early training and teaching in the public school informed her educational philosophy, for there she came to understand the importance of giving credence, in a coherent educational amalgam, to all the experiences that come a learner's way. She coupled that insight with the conviction that teachers must reach pupils on more than one level. She designed and concluded a ten-year project of school-related club activities that effectively increased the hours of Jewish instruction. The project demonstrated the efficacy of her basic belief that the child does not exist in a vacuum. Therefore, the Jewish school must be coherent with the secular school curriculum and integrate the Jewish with the secular, relating the Jewish child to the non-Jewish environment.[55] Braverman sought to achieve her goal by helping Jewish students read, think and study with Jewish material, much of it presented through art, music and drama. A practitioner as well as a theoretician, she provided the teacher and club leader with sample programs and implementation instructions that grew out of her certainty that Jewish learning comprises more than the formal classroom setting. She did not coin the term "informal learning." But she practiced it.

Although Braverman was able to increase instruction time and motivation in her synagogue schools through clubs and theater, she became dissatisfied with the structure of Jewish education and the realities that prevented dedicated Jewish teachers from achieving maximum results. She was impatient with a community, a board of education, a religious school committee, and a great mass of parents unaware of goals, vague about philosophy, with no purpose or design. At the same time, like Benderly, she opposed the all-day Jewish school, which, she believed, too frequently meant the transfer of the eastern European approach and method to the American scene.[56] She spoke to parent groups and cajoled school committees to make the one-day-a week program a better learning experience. Throughout her career, in her writings and lectures, she struggled with how to involve home and parents, how to reconcile the American and Jewish experiences, how to bring modernity to Jewish learning.

Braverman was a first-rate Jewish educator, motivated by her persuasion that Jews value education. Fully community-minded, without relinquishing her loyalty to the synagogue, she understood, as did Benderly and the leaders of the New York *Kehillah*, that bureaus of Jewish education propel the educational effort across the widest spectrum.[57] She was a perceptive theorist whose journals, articles, and notations on envelopes, paper napkins, concert programs, menus, and scraps of paper attest to her never-ending occupation with generative, broad questions of Jewish education's purpose, content, and context.

She was concerned about the Jewish education profession, probing always for a better system, a stronger theoretical base. She was acutely aware that the world around her was changing dramatically but that the Jewish school moved slowly because the Jewish community moved slowly, pursuing its own agendas as if the world outside did not matter. At the same time, she believed in a teacher's ability to effect change, that the Jewish teacher was Jewish education and was uniquely positioned to assure the school's viability, while depending on the community to provide infrastructure and materials. Like Benderly and Kaplan, she wondered why the teacher didn't enjoy the status he or she deserved and how to professionalize Jewish education. She answered then, as we do now, by emphasizing that adequate compensation, changing teachers' self-perceptions, and helping teachers become models of wholeness entail both communal and professional responsibility.[58] She goaded others, but led by example. To show her appreciation for teachers, she established the Fairmount Temple Faculty Recognition Award (Cleveland, June 1971), the David Yellin Teachers College Faculty Recognition Award (Israel, November 1976), and the Bureau of Jewish Education Creative Teaching Award (Cleveland, March 1980).

Braverman was a careful and strict observer of the classroom and held teachers responsible for how they discharge their obligations. Her reach and compassion encompassed all children as she tried to formulate an approach for those who fall behind due to absence, attitude, or different abilities. She pioneered with programs of individual help that first diagnosed the problem and then provided comprehensive remediation to strengthen the child by preventing failures, relying on summer school, and enlisting parents' cooperation via written notes and phone calls. Attempting to assist all who try to bring Judaism to young people structure their efforts, she identified a list of teachable moments like community children's programs, youth groups, vacation school, adult institutes, PTA meetings, festival celebrations, shut-ins, congregational groups, and religious school. Yet she was wary of gimmicks: "Aids are not substitutes for good teaching; they are *aids* for good teaching."[59]

She appreciated camping's potential, although concerning her first camp position she wrote, "The only training I had in preparation for this job was the course on theater I had taken at Western Reserve University." She later served as head counselor at camps Pinegrove in Massachusetts, Tabor in Pennsylvania, and Carmelia in Vermont. She believed that each girl in her Jewish camp became well prepared to face the problems of life — self-reliant, poised, confident, sure — and would ultimately become a valuable, intelligent member of the American Jewish community, an ambition she held for the children of her school as well. Here, as in other educational dimensions, she was ahead of her time as seen, for example, in an article on camping that reflects her educational philosophy and the lessons she learned about camping's contributions to personality and character development.[60]

Braverman's formula for good teaching rested on two fundamentals, respect for the individual and for the community. She discussed the first in the spirit of the progressive education of her day, "Individualize a child and give him an outlet for his creative ability."[61] While attending to the uniqueness of the individual, she was equally adamant about the place of group mores and values. She became judgmental and impatient when the education that defined her life lost sight of its deepest Jewish roots. She took one author to task because she wholeheartedly believed that every prayer should link children to religious concepts whereas the author had failed to attach the values to their Jewish sources.[62]

She spoke her mind in person and in print in defense of her certainty that Jewish education was sacred and too often taken for granted. She understood that it was a lifelong process decades before the term became popular. She expected all ages to enjoy Jewish education under all circumstances. She recognized nearly a century ago that too many parents, progressive and enlightened in their secular education, advanced no further than bar or bat mitzvah or confirmation, thus failing to appreciate the importance of continuing their children's education. Therefore, she placed great emphasis on adult learning. Jewish education, she believed, far from constraining young people, enriched them, making them better adjusted members of American society.[63] She appreciated the necessity and the difficulty of winning parents to the enterprise. She told them that Jewish education connected the child with humanity's richest spiritual treasures, the moral and ethical formulations of democracy, and a religious culture that ennobles human society. She knew the pitfalls in the appeal to parents: "What do you have to know to be a good parent? Nothing! What the child learns in the school you can unlearn in the home."[64] Speaking to the Reform Movement, she campaigned for the now well-understood principle that parents must be living examples of the faith the temple proclaims, that the transition from Orthodoxy is not to escapism but to a living Judaism and an undiluted education.[65]

The Play's the Thing

Braverman never wavered in her faith that the arts, drama especially, communicate Jewish values most enjoyably and, therefore, most expeditiously. Music and song feature prominently in her curricula as well as in her pageants. If words, music, stage directions were lacking, she wrote them. She tried to get others to recognize the importance of music in Jewish group activities. In her handbook for song leaders, she set out to arouse teachers about Israel as she was inspired, and to give them the resources they needed to captivate their students. She taught that song was central to the lives of ordinary Jews in Palestine; the *halutz* (pioneer) in Israel celebrates in song, songs "grown from the soil of *Eretz Yisrael*."[66] She urged teachers to recognize that holiday songs are not merely hymns of praise, but that holidays are stellar occasions to carry out the joyous repetition of songs that relate to the story of the holiday and individual characters of the festivals.[67] Many of her earliest publications extol the arts' pedagogic virtues and provide detailed instructions for others to follow.[68] At the same time, she extended her interest in the arts beyond the school and beyond the synagogue.[69] She frequently conveyed to others her faith in the power of Jewish stage shows, in which creative dramatics provide the best instrument for achieving the maximal educational aims. She knew what hard work it entailed, yet was confident that performance, thought through and written by the group itself, would produce unparalleled results.[70] She was alert for students who showed a flair for the arts and counted the artist, Joan Carl and the playwright Jerome Lawrence, a former Euclid Avenue Temple student, among her friends.[71] Lawrence acknowledged Braverman's significant influence on his Broadway career: "Libbie appointed me editor of the religious-school magazine, 'The Ner Tomid.' 'It's better to be a writer and a director (than an actor),' Libbie told me. 'Now you get to play ALL the parts.' With her blessing, with the warm wind of her love at my back, I've been trying to do that ever since."[72] At her death, Lawrence wrote, "Libbie's light shines down through the years, an impetus to idealism, a constant inspiration to care, not only for the everlasting light of Judaism, but for the perpetuity of the human race."[73]

From the moment New Amsterdam's Peter Stuyvesant met and imprisoned the Recife refugee immigrants in 1654, Jewish responses to the challenges of adaptation/assimilation have varied considerably in North America in an ongoing struggle with a dichotomy of nationality imposed by the majority culture. Braverman understood, appreciated, and factored questions of identity into her pedagogy. She was explicit about her own position, asserting that Jewish life in America should be neither superimposed on nor separated from American life but should adjust so as to make for a wholesome, well-integrated Jewish personality. She actualized Dewey's understanding that childhood is more than preparation for later life into ways to help Jewish children live fully as Jews in the present. That led her to club programs that extended hours, enriched curriculum, capitalized on gregariousness, strengthened temple bonds, channeled interests into Jewish life, promoted sympathetic attitudes to other Jews, provided varied and obvious Jewish experiences, developed lay leadership.[74] She provided curricula to help young people integrate their Jewish and secular worlds, yet was too much of a realist not to worry about the legitimate outside activities that so frequently resulted in postconfirmation separation from the synagogue. In confirmation-year programs designed to motivate continuation into the high school, she constructed appealing activities connecting Judaism and the American mainstream. She taught that learning can and should be fun for adults as well as children.[75] She counted on the excitement of the performing arts to merge the students' American and Jewish selves.[76] Braverman continued to believe this to the end of her life, convinced that even the complexities of modern life would respond to her formula, if educators would take it seriously and try it.

A Pioneer in Family Jewish Education

Braverman's focus on the total Jewish child led her to sweep the Jewish home into her fervent grasp. She knew well that the Jewish religious school could not function without the home, which must play the major part in the Jewish education of the child, providing subliminal learning and reinforcement. Not content with theory alone, she packaged a program to involve parents creatively and meaningfully in several ways: study groups designed to help parents understand the classroom learning; inviting parents to visit the school; enlisting parents to participate in school activities; providing conferences for individual parents and groups of parents; and reaching the home through printed materials.[77] Although such intercessions are fundamental to modern Jewish education, the program she presented seventy years ago created a new concept for educators to consider.

Braverman's pedagogy comprehended the importance of the Jewish home in a child's education. She concluded that home observances, customs, and practices embody the spiritual aims of Jewish education and cannot begin too early. Therefore the school has a stake in helping the home provide religious experiences that give meaning to religious values and abstract precepts.[78] An unwavering confidence that the home and parents are essential to build the ground for later Jewish learning motivated her meticulous attention to the form, setting, and substance of Jewish learning throughout her long, productive career.

If Not for Herself

Libbie Braverman smiled always (some say it was a Mona Lisa smirk), even when angry. She greeted me with her trademark smile when I last visited her in Cleveland's Montefiore Home a few days before she died in 1990 at the age of ninety. But her twinkling eyes disarmed, masking an unmovable will that buttressed strongly held opinions on just about any topic. She breathed Judaism, and it nurtured her. Zealous about the arts, Braverman discovered how to infuse them with Jewish meaning that appealed to her pupils and their teachers. Her schools echoed with plays, cantatas, and pageants on every imaginable Jewish theme. Essay, drama, and art contests pervaded her curricula and a variety of Libbie Braverman awards went to the winners. I watched her in action for nearly fifty years and worked beside her often. I respected and honored a complex, compelling, confidence-exuding, sometimes exasperating colleague blessed with limitless energy, loving Jewish knowledge and the Hebrew language, as comfortable on a lecture podium as in a classroom or teaching peers in small groups.

Braverman acknowledged God's plan for the universe, but claimed none for herself. She believed that her career emerged in spite of her lack of planning, that the variety of activities in which she found herself were the signposts that showed her the way. She was certain that the people she met and places she'd been were responsible for what happened to her. At the same time, she recognized that to enter open doors is, in fact, a plan. She believed that her "peculiar kind of preparation, the seemingly unplanned activities" led to her life's work. She didn't intend to become a Hebrew School teacher just because she went to Hebrew School. She didn't plan to produce plays just because she took a Shakespeare course. She did not envision carrying the torch for Women's Liberation. The only goal she acknowledges pursuing was to take teacher training at the Cleveland School of Education.[79] Early family influence, standards she absorbed from grandparents and parents, insatiable curiosity, high self-esteem, joy of Jewish life—these turned Braverman into one of the foremost and most prolific of twentieth-century Jewish educators.

Sure of herself and conscious of her worth, she unabashedly pushed her publications and advertised her availability for lectures and seminars without regard to travel cost, which she always billed along with her fee. She multiplied those efforts following her resignation from Euclid Avenue Temple in 1952. Her reward was a steady income from the large number of engagements she procured as lecturer, consultant, leader of interfaith workshops, and trainer of teachers at local and statewide institutes and at individual schools.

She insisted that friends and colleagues help her. For example, she urged the director of the Jewish Welfare Board lecture circuit to schedule appearances for her, suggesting places and topics.[80] She wrote to an extensive mailing list, reminding potential clients that she was available and that her background included many years of experience in Jewish education.[81] The American Association for Jewish Education, in a letter to all Jewish schools, advertised her availability and noted that she "is exceedingly skillful in conducting workshops for teachers and parents."[82] The Braverman archives contain voluminous correspondence growing from her suggestions to invite her back to places where she had spoken over the years. She demanded, "publish my *Holiday Handbook for Parents and Teachers.*" She told another colleague to use her *Activities in the Religious School and Supplement* in his school and to bring a copy for her to autograph when he visited Cleveland. She distributed her articles nationally and sent complimentary copies of her books to encourage educators to use them in their schools. She engaged a secretary to handle her growing volume of mail, make her travel arrangements, and manage her schedule. Publication of her autobiography *Libbie* brought a rash of book-signings as well as the proclamation of Libbie Braverman Week, March 29–April 5, 1987, by Beachwood, Ohio, mayor Harvey Friedman — at her suggestion.[83]

Braverman's image management was extensive. The archives overflow with personal appeals to market her availability and advertise her publications. The 1930s files and her scrapbook pages are replete with newspaper and magazine clips reporting on a multitude of addresses on Palestine and education, as well as committee activities, camp leadership positions, and her books. The files also contain many letters from schools seeking advice and materials and thanking her for consultations with the school and with teachers. Withal, she respected and listened intently to colleagues, attending Jewish educational conferences as often as possible, and saving her notes. In an unidentified and undated page of conference notes she wrote, "If the survival of Israel and the security of Soviet Jews are the most important international problems facing the Jewish Community, the future of Jewish education is the most crucial and decisive domestic issue confronting this generation of American Jews." She dedicated her life to that challenge.

Her self-promotion worked not only because of advertising, but because she had so much to offer, was an acknowledged expert, and excelled in public speaking, which played to her strong interest in drama. Diverse organizations wanted and appreciated her, among them United States and Canada Hadassah, Mississippi Valley Historical Society, Pioneer Women, Bonds for Israel, synagogues, Zionist Youth Commission, B'nai B'rith Women, Young Judea, Jewish Book Council of America, National Federation of Temple Sisterhoods, Jewish community centers, Rotary, Jewish National Fund, and various central agencies for Jewish education. Synagogue schools benefited from her curriculum talents, but so did others, as in her 1949 courses for the Hadassah School for Adults and her leadership of Cleveland's Federation of Jewish Women's Organizations. Her countless book reviews in many publications, especially the *Jewish Welfare Board Circle*, spanned her wide range of Jewish interests: biography, the arts, Hebrew, Zionism, literature, Jewish thought. She was a font of educational wisdom and Zionist history who knew that others admired her; she advanced her public image with the same energy and zeal she brought to all aspects of her life. Interviewer Carl Kovac told her, "'You're a fascinating woman.' 'Of course I am,' she replied. It wasn't that she lacked humility. It's simply that Mrs. Braverman is a woman who knows what she is all about . . . living proof that Judaism is not just a religion, It's a way of life . . . it's a continuous happening."[84] Kovac captured her essence: always on stage, always confident of the future, always advocating by her actions as well by her words for the things that commanded her loyalty.

Epilogue

Following Sig's death in 1960, Libbie built living memorials to support their interests and encourage excellence in others. She initiated the Sigmund Braverman Cultural Program at the Cleveland Jewish Community Centers as a "living memory to his high principles of Jewish culture."[85] She endowed a cultural lecture series in his name at Cleveland's Fairmount Temple. In 1963, she established the School of Architecture Sigmund Braverman Award at Haifa's Technion Institute and, in 1967, the Sigmund and Libbie Braverman Annual Board–Staff Institute at Cleveland's Jewish Community Center. There followed the Libbie Braverman Scholarship Fund in Memory of Sigmund Braverman at Israel's Hadassah Community College in 1978. She devised and organized the Sigmund Braverman Art Collection at the Cleveland Bureau of Jewish Education and arranged for it to acquire two commissioned Jewish sculptures in Sig's memory: in 1977, Pearl Amsel's *Teacher and Disciple* and, in 1979, David E. Davis's *The Tsadik*. In the presentation she observed, "According to Davis, the work symbolically portrays the concepts of saintliness and truth." Libbie noted in her autobiography, "A 'Tsadik' in honor of the 'tsadik,' Sigmund Braverman."[86] She later inaugurated the Sigmund and Libbie Braverman Annual Lectureship in Jewish Studies and Jewish Learning at the Cleveland College of Jewish Studies (May 1981). She maintained her involvement in all of the projects throughout her life.

At a posthumous dedication of one of Sig's temples, she said, "[He] believed [the synagogue] must integrate the Religious, the Educational and the Social functions, all rooted in Jewish history and Jewish tradition. . . . He dreamed the dream . . . he saw the vision. . . . I, too, saw the vision. I knew it when it was a spark in his eye."[87] They were of a single mind and one heart in comprehending the synagogue's importance to Jewish survival and its allegiance to learning and prayer. They shared a profound and abiding interest in Zionism and Jewish communal matters. She fondly observed that of their synagogue skills a writer once observed, "He builds them and she fills them."[88]

Five years after his death, reviewing her husband's papers, Braverman wrote that in his designs for well over forty synagogues and other Jewish institutional buildings she could sense his authentic voice and his wry humor, his devotion to his craft, and his commitment to Jewish ideals.[89] She spoke of him constantly, pointed with pride to his Cleveland buildings, and recalled their travels together. Though their careers required many separations, some of them lengthy, they cherished their vow to support one another's accomplishments and projects. Jewish learning, Jewish culture, and Jewish institutions framed the essence of two remarkable people whose gifts of soul and substance continue to bless the Jews in Cleveland, throughout the United States, and in Israel.

Libbie Braverman possessed multiple talents and an uncommon ability to conquer obstacles. Those privileged to work with and admire her said so. The Akron community had welcomed her as one of the finest leaders in Jewish culture and education. They were impressed that before the building was completed Braverman wore a fur coat and galoshes so that the first school session could take place; that she moved furniture and swept floors while establishing fine principles to govern the education program.[90] She remained true to those principles throughout her long and active life.

Of her many legacies, perhaps none is more significant than this: "Thus did Libbie influence and change the hundreds, the thousands of people she came in contact with, in classrooms, from lecture platforms, or through the pages of her books. Their attitudes to Judaism and Jewish culture and the Jewish nationalism, which we call Zionism, as well as patterns of family life, were shaped accordingly. These influences were passed on to second and third generations, increasingly remote from the original source, but still subject to the consequences of the first contact. And still these ripples make themselves felt."[91]

NOTES

I am indebted to the Western Reserve Historical Society, Cleveland, Ohio, and its staff, especially associate curator for Jewish history, Sean Martin, for facilitating access to the Libbie L. Braverman collections, nos. 4566 and 4812. I am grateful also to the Jewish Education Center of Cleveland and Director Seymour Kopelowitz for defraying research expenses.

    1. Libbie L. Braverman, *Libbie* (New York: Bloch, 1986), 3–5.
    2. Oral history, tape 1, side A, no. 490. All "oral history" citations refer to Braverman

interviews, January–February 1983, in the Jewish Women of Achievement Oral History Project conducted by the American Jewish Committee, Cleveland chapter.

3. Libbie and I were the only nonrabbinic Jewish Chautauqua Society lecturers in the 1950s and 1960s. We also worked together in a variety of teacher training programs for the Reform Movement, notably at the Union Camp Institute in Oconomowoc, Wisconsin, founded by Rabbi Herman Schaalman, then director of the UAHC Chicago region.

4. Cleveland Board of Education. Name-Change Notice.

5. "Who teaches a neighbor's child Torah is accounted the child's parent," Talmud: Nezikin/Sanhedrin 19b.

6. Oral history, tape 1, side A, nos. 345, 313.

7. Libbie Braverman. "Nathan Brilliant Memorial Address," July 1960. Libbie L. Braverman collections, nos. 4566 and 4812.

8. Braverman, *Libbie*, 141.

9. Poet, Hebraist, and educator, Friedland was the founding director of the Cleveland Bureau of Jewish Education. He served as director from 1924 until his premature death in 1939. Braverman, "Profile of a Pedagogical Giant," *Jewish Education* (Fall 1982).

10. As a former Bureau director, I appreciated Libbie's advice, although sometimes it could be an unwelcome intrusion. Some of my predecessors were less accepting.

11. Unidentified news clip, June 15, 1952; oral history, tape 1, side A, no. 689; letter from Rabbi Eric Friedland, Chicago. June 23, 1952; letter from Rabbi Jack J. Cohen, Jewish Reconstructionist Foundation, July 2, 1952.

12. Libbie Braverman. "Nathan Brilliant Memorial Address," July 1960.

13. Nathan Brilliant left Euclid Avenue Temple in 1946 to direct the Cleveland Bureau of Jewish Education, becoming the first Reform educator to head a major communal agency. I was the second, following the same path in 1978, from Fairmount (formerly Euclid Avenue) Temple.

14. Emanuel Gamoran was the founding director of the Commission; he served from 1923 until his retirement in 1958. He was associated with the Commission until his death in 1962.

15. Nathan Brilliant and Libbie L. Braverman, *Religious Pageants for the Jewish School* (New York: UAHC, 1941, 1943); Brilliant and Braverman, *Supplement to Activities in the Religious School* (New York: UAHC, 1950); and Brilliant and Braverman, *Activities in the Religious School* (New York: UAHC, 1951).

16. Brilliant and Braverman, *Activities in the Religious School*, vi.

17. Braverman, *Libbie*, 142.

18. *Akron Beacon Journal*, January 1953; *Connecticut Jewish Ledger* (n.d., 1966).

19. Braverman's four major works were *Children of Freedom* (New York: Bloch, 1953); *Teach Me to Pray*, with David I. Cedarbaum, 2 vols. (Chicago: Board of Jewish Education, 1955, 1957); *Children of the Emek* (1937; New York: Bloch, 1962); and *The Six-Day Warriors*, with Samuel M. Silver (New York: Bloch, 1969).

20. The 1869 Philadelphia conference of Reform rabbis asserted "universalism as the union of all the children of God." The 1885 Pittsburgh platform declared, "We consider ourselves no longer a nation but a religious community." Reform's journey to Zionism began with the 1937 Columbus platform.

21. Oral history, tape 1, side B, nos. 904–1069.

22. For example, Braverman, "The German Situation in Relation to Palestine," address to the Jewish Women's Federation Symposium, October 20, 1933; report on an address to Hadassah on her recent return from two months in Palestine, *Detroit Jewish Chronicle*, September 1934.

23. *Monthly Bulletin*, Cleveland Hadassah, November 1937.

24. Letter from Henry Montor, October 6, 1953, congratulating her on organizing a highly successful Cleveland Women's Bond Event.

25. Cited in *Cleveland Jewish News*, August 1, 1986.

26. Braverman, *Libbie*, 99.

27. *Review and Observer*, September 1931, reported her forthcoming address to a Junior Hadassah meeting on the topic "a visitor's impressions of the World Zionist Congress and Palestine."

28. Jewish National Fund Women's Committee Report. November 23, 1936.

29. *Cleveland Plain Dealer*, September 13, 1939.

30. "They Rely on Us," Cleveland Hadassah, *Monthly Bulletin*, October 1939.

31. Cleveland Hadassah, *Monthly Bulletin*, January 1948.

32. Diary entries, undated, but probably around 1948.

33. Letter from Si (Isaiah) Kenen, June 30, 1948.

34. Letter from Rabbi Philip L. Lipis, Highland Park Ill., March 3, 1953, expressing hope that space remained for young people from his community.

35. *Cleveland Jewish News*, September 1967.

36. *Cleveland Jewish News*, June 1972.

37. *Cleveland Plain Dealer*, May 28, 1985.

38. Libbie L. Braverman, *Palestine Program* (New York: Young Judea, 1936), foreword.

39. The pageant was "inspired by the remarkable self-restraint exhibited by the Chalutzim during the disturbances in Palestine." With Nathan Brilliant, Cleveland, Euclid Avenue Temple, undated, but in the late 1930s.

40. *Cleveland Plain Dealer*, September 27, 1931. One of the earliest of the twin stories was "On the Yarkon: Meet the Twins," *Young Judea*, October 1935.

41. "Teacher Writes Book," October 1937, interview with Libbie about *Children of the Emek*, author and venue unknown.

42. Israel S. Chipkin, *Young Judea Leader*, October 1937, 15.

43. Braverman, Workbook for *Children of the Emek*, (Cleveland: Bureau of Jewish Education, 1950).

44. Braverman, "The Jewish Assembly," Religious Teacher's Association of Ohio-Michigan-Indiana, 1952.

45. Oral history, tape 2, side B, no. 829.

46. Review in *Jewish Welfare Board Circle* (January 1954).

47. Braverman, *Children of Freedom*, foreword.

48. *American Examiner*, November 4, 1969.

49. Introduction in Braverman, with Nathan Brilliant, *Devices for Teaching Hebrew Reading*, (Cleveland: Bureau of Jewish Education, n.d.)

50. Braverman, *Hebrew Study in the One-Day-a-Week School: A Guide for Teachers* (Cleveland: Euclid Avenue Temple, 1955).

51. Braverman, *Curriculum* (Cleveland: Euclid Avenue Temple, ca. late 1940s).

52. Review of Lillian S. Abramson and Lillian T. Liederman, *Jewish Holiday Party Book* (New York: Bloch, 1955), *Pedagogic Reporter* (Spring[?] 1955).

53. *Jewish Education* (January–March 1935): 49–51.

54. Braverman, "Nine Purim Games," in *Games of All Kinds for the Jewish Club* (New York: National Jewish Welfare Board, n.d.), 11–12. Braverman, *A Holiday Handbook* (Oakland, Calif.: Jewish Education Council, n.d.); Temple Sinai, Stamford, Conn., re-

issued this apparently well-received source book of introductory materials for Shabbat and holidays in an expanded version. Braverman, with Nathan Brilliant, *A Passover Seder in Action and Pictures* (Buffalo, N.Y.: Bureau of Jewish Education, n.d.). Braverman, with Renee Shulman, *On the Wings of a Century* (Cleveland: Euclid Avenue Temple, 1942); this was a dramatic pageant to celebrate Euclid Avenue Temple's one hundredth year. Braverman, with Nathan Brilliant, *A Modern Haggadah* (Cleveland: Euclid Avenue Temple, 1938). "A Program for a Hanukkah Assembly," *Jewish Teacher* (November 1933): 10ff. Braverman, *Chanukah: A Manual of Suggestions for Parents, Teachers, and Club Leaders* (Cleveland: Euclid Avenue Temple, n.d.).

55. Braverman, "Club Activities in the Religious School," *Jewish Education Magazine* (January–March 1937): pp. 20ff. Originally presented at a convention of the Jewish Religious School Teacher's Association of Maryland, Va., and Washington, D.C., which she twice served as president. She was also a president of the Ohio Michigan Indiana Religious School Teachers' Association.

56. Undated handwritten page with many shorthand notations.

57. Notes scribbled on program booklet of a Jewish National Fund gathering honoring Ohio congressman Charles A. Vanik, March 9, 1975.

58. Miscellaneous jottings, undated and scattered throughout Libbie's papers.

59. Diary entries, undated, but probably around 1948.

60. Braverman, *Libbie*, 61, 64; "Individualizing the Camp," *Camping Magazine* (n.d.).

61. *Cleveland College Life*, January 25, 1932.

62. Review of Samuel Halevi Baron, "Children's Devotions" (New York: Bookman, 1954) in the *Jewish Welfare Board Circle*.

63. Undated address to Cleveland Hadassah.

64. Diary entries, undated, but probably around 1948.

65. Miscellaneous jottings, undated and scattered throughout Libbie's papers.

66. Braverman, *Come, Let's Sing* (New York: Hadassah Education Department, ca. late 1930s).

67. Undated journal entry.

68. A typical example, Braverman, with Nathan Brilliant. "Maimonides Octocentennial Pageant" *Jewish Teacher* (April 1935): pp. 24ff. The pageant provided lessons about Maimonides in five scenes. Similarly, Braverman, with Nathan Brilliant, "Proclaim Liberty throughout the Land: A Pageant of Freedom to Celebrate the Birthdays of Washington and Lincoln" *Synagogue* (January 1939): 9, demonstrated that she saw a natural connection between Jewish teaching and American civic values.

69. *Independent and Review*, June 1934, reported that Libbie had become the founding president of the Anglo-Jewish Art Theater.

70. Braverman, "Dramatics in the Synagogue Center" *Synagogue Center* (March 1942): 7ff.

71. Correspondence files, 1975–87. Libbie often told me of her particular attachment to Lawrence and her pride at having discovered him first. Jerome Lawrence (1915–2004) wrote or collaborated on dozens of screen, stage, and TV adaptations, including *Auntie Mame* and *Inherit the Wind*.

72. Braverman, *Libbie*, x.

73. Letter from Jerome Lawrence, November 14, 1991.

74. Braverman, "Club Activities in the Religious School," *Proceedings of the Eighth Annual Institute of the Jewish Religious School Teacher's Association*, November 1936.

75. Braverman, with Nathan Brilliant, "Laying the Groundwork for Temple Affiliation," *Jewish Teacher* (June 1940); Braverman, *Libbie*, 65.

76. Braverman, *With Lifted Hands: A Choral Pageant Concerning Jews in America* (New York: National Federation of Temple Youth, 1954); Braverman, with Sam Silver, *They Helped Build America* (Stamford, Conn.: Temple Sinai, 1954); Braverman, "Three Hundred Years — Thirty Anniversaries," pageant written in cooperation with David I. Cedarbaum, Hyman Reznick, Yosef A. Schub, in *The American Jewish Tercentary, 1654–1954: Teaching Units*, ed. David I. Cedarbaum (Chicago: Board of Jewish Education, 1954); Braverman, *Three Hundred Years: A Confirmation Choral Reading* (Cleveland: Community Religious School, 1955).

77. Braverman, with Nathan Brilliant, "Relating the Parent to the Jewish School," *Jewish Teacher* (November 1939): 18ff.

78. Braverman, "Religious Values Caught or Taught," *Religious Education* (September–October 1956).

79. Braverman, *Libbie*, 89–90.

80. Letter to Samuel Freeman, June 1953.

81. Promo on Libbie's letterhead, June 11, 1953.

82. Letter from Judah Pilch, executive director, December 4, 1952.

83. Letter to Jacob Behrman, Behrman House Publishers, September 2, 1952; letter to Rabbi William Silverman, Nashville, Tenn., undated, but probably 1952. Without prompting, and calling it a tribute from a former student to an esteemed teacher, Cleveland Heights, Ohio, mayor Beryl Rothschild, declared December 20, 1985, Libbie Braverman Day in honor of Libbie's eighty-fifth birthday.

84. *Cleveland Plain Dealer*, October 24, 1974.

85. Letter to George Goulder, June 6, 1960.

86. *Cleveland Jewish News*, November 4, 1977, and October 10, 1979; Braverman, *Libbie*, 161.

87. Excerpted in *Voice*, Temple Beth El, Baltimore, January 16, 1973.

88. Undated publicity sheet Libbie circulated as a bio and to solicit speaking engagements.

89. *Cleveland Jewish News*, June 25, 1965.

90. From a tribute given at Temple Israel, Akron, Ohio, April 18, 1953.

91. Carl Alpert, "Libbie Braverman: A Personal Tribute," Haifa, Board of Governors, October 1991.

5 : Mamie Gamoran

Modeling an American Jewish Life

1900–1981

Mamie Gamoran, circa 1950s.
Courtesy of Hadassah, The Women's Zionist
Organization of America, Inc.

In 1967, the Union of American Hebrew Congregations (UAHC) published *Talks to Jewish Teachers*, a slim volume by Emanuel and Mamie G. Gamoran that presented a distillation of Emanuel Gamoran's lectures delivered over his thirty-five year tenure (1923–58) as director of the Reform Movement's Commission on Jewish Education. Manny, as he was better known, began the project soon after he retired, but died before the book could be finished. His wife, Mamie, completed the project, editing his work as she had throughout their thirty-nine years of marriage. She also wrote seven of the chapters from the notes he left behind. This last collaboration is just one of countless examples of how deeply intertwined their lives were, personally and professionally like other Benderly-inspired couples, such as Rebecca and Barnett Brickner. This essay affords Mamie Gamoran her due. Through the Jewish textbooks she wrote, she was able to disseminate her husband's views, planting them firmly in homes and synagogue schools. Believing that she and her husband had fashioned an ideal American Jewish life, she used their experience as a model for much of what she wrote. As Alexander M. Schindler comments in the foreword to the book, Mamie was Emanuel's coauthor in everything, "the companion not just of his life, but of his work these many years" (Gamoran and Gamoran, 1967, iv–v).

Mamie Goldsmith Gamoran (1900–1984) was a prolific author of Jewish children's books and an active Jewish lay leader in Hadassah and many other Jewish organizations. Through her writing, she turned her personal life into a model for American Judaism: a comfortable synthesis of the Jewish and the American, blending Zionism and American citizenship, Reform Judaism with a high degree of Jewish literacy in order to create a Jew who could be comfortable in any Jewish setting. While she wrote throughout her life, she defined herself first and foremost as wife and mother, in a supporting role to her husband as educational leader within the Reform movement. Indeed, the family history that she penned toward the end of her life makes scant mention of her writing or almost two decades of service on the national board of Hadassah and her many other accomplishments. The memoir is interspersed with many references to her husband's work, but there is little about the eight textbooks, or the many pageants, ceremonies, guides, poems, stories, and other materials that she wrote. While the detail is lacking, she hints at how important this aspect of her life was when she notes: "Writing, indeed, has provided me with the greatest learning opportunity of my life" (M. Gamoran, 1984, 130).

Twenty-two years after Mamie's death, her daughter-in-law Judith Halperin Gamoran reminisced about Gamoran's constant writing. "She would write a poem for every occasion. She always made time to write. I found note-book after notebook, where she was sitting on the subway and making verbal sketches. I think if she hadn't been married to Emanuel Gamoran, she would have become a novelist" (interview, 20 June 2006).

Sadly, not realizing the potential value of her diaries and notes, her children destroyed them soon after her death. Aside from her own family chronicle interspersed with a few stories, poems, photos, and documents, there are few resources available to uncover the details of Mamie Gamoran's life. There is almost no one alive today who worked with her or has any sub-stantive memories of her activities. The Union of Reform Judaism (successor to UAHC) did not retain records of correspondence or other documents about her publications. The American Jewish Archive at the Hebrew Union College in Cincinnati has a smattering of letters, an undated story she wrote about Samson Benderly, and her family history. The Hadassah archives contain a rich vein of information about her active life after she was widowed. But, as to her almost four decades of collaboration with her husband, we can only turn to the books themselves.

Mamie Gamoran's family history includes a detailed accounting of the genealogies of the many branches of her family and a listing of the accom-plishments of her children, nieces, nephews, and cousins. There are glimpses of Gamoran as a young girl, as a loving wife and mother, as a constant and cheerful hostess, as a committed Zionist, and as an active Jew. She readily gives her husband the bulk of the credit for developing and embodying a philosophy of Jewish education that shaped their lives. To be sure, Emanuel Gamoran had trained under John Dewey and William Kilpatrick, certainly among the most influential educational thinkers of the twentieth century. He was yeshivah-trained and was also a disciple of Samson Benderly and Mor-decai Kaplan. Unlike her husband who came from a home rich with Jewish tradition and practice, Mamie Gamoran came from a highly assimilated Ger-man Jewish home with much less Jewish background or Jewish education. She earned a diploma from a commercial high school and a certificate from the night school of the Teachers Institute. She had no university training, nor she did she consider herself a Jewish studies scholar or historian, having only a cursory exposure to Jewish texts. Her writings reveal her as an admir-ing wife, filled with deep respect for her husband's ideas and passions and fully committed to helping him carry out his vision. And from all outward appearances, it was his vision that dictated choice of subject matter and focus of content in her work. Emanuel Gamoran was the visionary, but Mamie Gamoran was the translator of his ideas through the textbooks that became a staple in Jewish classrooms for more than forty years.

Gamoran's work has merit on its own even if it was inspired by her hus-band's vision. And surely, with such joint intellectual activity and close col-laboration, she had an impact on him as well. While she frequently described

Manny as "my more than editor," she too, served as editor and critic for her husband's work. She reminisced about their joint project, *Talks to Jewish Teachers*:

> I was revising much of his material and adding some ideas of my own. One day I said to him, "Do you think, when the book comes out, it should say, 'By Emanuel and Mamie G. Gamoran?'" He thought and said, "Let's talk about it." That was all he said at the time. A few mornings later, as he was about to leave for the office, I said, "Would you like to see what I did yesterday?" "Yes," he replied and took off his coat. We sat down on the sofa and read it together. Whatever it was, it must have been good. He turned to me and said, "This is why the book must be 'By Emanuel and Mamie G. Gamoran,'" and kissed me. That night he died. (M. Gamoran, 1984, 147)

This chapter explores how Mamie Gamoran translated her husband's vision for Jewish education into textbooks and stories that served more than two generations of American Jewish children. During the course of his tenure at the Commission on Jewish Education, Mamie Gamoran published eight different textbooks that propelled Emanuel Gamoran's initiative to establish an extensive library of graded curriculum and textbooks for use in Jewish schools. Her textbook career ended with her husband's death, but Gamoran continued to write, edit, and publish smaller works, like booklets, guides, school programs, and confirmation services for a variety of other organizations and publishers until just a few years before her own death in 1984.

After offering a brief biography of Mamie Gamoran, I discuss the principles of her husband's philosophy of Jewish education. Through an analysis of two sets of textbooks—her three books that focus on Jewish holidays and customs, and her three-volume Jewish history series, I elucidate not only the vision of Jewish education articulated by her husband, but also how Mamie Gamoran translated it for teachers and students

Early History

Mamie Goldsmith Gamoran's earliest history would hardly suggest her future path as a Jewish children's textbook writer and Jewish activist. She was born at the turn of the twentieth century to a father of German Jewish origins who was born in South Africa and immigrated to America as a young man in 1888. Her mother's family arrived even earlier, in the 1860s. In her family history Gamoran notes that her father spoke unaccented English, rather a rarity among immigrants in those days. She also notes that her father's youthful travels "were not conducive to strong Jewish attachments," and he had minimal Jewish knowledge and few ritual practices (M. Gamoran, 1984, 35).

Mamie was named for her mother who died of pneumonia seven days after her birth. She was the youngest of four children. Her father married Matilda Bauer, a German Jewish immigrant who became known to the children as Mama. The family's early years were spent in Yorkville, a neighborhood that Mamie Gamoran described as a mix of German and Italian immigrants with relatively few Jews. German was the language the family spoke at home, not Yiddish. Her family's religious life was limited to observing the High Holidays and having a *seder* in English. They rarely attended synagogue. When Matilda's sister died in 1912, Matilda began to light Shabbat candles, and Mamie's father would recite *kiddush* on Friday night in "rather halting Hebrew" (M. Gamoran, 1984, 36).

When Mamie was ten, the family moved to the Bronx. She graduated grammar school as salutatorian and began high school, transferring after a year from the academic to the commercial branch due to the family's economic situation. But before she transferred, a classmate invited her to join a Jewish girl's club, "where they help you to be a Hebrew teacher" (M. Gamoran, 1984, 41). She describes it as a rather spontaneous decision that changed the course of her life: "Nothing was farther from my mind, but I went along to a meeting of the Bronx group of the Association of Jewish High School Girls. I liked it and was given permission at home to join. This was just short of miraculous — we didn't hold with clubs, etc." (M. Gamoran, 1984, 41).

This girls club was part of the League of Jewish Youth, an organization founded by Samson Benderly. Gamoran's involvement in the league had a profound impact on her. It was the place where her Jewish passions and commitment were first developed. It was where she first tested her leadership capabilities, where she became a Zionist, and when she began attending synagogue services. It was also where she first published her writing. While her family chronicle references little of her work, Gamoran proudly notes that a poem she wrote appeared in the first issue of the youth group's newspaper *Hed Ha'Galil* (Echo of the Galilee).

The league was also where she met Emanuel Gamoran, her future husband, who served as a youth group adviser. They did not begin to date until somewhat later, when she was a student at the Israel Friedlander Extension Classes of the Teachers Institute of the Jewish Theological Seminary, led by Mordecai Kaplan. Mamie Goldsmith was among the six young women who comprised the first graduating class in 1922. While enrolled there, she began to work as a special assistant to Samson Benderly at the Bureau of Jewish Education. At that time, Emanuel Gamoran was finishing his doctorate at the Teachers College of Columbia University, while also working for Benderly, as well as teaching at the Teachers Institute. He became a constant presence in her life, in school and at work, so it was not surprising that they started dating. In her memoir, Gamoran coyly writes that at first she didn't date Manny exclusively; indeed, she suggests there was considerable competition for her heart. But something must have tipped the scales in his favor, because in February 1922 they became engaged and were married in December of that year.

Emanuel Gamoran came from a much more traditional eastern European, Yiddish-speaking, kosher home, all quite foreign to his wife. The young couple must have been quite anxious about how their parents would get along. She writes, "The families strained to meet and to communicate. Both groups were meeting Jews who were different from those whom they usually met and probably felt this was what happened in America" (M. Gamoran, 1984, 61). Perhaps this personal struggle forged the couple's commitment to pluralistic forms of Jewish expression and made it a defining featuring of their work.

Just before they married, Emanuel Gamoran was offered the position of director of the Commission on Jewish Education for the Reform Movement. Initially he refused, stating he was not a good fit believing as he did that the Reform Movement's one-day-a-week Sunday school was insufficient to assure Jewish continuity in America. But the leadership persisted; after he was convinced that the Commission hoped to intensify Jewish education, Gamoran accepted the job. The prospective director had set the conditions under which he would take on the directorship: that he spend the first six months in New York to "get acquainted with the group," followed by a year in Cincinnati, the UAHC headquarters at the time, and then take a one-year leave without pay to travel in Europe and study in Palestine. From the outset, Gamoran clearly articulated his ideological commitments to Jewish living and to Zionism, qualities that made him distinct from and at times at odds with many of his Reform colleagues (Krasner, 2002). His educational vision included the strengthening of Hebrew and a reinjection of Jewish observance into Reform Judaism through recovery of traditions and customs (Grand and Gamoran, 1979).

The sojourn in Palestine was something of a rite of passage for almost all members of Benderly's inner circle. Mamie Gamoran writes: "Most of the men in the office of the Bureau of Jewish Education went to Palestine for a sort of postgraduate course" (M. Gamoran, 1984, 105). The Gamorans spent two months traveling in Europe and almost ten months living in Palestine, experiences that surely were life-shaping events for them both. Aside from traveling, meeting people, and experiencing firsthand the "rebirth of the Jewish national spirit in Palestine," one of Mamie Gamoran's main preoccupations was learning Hebrew, She and her husband had decided they wanted to create a Hebrew-speaking home. Hillel Gamoran, the Gamorans' middle son, recalls that his parents did not insist that Hebrew alone had to be spoken in the Gamoran household. Nonetheless, he recalls, "There was a lot of Hebrew in our home. Until [my] high school graduation, my dad had Hebrew lessons with me and my brother for an hour after dinner. Even when I was an adult with my own family, he would come [to] visit, and we would study together" (interview, 20 June 2006).

Gamoran, like so many of the women profiled in this volume, had become a passionate Hebraist and Zionist. Indeed one of the last things she wrote was a small pamphlet called *The Hebrew Spirit in America* (1975) for the Histadrut Ivrit, a nonprofit organization dedicated to advancing Hebrew language and culture in the United States.

The Gamorans' return from Palestine to Cincinnati coincided with their starting a family. Between 1926 and 1933, they had two sons and a daughter. They were members of both Reform and Conservative congregations, and it was at the latter that they chose to celebrate the b'nai mitzvah of their sons. Their first-born, Carmi, never attended religious school, but the younger two went to Sunday school at the Reform Isaac M. Wise Temple and were later confirmed there. All three children were also taught at home, Carmi and later Hillel with Manny; Judy with Mamie. The boys played baseball, tennis, and basketball, Carmi had a paper route, and Judy played violin in her high school orchestra. The Gamorans were fully American and fully Jewish,

While Gamoran credits her husband with making "the character of our home" (M. Gamoran, 1984, 131), together they created a hospitable and open house where all Jews could feel comfortable and welcome. She describes their Jewish life as somewhat of an anomaly:

> We were associated with the Reform movement; we spoke Hebrew to our children. We were liberals in our thinking, in our children's education, in our religious practices. Nevertheless, we erected a *suka* on our wide, open porch each *Sukkot* holiday, and served wine, tea and cake to as many as two hundred visitors. Some guests shook the *lulav* and said the blessings for the first time. . . . I used to say jokingly, "The Reform say we are Orthodox and the Orthodox say we are Reform." But we wanted to be Jews without a label. (M. Gamoran, 1984, 133)

Jonathan Krasner points out that what drove Emanuel Gamoran was his desire to educate for more "Jews without a label" even as he situated himself within a denominational framework (Krasner, 2002). One of the most far-reaching ways he promoted this agenda was through the development of an extensive series of textbooks and curricular materials that in the mid-twentieth century were the "industry standard." They were used in synagogue schools across the denominational spectrum, by Conservative, Orthodox, and Reform schools. There was little competition in the Jewish education textbook market at that time, and the UAHC press quickly gained a reputation for innovative and engaging materials. Mamie Gamoran became a textbook author early on, selecting and arranging two anthologies of biblical writings, *The Voice of the Prophets* (1929) and *With Singer and Sage* (1930). Not until her children were a bit older, in the late 1930s, however, did she begin to create original works. Once she began writing, she was in constant production. Between 1939 and 1960, she wrote six different textbooks for the UAHC press, numerous smaller publications such as specialized curricula and programs, and countless book reviews for her husband's bimonthly publication the *Jewish Teacher*.

Vision Drives Practice

Gamoran wrote poems and stories from girlhood, but she grew as a writer intellectually, socially, and religiously through her association with her husband, who in turn was influenced by many of the most powerful early twentieth-century thinkers in general and Jewish education. We have a clear record of Emanuel Gamoran's vision and how he translated it into curriculum and policy through his many UAHC publications and his articles in the journal *Jewish Education* and elsewhere (Krasner, 2002). Two volumes in which Emanuel Gamoran's philosophy of Jewish education can be found are in *Talks to Jewish Teachers* (Gamoran and Gamoran, 1967) and in *Emanuel Gamoran, His Life and Work* (Grand and Gamoran, 1979), a memorial volume that includes tributes written by his former colleagues and a collection of his essays on education. His work and influence have also been discussed by Olitzky (1984) and Krasner (2002).

Emanuel Gamoran's philosophy of Jewish education evolved through his association with Dewey and Kirkpatrick at Columbia University, Kaplan at the Teachers Institute, and Benderly at the New York Bureau of Jewish Education. He promoted a values-driven curriculum that he believed should "be subjected to the criteria arising from the needs of American life" (E. Gamoran, 1924, 64). Thus he fully subscribed to Benderly's and Kaplan's vision of "socialization and survival in a pluralistic American Jewish framework" (Krasner, 2002, 168). He was deeply committed both to the Jewish religion and the Jewish people, and emphatic in his belief that no one form of Judaism should be privileged over another. He was an avowed Zionist but fully enmeshed in American democratic values and life. He consistently advocated a program of Jewish education that would reflect a cultural synthesis of Jewish values adapted to American life.

In practical terms, Emanuel Gamoran defined the aim of American Jewish education "to enable our children to participate intelligently and effectively in American Jewish life." He wanted "to prepare our children for meaningful and intelligent participation in Jewish life at home, in the school, the synagogue, and the community, and to develop the skills and appreciations that are needed for effective participation" (Gamoran and Gamoran, 1967, 4). He believed that Jewish education should meet learners' needs; he identified them as psychological security in their Jewish identity, socialization into the home, school, synagogue, wider Jewish community, and satisfaction in Jewish life from a spiritual, cultural, and aesthetic point of view (E. Gamoran, 1952).

Mamie Gamoran introduced American Jewish youngsters, and by extension their teachers and parents, to her husband's educational vision, priorities, and values. Her first original work for the UAHC Press was *Hillel's Happy Holidays* (1939), a book designed to teach customs and holidays to young children. In *Talks to Jewish Teachers*, the Gamorans maintain that customs and ceremonies are the "perfect" subject to be taught in the Jewish school (1967, 97). Perfect because they were an ideal vehicle to increase children's participation in Jewish life at home and in the synagogue. Perfect because the children would bring their parents along. Perfect, also, because customs and ceremonies could be the key to Jewish cultural literacy, an introduction to Bible, rabbinic thought, and Jewish history. Then too, teaching customs and ceremonies would foster respect for Jewish diversity, for other Jews who practice unfamiliar holiday rituals. These aims provide the structure for the book, with great emphasis on the last, of the objectives, namely the promotion of Jewish unity over denominational superiority (Krasner, 2003). In his "Notes to Teachers and Parents," the introduction to *Hillel's Happy Holidays*, Emanuel Gamoran posits that the object of the book is "to provide the kind of material which will acquaint Jewish children not only with those customs and ceremonies which they may themselves practice at home or in the synagogue, but also to develop on their part a sympathetic attitude to the customs observed by other Jews" (M. Gamoran, 1939, viii).

Through simple albeit didactic prose, Mamie Gamoran takes her readers into the Jewish calendar via a family mirrored after her own. Her story presents a world infused by a rich and engaging Judaism that draws on home life, extended family, synagogue, and the broader Jewish world. The action centers on Hillel, a seven-year-old middle child, modeled after the real-life Hillel in the Gamoran family. Hillel is a member of what we would call today a highly affiliated family, fully engaged in Jewish life while deeply rooted in American life. Hillel's family belongs to a Reform Temple and regularly attends Shabbat and holiday services. The family is far more ritually observant than a typical Reform Jewish family of that time. The author never divulges Hillel's father's occupation, but he is a knowledgeable Jew and engaged parent, quizzing his children about holiday facts and telling them stories about Jewish life, past and present.

Hillel's life centers on his own family's Jewish holiday celebrations throughout the year. Children also learn about Jewish pluralism through his relatives and neighbors. Hillel and his siblings help build a *sukko* and search for leaven on the eve of Passover at his Conservative cousins' home.[1] They accompany them to celebrate *Simchas Torah* at their Conservative shul. Hillel makes friends with Stanley, the boy next door; he brings Stanley *shalach manos* (gifts of food) for Purim and invites him to his home for a seder, since Stanley's own family does not celebrate Passover. Later we see that Hillel's efforts at "Jewish outreach" result in Stanley joining Hillel at Sunday school at their Temple. The story even includes a visitor from Palestine who coincidentally appears at *Tu B'shevat*, the holiday that became linked to raising money for planting trees in Palestine. It is worth noting, that even without any overt expression of Zionist sentiment in the story, Mamie Gamoran, and by extension her husband, were subject to criticism from a vocal faction within the Reform movement for this mild reference to Palestine (Krasner, 2002). Nonetheless, Gamoran continued to include positive references to Palestine and later the state of Israel throughout her UAHC writing career.

All the elements of Emanuel Gamoran's philosophy are incorporated into these tales of the Jewish calendar. Mamie Gamoran depicts a family that loves Jewish living and Jewish learning, a family that is as comfortable in their cousins' Conservative synagogue as they are in their own Reform temple, a family that reaches out to assimilated Jews who haven't yet experienced the beauty of a rich Jewish life. Throughout the stories, she illuminates an idealized American Jewish identity: a family that has ties to Palestine and is deeply connected to Jewish history while remaining fully rooted in American soil.

These elements remain central in later books on Jewish customs and ceremonies. Shortly after *Hillel*, she wrote *Days and Ways: The Story of Jewish Holidays and Customs* (1941), intended for the older elementary grades. Rather than employing the device of a fictional family, Gamoran addresses the reader directly in an anthology of stories about how the holidays developed. The book also includes details about the holiday cycle and instructions about how to observe the holidays, including blessings in both Hebrew and English. The final two chapters of the book take her readers on a guided tour of a Jewish home to introduce some of the laws of kashrut and ritual items such as a *mezuzah*, a *mizrah* (a wall-hanging to denote east, the direction of Jerusalem), a *tzedakah* (charity) box, *yarmulke, tallis*, and *tefillin*. Like *Hillel's Happy Holidays*, Jewish unity is the subtext. In his introductory "Notes for Teachers and Parents," Emanuel Gamoran points out that one of the aims of this book is to familiarize the readers with a full range of Jewish customs and ceremonies that they may or may not practice so that they can "enter sympathetically in to the lives of other Jews." He continues, "We feel such procedure is essential in our education, if we are to attain even a modicum of unity in Jewish life" (M. Gamoran, 1941). If anything, the emphasis on experiencing and accepting all forms of Judaism is more pronounced in this volume. For example, in the chapter on the fall holidays of *Sukkot, Shmini Atzeret*, and *Simhat Torah*, Mamie exhorts: "If your parents are members of a Reform temple, you should visit a Conservative or Orthodox synagogue in your city to see this *Simchas Torah* celebration" (M. Gamoran, 1941, 64). She makes a similar suggestion for *Tisha B'Av*. Similarly, she tells readers who belong to a Conservative or Orthodox synagogue to "visit a Reform temple on the eighth day of *Sukkos*, to witness a combined *Sh'mini Atseres* and *Simchas Torah* celebration" (65).

In addition to promoting interdenominational harmony in *Days and Ways*, Gamoran also places great emphasis on cultural synthesis. *Sukkos*, as she refers to the harvest festival, is compared to Thanksgiving; in her chapter on *Chamisho Osor Bi-Sh'vot*, the legend of Johnny Appleseed is compared to the rabbinic tale of Honi planting trees; the American Civil War serves as a basis for understanding Passover; and in discussing *Lag Bo-omer*, Gamoran likens Bar Kochba to Superman (M. Gamoran, 1941). More than twenty years after *Hillel's Happy Holidays*, Gamoran wrote her last UAHC book, *Hillel's Calendar* (1960). Here, she returns to the story form and revisits Hillel, now as a nine-year-old boy. By the time this book was published, her husband had retired, but his influence remains. Jewish unity and the American Jewish synthesis are still her central themes. In fact, as Gamoran moves her readers through the calendar year, they do not merely experience the Jewish holidays, but they also learn how Hillel's family finds Jewish echoes and significance in American holidays as well. In her acknowledgments, Gamoran notes that she hopes that the readers "will begin to realize the common traditions of their American and Hebraic background." This sentiment clearly reflects one of the core aims articulated in *Talks to Teachers*; the Gamorans state that Jewish education "should strengthen our pupils' zeal for such values as democracy, social justice, human freedom, and world peace, while emphasizing how they are derived from Jewish tradition as well as from other sources" (Gamoran and Gamoran, 1967, 5). Thus, on Columbus Day, students learn about Columbus's Jewish mapmaker and the first man to step foot on the New World, a Jew named Luis de Torres. On Thanksgiving, they discover that the Pilgrims mirrored their harvest celebration after the biblical festival of *Sukkot*. Readers meet Hillel's cousin, Dan, a soldier in the U.S. army whose presence leads to a discussion about how Jewish chaplains were first appointed to the U.S. Army by Abraham Lincoln. On Israel Independence Day, Hillel and his siblings make a list comparing ways in which Israel and the United States are similar and different. And on Flag Day (June 14), a parade prompts Hillel to ask his father who had the first flag. This leads to a discussion about biblical references to flags. As the family walks to their car after the parade, Hillel remarks: "I didn't think we would talk about the Bible on Flag Day." His mother replies: "Most Americans love the Bible. Jews and Christians study it, and follow its teachings." And father (like Emanuel Gamoran) has the last word, saying: "Long ago . . . a wise rabbi said, 'Look in the Bible and look again. You will find everything in it' — even flags. Flag Day is a very good day to talk about the Bible" (M. Gamoran, 1960, 179).

As summer comes around, Hillel goes off to overnight camp for the first time. Gamoran never explicitly states that this is a Jewish camp, but in a bunk spat over whether Hillel can hang up his Hebrew calendar, one of the boys recalls that they had a special program the year before on *Tisho B'Ov*, a Jewish holiday that falls in the summer. The boys get a lesson in democracy when their counselor gets the boys to vote on whether Hillel can put up his calendar. The vote passes four to one, with Hillel abstaining. All is reconciled when the counselor points out that the Jewish calendar also marks the Fourth of July, American Independence Day.

The New Jewish History

Although the teaching of customs and ceremonies was pedagogically effective, even dearer to Emanuel Gamoran's heart was the teaching of Jewish history. Indeed, his first foray as a textbook editor was Lee Levinger's *History of the Jews in the United States*, published in 1930. This was the first American Jewish history textbook, and it was in use through many editions well into the 1960s. After World War II, Mamie Gamoran undertook to write a more comprehensive history of the Jewish people. Published in three separate volumes between 1953 and 1957, the books span the course of Jewish history from Abraham until the present day. It is fascinating to compare the breadth of this work with Behrman House's contemporary publication, *The History of the Jewish People*, vol. 1, *Ancient Israel to 1880s America* (Sarna and Krasner, 2006), a slim 170 pages including the index. Even without Book 3, *From the Discovery of America to Our Own Day*, Gamoran's work is more than two and a half times as long as this newer volume. Certainly, stylistic changes are most evident; the contemporary work is filled with short narrative passages, colorful graphics, maps, reflection questions, and activities to help the reader analyze and relate to the historical data. Gamoran's books also have illustrations as well as discussion questions and suggested activities at the end of each chapter, in a style consistent with similar works from the 1950s. What is distinctive about Gamoran's text is the amount of detail she provides and her orientation to Jewish history. Given her husband's priorities, it is not surprising that the first chapter about specific subject matter in *Talks to Jewish Teachers* is devoted to why Jewish history should be taught:

1. To transmit a knowledge of the growth and development of the Jewish people
2. To develop positive attitudes towards Judaism and the Jewish people — a Jewish consciousness
3. To establish an understanding of Jewish life today so that students are prepared for, and desirous of, participating in it. (Gamoran and Gamoran, 1967, 24–25)

Emanuel Gamoran's approach to Jewish history as a means of building Jewish identity and harmonizing Jewish and American life is consistent with the values of his era (Gold, 2004). Much more time and attention was dedicated to the teaching of Jewish history in Jewish schools during the interwar period and first two decades after World War II than in contemporary religious schools. Analysts of the period suggest that Jewish history was embraced as a strategy to counteract forces of assimilation brought about by the rapid suburbanization of American Jews and an attendant loss of organic Jewish community. History was seen as a way to reinforce a sense of Jewish self-esteem and to counteract antisemitism and negative depictions (Sheramy, 2003). The Gamorans observe, "We want our pupils to be challenged by our story, to find it dramatic and to realize that the Jewish people have made important contributions to the peoples with whom they have lived, and to the world" (Gamoran and Gamoran, 25). In another Jewish history textbook of the same era Deborah Pessin writes, "Jewish history, perhaps more so than any other single subject, is the vehicle for conveying to the child the achievements of his people and for inculcating within him a pride in being a member of his group" (Pessin, 1956, 142–43).

To achieve this goal, Mamie Gamoran constructed her textbook around Jewish heroes and heroic deeds. In contrast, the Sarna and Krasner (2006) history focuses more on events than on individual people, though occasionally a key figure such as the Prophet Elijah or Judah Maccabee is highlighted in an insert. In Gamoran's narrative, the hero is almost always at the center. Mamie Gamoran credits her husband with providing her with a threefold focus: "drama, achievement, and spiritual values" (M. Gamoran, 1953, ix). Emanuel Gamoran articulates his purpose in greater detail in his editor's introduction to *Book 1—From Abraham to the Maccabees*: "Above all, the author sought to keep in mind the desirability of creating positive attitudes on the part of our children. They are to be led to feel that the history of their people is an unfinished story in which they will participate; that it is dramatic and challenging and that the Jewish people have made important contributions to the world and to the peoples in whose midst they lived" (vii).

The style and content of *The New Jewish History* are consonant with other textbooks of the same period, both in Christian and Jewish education. Gamoran's method is a "functional" one. She selects and crafts stories that will "best serve the purposes of ethical training in a modern, American setting" (Gold, 2004, 109). Like other authors of the time, her biblical characters are painted in bold strokes and depicted as moral exemplars. She smoothes over any ambiguous or questionable behavior, qualities that are plentiful in the original text Thus, she describes Abraham, the father of the Jewish people, as "honest and just" in all his dealings (M. Gamoran, 1953, 19). She introduces the reader to Moses with: "The name Moses, stands out like a great shining light in the midst of a dark night" (32). David is heralded in an equally unambiguous manner: "At this moment a new figure comes into Jewish history. This figure is so dramatic, so fascinating and above all so beloved, that since his day no one has ever taken his place in the hearts of the Jewish people. This exciting person was David, the shepherd boy who became king" (86).

It is also interesting to examine what she leaves out of her detailed account. Omitting portions of the Bible that were perceived as overly complex or that might create dissonance was a typical feature of children's textbooks of the time (Gold, 2004). Indeed, this practice continues today with books such as *A Child's Bible* (Rossel, 1996), which omits any mention of Hagar and Ishmael, and employs midrash (rabbinic exegesis) to whitewash questionable behavior. For instance, in Gamoran's work, absent are the stories of the binding of Isaac, the selling of Joseph, the episode of the golden calf, the multiple rebellions in the wilderness, God prohibiting Moses from entering the land of Canaan, and of course, David's numerous infidelities.

These omissions suggest a desire to gloss over some of the more troubling biblical passages that may not create such "positive attitudes" about Jewish characters or convey the desired message of Jewish achievement and spiritual values. While some authors of the time may have excised anything at all "repugnant to the moral character of the pupil" (cited in Gold, 2004, 110), Gamoran does not entirely steer clear of conflict and questionable behavior. She describes Saul as sick and angry when he seeks to kill David. She records that Solomon used forced labor to build the Temple. And, she notes that there was injustice, corruption, and idolatry during the times of the Prophets. These examples seem to fit well within the guidelines for teaching the Bible suggested in *Talks to Jewish Teachers* that encourage teachers to confront the less than perfect actions of these biblical characters: "Their faults make them human. Their problems and the solutions they found become understandable" (Gamoran and Gamoran, 1967, 27).

Gamoran readily attributes the Bible to human authorship and frequently mentions places where there is insufficient evidence to support certain accounts, such as Joshua's conquest of Jericho. She comments that scholars question the claim that Solomon authored the Book of Proverbs, Song of Songs, and Kohelet (Ecclesiastes), and that Isaiah was a single prophet. She also describes the Book of Ruth as a didactic tale, designed as a kind of social protest against the vow many Judeans made to expel all the foreign women after their return from Babylonian exile (Ezra 10:3). Yet, while she assumes this critical stance, she also notes that the Bible can be read as "a record of events which happened to the Jewish people" and encourages her readers to think of the men and women of the Bible "as real people, who lived an everyday life, who ate and slept, who were happy and sad at different times" (M. Gamoran, 1953, 5).

Given this treatment of the Bible as a form of history, God seems to play a somewhat minor role in the unfolding of events. Once again, this reflects a common trend of the era to minimize God's role and present stories with supernatural elements as "legends" (Gold, 2004, 101). This perspective is most apparent in Gamoran's naturalistic depiction of biblical miracles. In *Talks to Jewish Teachers*, the Gamorans advise that miracles should be explained as misinterpretations of natural phenomena (Gamoran and Gamoran, 1967). Thus, no mention is made of the angel of God who appears to Moses out of a bush that burns but is not consumed (Exodus 3:2). Rather, Gamoran writes, "Moses *believed* that God called to him and gave him that great task" to take them out of Egypt (34, emphasis added). They remove God's direct hand in the ten plagues as well: "The Bible tells how one misfortune after another struck Egypt. . . . At last the Pharaoh was convinced that the God of the Hebrews had sent the plagues and that only when they left would good fortune come once more to his country" (34–35). And she notes that the parting of the Sea of Reeds "*seemed* like a miracle, and that is how it was related again and again to their children and descendents" (36, emphasis added).

When Gamoran moves out of the biblical era in Book 2, she no longer questions the historicity of events and, instead, crafts her narrative without editorializing about sources and authorship. These volumes are a testimonial to her long-standing commitment to communicate the idea of cultural synthesis as developed by Benderly and Kaplan. Ben Rosen, executive director of the American Association for Jewish Education (the precursor to today's JESNA [Jewish Education Service of North America]) expressed this ideal in 1949: "The unmistakable obligation of Jewish education today, as never before, is to synthesize the ideals of Jewish religion and American democracy . . . [and] to build better Americans and better Jews at a time when we are in desperate need of both" (quoted in Sheramy, 305).

In her history textbooks, Gamoran continues to draw analogies between contemporary American issues and events in Jewish history. For example, she cites changes in immigration and racial laws in America to describe how societies change over time. She compares the lawmaking practices of the academy at Jabneh with the workings of the U.S. Supreme Court. She employs Franklin Roosevelt's Four Freedoms as a lens to study the golden age of Spain, sending a message that Jews were at home in America, and this was yet another golden age.

Gamoran is also intent on teaching teachers to use some of the principles of progressive education. Her questions and activities at the end of each chapter are designed not only to promote Jewish cultural literacy, but to inspire creativity and critical thinking as well. For example, she encourages the students to act out a five-minute play about the escape of Rabbi Jochanan ben Zakkai after the destruction of the Second Temple (M. Gamoran, 19). She asks the students to consider whether the Jewish people were more successful under the Maccabean kings, King Herod, or the Sanhedrin, asking them how they would measure "success" (81). She instructs them to write a short composition about the Mishna, including its divisions and the names of some of the rabbis who helped prepare it (122). She has the students compare and contrast daily life and the role of leadership in Palestine and Babylonia during the time of the Talmud (134). And, she urges them to stage a debate between a Karaite and his rabbinic opponent on the authority of rabbinic interpretation (166). Gamoran's vision included both academic rigor and a respect for the natural curiosity and playfulness of the children for whom she wrote.

After Manny

In 1951, the UAHC moved its headquarters from Cincinnati to New York, and the Gamorans followed. Mamie Gamoran doesn't provide much detail about this stage of her life in her memoir. But, she certainly alludes to how pleased they were with the move when she writes, "we were returning to many old friends and family in New York. And we were living at the center of Jewish life in America" (M. Gamoran, 1984, 145). In 1954, they returned to Israel for the first time since their long sojourn there in the 1920s to visit son Hillel and his new wife, Judith, who were following in his parents' footsteps by spending a year there (Hillel Gamoran interview, 20 June 2006). In 1961, the Gamorans traveled to South Africa at the invitation of the Association of Reform Temples in South Africa. In a report to Hadassah about their six-week visit, readers acquire additional evidence of their close collaboration; Mamie Gamoran uses the plural "we" in describing the fifty-plus talks they gave demonstrating teaching techniques and speaking on topics like American Jewry, education, and youth (M. Gamoran, 1961). We know she gave at least one speech to a woman's group, but Mamie Gamoran doesn't elaborate on what she means by "we." Did she help her husband prepare the talks, or did she participate in their delivery as well? Given that they had already begun their work together on *Talks to Teachers* by this time, we can surmise that she was a significant partner in the formulation and articulation of these ideas, whether or not she was a copresenter.

Emanuel Gamoran retired from the UAHC in 1958 and died unexpectedly in 1962 when he was sixty-six, shortly before the Gamorans' fortieth wedding anniversary. His wife's publishing position at the UAHC press ended with her husband's retirement. Eugene Borowitz succeeded Manny as director of the Commission on Jewish Education. He recalls that there was some grumbling over Gamoran's practice of employing both his wife and sister as authors, even though he submitted their manuscripts for blind review.[2] Borowitz suggests that after Gamoran's retirement, his wife may have been considered an "educational has-been." He notes that a competitive publisher, the American Council for Judaism, had been quite active during these years and "the Union was under attack to recapture the leadership" (Borowitz, email correspondence, 26 June 2006).

While Mamie Gamoran never wrote anything quite as substantive as *The New Jewish History* after her husband died, she did continue to produce a selection of materials for different Jewish education publishers including KTAV, the United Synagogue for Conservative Judaism, and Histadrut Ivrit, as well as articles for *Hadassah Magazine*, the *Reconstructionist*, and the *Jewish Spectator*. Like her earlier works, these materials inculcated the possibility of a rich Jewish life within an American milieu. Yet it appears that at this stage of her life, writing became a secondary to her leadership in Hadassah and related Zionist and Jewish educational activities. Like so many other women of this era, Gamoran found in Hadassah an ideology that complemented her professional and personal interests.

Gamoran had been quite active in Hadassah during her Cincinnati years as well, both as a lay leader and a teacher. By the time she moved to New York, her children were grown, and she had more time to devote to organizational activities. She soon became a member of the national board of Hadassah and devoted herself fully to its mission in a variety of ways for over twenty years. Hillel Gamoran recalls: "When my father passed away, [Hadassah] was her life. She would go to the office every day. She was the Hebrew chairman; [she] wrote the Hebrew column in the Hadassah newsletter for many years" (interview, 20 June 2006).

A Hadassah report from 1976 lists Mamie's impressive résumé of organizational roles. These include:

Member, National Board of Hadassah
Member of the Board of the Women's Division of the Zionist
    Organization of America
National Chairman of Machon Szold (Hadassah)
Former National Chair of Hebrew Studies, Film, Performing Arts
    Bureau and Program Departments (Hadassah)
Past president Federation of Jewish Women's Organization of
    Cincinnati
Former Vice President Jewish Community Council of Cincinnati
National Vice President Hebrew Federation of America
Hadoar Editorial Board Member
Secretary, Herzliah Teachers Institute

During the 1960s and 1970s, Gamoran traveled extensively to Israel for Hadassah, leading numerous groups, and attending conferences and seminars. The Hadassah archives have records of her promoting foster parenting in Israel in the early 1960s, participating in the World Zionist Congress in 1964, speaking at a meeting of the Israeli Society for Biblical Research in 1965, and working throughout the 1960s and early 1970s in helping to establish Machon Szold, a Hadassah-sponsored behavioral sciences research institute in Israel. She frequently combined visits to her children and grandchildren with meetings for Hadassah and related organizations.

It seems only the inevitable process of aging slowed her down. The archives include several letters to friends in which she apologizes for not being able to lead a group trip to Israel or participate in a meeting because of illness. In

1982 at the age of eighty-two, she gave up her last official role for Hadassah when she submitted her resignation as chair of the Research and Archives Department. At that time, she also stopped writing; she no longer had the stamina. As Hillel Gamoran writes in *Family History*, "By 1982 her strength was waning; she could no longer sit at the typewriter for an extended period of time" (M. Gamoran, 1984, preface).

Mamie Gamoran died on July 29, 1984. Shortly thereafter, her son, Hillel, wrote a letter to the National Board of Hadassah in appreciation for their many notes of condolence. He concludes: "At the center of mother's life was Hadassah, the work it does in Israel for the young and the sick, and the education and Jewish identification it provides for thousands in America. She loved Hadassah. She loved working for Hadassah. She loved the women of Hadassah. She counted them among her closest friends" (H. Gamoran, 1984).

Conclusion

As a young rabbinical student coming to Cincinnati in 1942, Eugene Borowitz recalls Mamie Gamoran as "a pleasant human being with whom it was a pleasure to talk and a housewife who had written some children's books" (email correspondence, 26 June 2006). To a young man of that era, Mamie probably did seem to fit within conventional images of wife and mother, and from all the evidence it appears that she was fully content in fulfilling these roles. But though she may have relished the roles, she was not limited to them. She was much more than wife and mother.

Gamoran sustained and harmonized four key passions throughout her lifetime. First, was her love of her husband and her family. There was also her love for Jewish living and Jewish learning. Her passion for Israel and Hebrew were constants as well; they seemed to take a more prominent role when Hadassah became such a major part of her life after her husband died. And her passion for writing brought all these other passions together.

To be sure, Mamie was Manny's partner, influencing him as he influenced her. But, her life also stands apart from his, through her prolific writing and through her decades of dedicated activism and leadership for Hadassah. While we may not be able to discern whether it was her voice or her husband's that was more dominant in her writings, in the end, it doesn't matter. She directed her energies and talents to topics that mattered to them both. They were inspired by the same ideas and shared the same passions. They also shared the same values and priorities for their home life and for their work.

As a writer, Gamoran was an active participant in helping her husband achieve his dream of creating a library of textbooks for use in the Jewish school. In her books, she translated their shared vision into materials that she hoped would define and promote American Jewish life rich in ritual observance, fully tolerant and accepting of all forms of Jewish practice, deeply knowledgeable of Jewish history, and wholly committed to participating in the ongoing story of the Jewish people. And as a writer and active lay leader, she herself contributed significantly to the story as well as changing the nature of Jewish education across the denominations. A proud Zionist, a proud American, a Reform Jew with a high standard of cultural literacy and religious practice, and a committed pluralist, Mamie Gamoran was confident in the power of Jewish education to re-create the American Jewish family.

NOTES

1. Mamie's use of Ashkenazi-style transliteration throughout her work was consistent with the times.

2. Manny's sister, Rose G. Lurie, wrote three books for the UAHC Press during the 1930s.

REFERENCES

Gamoran, E. 1924. *Changing Conceptions of Jewish Education.* Vol. 2. New York: Macmillan.

———. 1952. Jewish education in a changing Jewish community. *Jewish Education* 23(3): 12–15.

———. 1964. Jewish education in a changing community. *Jewish Education* 34(2): 87–95.

Gamoran, E., and M. G. Gamoran. 1967. *Talks to Jewish Teachers.* New York: Union of American Hebrew Congregations.

Gamoran, Hillel. 1965. Letter to Hadassah. Hadassah Archives, RG12/Corporate Governance, Documentation and Structure, Series: National Board Materials.

Gamoran, M. G. 1929. *The Voice of the Prophets.* Selected and arranged. Cincinnati: Department of Synagogue and School Extensions of the Union of American Hebrew Congregations.

———. 1930. *With Singer and Sage.* Cincinnati: Union of American Hebrew Congregations.

———. 1939. *Hillel's Happy Holidays.* Cincinnati: Union of American Hebrew Congregations.

———. 1941. *Days and Ways: The Story of Jewish Holidays and Custom.* Cincinnati: Union of American Hebrew Congregations.

——— 1948. Confirmation service. New York: United Synagogue Commission on Jewish Education.

———. 1953. *The New Jewish History,* Vol. 1. New York: Union of American Hebrew Congregations.

———. 1956. *The New Jewish History,* Vol. 2, New York: Union of American Hebrew Congregations.

———. 1960. *Hillel's Calendar.* New York: Union of American Hebrew Congregations.

———. 1961. Unpublished report to Hadassah on South Africa trip. Hadassah Archives, RG12/Corporate Governance, Documentation and Structure, Series: National Board Materials.

———. 1975. *The Hebrew Spirit in America.* New York: Histadrut Ivrit of America.

———. 1982. Learning and teaching. *Jewish Education* 50(3): 12–16.

———. 1984. A family history. Manuscript, in the American Jewish Archive, Cincinnati.

Grand, S., and M. G. Gamoran. 1979. *Emanuel Gamoran: His Life and Work*. New York: Emanuel Gamoran Memorial Fund.

Gold, P. S. 2004. *Making the Bible Modern: Children's Bibles and Jewish Education in Twentieth-Century America*. Ithaca: Cornell University Press.

Krasner, J. B. 2002. Emanuel Gamoran: Jewish pluralism and Reform Jewish education. In Representations of self and other in American Jewish history and social studies schoolbooks. PhD diss., Brandeis University, Waltham, Mass.

———. 2003. A recipe for American Jewish integration: *The Adventures of K'tonton* and *Hillel's Happy Holidays. Lion and the Unicorn* 27 (September 2003): 344–61.

Levinger, Lee. 1930. *History of the Jews in the United States*. Cincinnati: Union of American Hebrew Congregations.

Olitzky, Kerry M. 1984. A history of Reform Jewish education during Emanuel Gamoran's tenure as Educational Director of the Commission on Jewish Education of the Union of American Hebrew Congregations, 1923–1958. DHL diss., Hebrew Union College–Jewish Institute of Religion, New York.

Pessin, D. 1956. The teaching of Jewish history. In *Readings in the Teaching of Jewish History*, ed. Azriel Eisenberg and Abraham Segal, 141–46. New York: Jewish Education Committee.

Rossel, Seymour. 1996. *A Child's Bible*. West Orange, N.J.: Behrman House.

Sarna, J. D., and J. B. Krasner. 2006. *The History of the Jewish People*. Vol. 1: *Ancient Israel to 1880s America*. Springfield, N.J.: Behrman House.

Sheramy, R. 2003. "Resistance and war": The Holocaust in American Jewish education, 1945–1960. *American Jewish History* (91): 287–313.

6 : Sadie Rose Weilerstein through the Looking Glass

K'tonton and the American Jewish Zeitgeist

1894–1993

Sadie Rose Weilerstein reading to children in the library of the Board
of Jewish Education of Greater Washington, circa 1988.

Courtesy of Deborah Weilerstein

When young fans asked children's author Sadie Rose Weilerstein whether her beloved four-inch-high K'tonton character was real, she wasn't sure how to answer: "If I say 'yes,' I confuse the children. But if I say 'no,' then K'tonton is insulted," she explained. "There are all kinds of 'real,' and K'tonton is very real to me. I hear him talking; he tells me what to write. My husband and I called him our fifth child."[1]

This charming anecdote reveals far more than a writer's eccentricities. To be sure, Weilerstein was a confirmed romantic who, by her own admission, went through life with her nose in her books and her head in the clouds. She found it difficult to concentrate on day-to-day chores like cooking. Her children used to joke that "her favorite flavor was burnt."[2] But she was extremely zealous when it came to guarding the integrity of her creations, even if it meant locking horns with her editors. One veteran of these battles, David Adler, formerly of the Jewish Publication Society (JPS), recalled Weilerstein's stubbornness, but added: "K'tonton was so real to her. And that's why he was real to her readers."[3]

The very premise of a Jewish Tom Thumb owed much to the established pantheon of fantasy literature. Indeed, Weilerstein tipped her proverbial hat to Hans Christian Anderson, Henry Fielding, S. Y. Agnon, and other sources of inspiration in the foreword to her first K'tonton volume, *The Adventures of K'tonton* (National Women's League, 1930). K'tonton, she wrote, "wishes to say *Shalom* to the many Thumblings who have preceded him."[4] Her whimsical tales and animated style were apparently too much for the reviewers at the Jewish Publication Society, who rejected her manuscript. One of them said the stories were "unreadable," "without probability," "without charm," and "without fact." In actuality, those early stories borrowed heavily from the everyday experiences of her son Herschel, while in later years, Weilerstein rounded out K'tonton's character by drawing upon the personality traits of her husband, Reuben. K'tonton's adventures were spun from "bits of reality that emerge into a story," Weilerstein explained.[5] As a reviewer of one of her subsequent K'tonton books put it: "If one forgets the initial improbability of a child four inches high, everything else about the book is entirely realistic."[6]

The reality that Weilerstein captured was not disembodied from time and place. If the appeal of her books derived in large part from her gifts as a storyteller, their power came also from her ability to capture the zeitgeist. Weilerstein's early books exemplified the balancing act that American Jews sought to perform between the prevailing assimilationist ethos and their allegiance to Jewish continuity. But they also underscored the growing realization that the unprecedented freedom that American Jews found on these shores could result in the dissolution of their religious and ethnic distinctiveness. Many of her characters, including K'tonton, were archetypes of American Jewish acculturation. By the mid-1960s, the organized Jewish community's concern had shifted from Americanization to survival. Likewise, Weilerstein's later volumes explored pathways of Jewish identification and cultural synthesis for a generation that took its Americanism for granted.

Of Mothers and Daughters

Sadie Rose Weilerstein was born to Bernard and Tillie (née Berger) Rose on July 28, 1894, in Rochester, New York. The Roses had emigrated from Lithuania in the 1880s. By the time Sadie and her three siblings were growing up, Bernard owned a factory and the family was well integrated into American society. The Roses encouraged all of their children, male and female, to attend college. Sadie graduated from the University of Rochester in 1917. She taught English to children at the Rochester School for the Deaf for about three years before marrying a young Jewish Theological Seminary–trained rabbi, B. Reuben Weilerstein in 1920. The couple met when Reuben came to Rochester to audition for a rabbinical position at Temple Beth El, the Conservative synagogue where the Rose family worshipped. Since the Roses were one of the few families who kept strictly kosher, they often put up "official" synagogue guests like Weilerstein.

Upon their marriage, the Weilersteins moved to Brooklyn, New York, where Reuben assumed the pulpit of Temple Emanuel in Boro Park, and, later, Temple Petach Tikvah, in the Eastern Parkway section. In 1929, the family moved again, this time to Atlantic City, New Jersey, where Reuben accepted a position at the Jewish Community Synagogue. He served there as rabbi (and after 1959 as rabbi emeritus) until his death in 1963. Sadie was an engaged *rebbetzin* (rabbi's wife) who was also active in community affairs and in Hadassah, the Zionist women's organization. The couple had four children, Herschel, Judy, Deborah, and Ruth, three of whom eventually settled in the Washington, D.C., metropolitan area. With some reluctance, Sadie moved to Rockville, Maryland, in 1978 to be closer to her family. She continued to write well into her nineties and died a month shy of her ninety-ninth birthday, on June 23, 1993.[7]

By all accounts, Sadie's mother, Tillie Rose, was a powerhouse of a woman, "a real *balabusteh*" (the Yiddish equivalent of domestic goddess) in the words of one of her granddaughters.[8] She was committed to a number of causes, including the women's suffrage movement. She worked alongside Susan B. Anthony and helped raise the necessary funds to compel the University of Rochester to admit women into degree-granting programs. Sadie's brother played the bugle during suffragette marches.[9]

Tillie was also active in Zionist affairs. In 1914, the National Convention of the Federation of American Zionists took place in Rochester. Tillie eagerly attended the sessions, including a Sunday afternoon conference of the eight Daughters of Zion chapters, presided over by Henrietta Szold, during which the group's name was changed to Hadassah and the decision was made to establish a central committee for the national organization in New York City. That same evening, Szold and other delegates founded a Rochester chapter of Hadassah in the Roses' living room, and for many years Tillie Rose remained its driving force. "Mama was never an unquestioning follower. There were times when she was a dissenter, even in Hadassah," Weilerstein said.[10]

The Roses hosted a number of convention delegates in their Avenue A home, including the inspirational Zionist emissary and organizer Bella Pevsner. When delegates complained that the city lacked a satisfactory kosher restaurant, Pevsner reportedly said, "I'll take you to a good place." A group of delegates followed her back to the Rose home where Tillie prepared a scrumptious meal with no advance notice. Apparently, many of the guests assumed that they were eating in a boarding house and offered to pay Rose at the end of the meal. The proffered payment was refused, of course, but Tillie continued to entertain dinner guests throughout the convention. Weilerstein, who was nineteen at the time, mostly recalled waiting on company and washing dishes. But she marveled at how her mother "managed to serve so many guests with no advance warning and without missing a session. Being an easy hostess at long or short notice was one of Mama's many gifts."[11]

Weilerstein also recalled her mother's devotion to Szold, an admiration that began long before she became a public figure. "Miss Szold's integrity, her quiet thoroughness, her gift for getting things done, her insistence on principle as a guide to action were qualities Mama understood and valued." Weilerstein shared her mother's high regard for the Hadassah founder. "Miss Szold spoke quietly, logically, with no attempt at oratory or dramatics. I liked her way of speaking. She seemed to respect the intelligence of her hearers."[12] Years later, Szold would return the compliment. In a letter to Carmel Finkelstein, wife of JTS (Jewish Theological Seminary) chancellor Louis Finkelstein, Szold wrote:

I cannot recall any attempt to bring Jewish children the content and form as so subtly charming, and I think, therefore, so effective [as *The Adventures of K'tonton*]. Besides, the authoress is a mistress of a style in every way adapted to the subject and the child reader. There is no writing down to what is erroneously in my opinion considered a child's comprehension of language. The simplicity of the style is attractive to the grown-up as I am sure, it must be to the child reader.[13]

It was precisely those managerial qualities that Tillie Rose and Henrietta Szold shared, that Sadie Weilerstein claimed she lacked. Instead, Weilerstein portrayed herself as a romantic. Under the influence of her father, she developed a keen appreciation for nature. Bernard Rose would take his daughter on bird watching outings, leisurely "*Shabbos* walks" along the steep banks of the Genesee River Gorge and through the Indian trails that lay beyond the falls.[14] As a young mother in Brooklyn, in an era when aspiring middle-class housewives prided themselves on the cleanliness or orderliness of their homes, Weilerstein had little patience for housework. She rushed through her chores so that she could take young Herschel out into the fresh air. Often mother and son would sit on the stoop of their apartment house, and she would tell him stories. Her reputation as a storyteller spread and she soon developed a following of neighborhood youngsters who came by to hear her tales.[15]

Weilerstein liked to say that she owed her writing career to her mother; were it not for Tillie Rose's persistence and proactive disposition, the stories Weilerstein concocted to amuse and edify her children would never have been published. During her visits to the Weilerstein home, Rose often listened as Weilerstein regaled young Herschel with her tales. Without consulting her daughter, she determined to ascertain their quality and marketability. "With my mother there was no gap between the thought and the act. On her next visit she took the stories I wrote and marched off to the New York Public Library [NYPL] demanding to know whether the stories were good."[16]

Joshua Bloch, librarian of the NYPL's Jewish division, referred Rose to Viking Press, which in turn steered her toward Bloch Publishing, a Jewish-owned publishing house that specialized in textbooks and other Jewish educational materials. The stories were ultimately accepted for publication and the result, six months later, was Weilerstein's first volume *What Danny Did* (Bloch, 1928).

The book's reviews in the press were overwhelmingly enthusiastic across the spectrum, from the English language organ of the German Jewish elite, the *American Hebrew*, to the Yiddish Orthodox *Jewish Morning Journal*.[17] The book was also favorably reviewed in the *United Synagogue Recorder*. Weilerstein came to the attention of Carrie Davidson, the founding editor of the National Women's League of United Synagogue magazine *Outlook*, whose husband Israel Davidson was a professor of medieval Hebrew literature at the Jewish Theological Seminary. Davidson published Weilerstein's earliest K'tonton story in 1930. "If it were not for Carrie Davidson, the first editor of Women's League *Outlook*, my K'tonton stories might have remained stories I told my own children. She kept after me, because she needed items for her children's page in the magazine. Finally, I wrote down the first K'tonton story."[18]

An Accidental Writer?

Weilerstein's eagerness to assign credit to others for launching her writing career is curious. While we have no reason to doubt the veracity of these anecdotes, one cannot help wondering why she seemed to revel in them. Was she reaching for a trope that would allow her to preserve an aura of middle-class conventionality? At first glance, this seems unlikely. Weilerstein was hardly a maverick career woman in the mold of school superintendent Julia Richman, labor organizer Rose Schneiderman, or even Henrietta Szold. In pursuing her writing she was joining the ranks of many other rabbis' and educators' wives who made virtual careers out of their involvement on the local and national levels in organizational work, institutional development and publications, often in a leadership capacity. Yet, as historian Shuly Rubin Schwartz pointed out in her study of the American Jewish *rebbetzin*, many of these women—particularly those who drew on their homemaking expertise to aid other homemakers—"actively conflated the boundaries" between the public and private realms. Weilerstein's labors to fill the void in juvenile Jewish children's literature, providing mothers with resources to "enrich their children's Jewish upbringing," certainly place her within this category.[19]

Weilerstein's pains to portray herself as an unintentional author only reinforced an impression of liminality between her personas as mother and writer, as did her tendency to locate her writing within the ambit of her motherly duties. Weilerstein habitually told interviewers that she began her writing career "by accident," making up Jewish-themed stories to tell her son only after a fruitless hunt for analogous published material.[20] "I came to write my first books out of a need," she wrote in her entry for the reference volume *Something about the Author*:

> Our four-year-old son had a shelf full of books, poems, stories and picture books about pets, farm animals, circuses and zoos, subways, taxis, steam shovels, the varied activities that filled his day. But when he shined the Sabbath candlesticks until he "could see his face in them"; when he used his tools, small but sharp, to help build a *sukkah* (harvest booth) "for real, not make-believe"; when he celebrated the whole round of Jewish holidays, each with its exciting preparations and rituals, there was no book to give him back his experience. Experiences take on an added dimension when you relive them in a book, so I "made up" the stories he needed. Eventually they were written down and got into a book, *What Danny Did*.[21]

The final sentence practically eliminates any sense of personal agency, as if the book wrote itself.

In reality, however, Weilerstein was no accidental author, and she published her first children's story long before she was a mother. From the time she was very young, her parents cultivated within her a love of books. "We were a reading family. Every Friday night, we would read to each other after dinner. While washing the dishes, my sisters and I would take the parts of the sisters in *Little Women.*" By the age of seven she was reading from the *Complete Works of Henry Wadsworth Longfellow.* Weilerstein's first foray into fiction writing came in grammar school. She composed her first fairy tale for the Sweet Violets Club, a group she organized whose members alternated reading their own stories. While summering at the family's vacation home on the shore of Lake Ontario, Weilerstein organized another social club with her friends. When it was her turn to host, she entertained her guests by reading from her own stories. In high school, Weilerstein continued writing for various school publications and while in college she became a published children's author. Her first story, titled "How Sorkie Came to America," appeared on the children's page of the *American Hebrew.*[22]

Weilerstein was also a very deliberate writer. She was constantly editing and reediting her work and she gave deep thought to the writing process. She consciously modeled her early stories on the Bank Street School style with its onomatopoeic words, repetition, and refrains. "The stories are pattern stories, not with a plot but a pattern," she explained. "They have a lot of repetition of sound effects. They are talk-along, sing-along, act-along stories." She demonstrated the technique in 1981 in a nationally broadcast radio interview: "Fish for *Shabbat,* flippedy-flop, mother will chop it, chop, chop, chop."[23] She was also careful to avoid making her stories heavy-handed and overly moralistic. She thought very little of books like *Hillel's Happy Holidays* by Mamie Goldsmith Gamoran, which in her view sacrificed artistry for didacticism. "I didn't set out to teach in my stories. Judaism was part of my life, and I loved it and wrote about it."[24]

In intimate settings, Weilerstein was more candid about the pride that she took in her work. "My mother used to say that she invented [Jewish] holiday stories," her daughter Deborah Weilerstein remembered. She was also not afraid to display a modicum of writer's vanity. "She cared a lot about her reviews. It meant a lot to her in particular to be reviewed in the non-Jewish press and magazines. She was ecstatic to receive a review in *Horn Magazine.*" She was also deeply moved when in 1980 the Association of Jewish Libraries presented her with the Sydney Taylor Body-of-Work Prize. Weilerstein carefully filed away her review clippings and selected fan mail. Another daughter, Ruth Breslow Young recalled that her mother was "a perfectionist" and "her own best critic."[25] She often did her best writing late at night and into the early morning hours. She would keep a pad by her bed and would sometimes awake at two or three o'clock in the morning and jot down an idea that came to her while she was dreaming or semiconscious. "When I can't sleep, I get up and write . . . whatever comes into my head. . . . It's called automatic writing. Sometimes the next day I tear it up and throw it away, but many, many times I keep it and improve it."[26]

The Adventures of K'tonton

K'tonton, a pious, pint-sized mischief-maker described as "a little Jewish Tom Thumb," was introduced to the world in the pages of the Conservative movement's Women's League for Conservative Judaism magazine, *Outlook*, in September 1930. Three years later, Weilerstein had accumulated enough stories for a book. But when she was unable to find a publisher, the Women's League agreed to publish the collection, and *The Adventures of K'tonton* appeared in 1935.[27]

K'tonton was inspired in part by S. Y. Agnon's story about a tiny medieval rabbi, Gadiel Hatinok, who saves a Jewish community from a blood libel. Weilerstein recalled that one evening her husband was reading the story aloud to her when their five-year-old son inquired about the fictitious rabbi. Rather than delve into the frightening details of ritual murder accusations, Weilerstein claimed that she "turned the tiny person into a thumb-sized boy much like himself, except for size, who took a ride on a chopping knife and wished he hadn't." Weilerstein's husband appropriately named the character K'tonton, which means "very tiny" in Hebrew.[28] Weilerstein was also inspired by other stories of thumblings, including Hans Christian Andersen's "Thumbelina" and the Grimm Brothers' "Tom Thumb." She paid tribute to "the many Thumblings who have preceded" K'tonton and acknowledged "her indebtedness to all of these" in the preface to *The Adventures of K'tonton*.[29]

To later generations of Conservative readers, K'tonton's ethnically homogeneous milieu might have appeared quaint. The only gentile in his Brooklyn neighborhood seemed to be the fat Irish policeman.[30] His parents attended a traditional synagogue with a women's gallery. K'tonton also celebrated somewhat obscure Jewish festivals like Lag Ba'Omer along with the more widely observed holidays like Passover and Hanukkah. But K'tonton, as drawn by Jeannette Berkowitz, was well on his way to cultural integration. For the most part, the *arba kanfot* (ritual fringes) that he wore under his shirt remained tucked away from view. And although he donned a big *yarmulke* on his head for holidays and ceremonies, he went bareheaded when he was at play.

K'tonton's family was also on the road to middle-class respectability. They already internalized America's "cult of true womanhood"; a clear division of labor existed between K'tonton's stay-at-home mother and his working father. While their community was ethnically homogeneous, the family did not live in an urban ghetto enclave.[31] Nowhere in the volume does Weilerstein specify the type of dwelling in which the family lives. But clues in various stories indicate that K'tonton's family lives in a house rather than an apartment building, possibly a brownstone. Perhaps, K'tonton's was one of the many families that migrated during the 1920s to new middle-class Jewish neighborhoods or "gilded ghettos" in Brooklyn and the Bronx.[32] In terms of their level of religious observance, they appeared to resemble the so-called reasonable or modern Orthodox or traditional Conservative. The dividing line between the two movements was still very murky in the 1920s and early 1930s. Such Jews placed high value on the observance of Sabbath, festivals, dietary laws, and synagogue worship, but tried to remain as unobtrusive as possible in the public domain. Like K'tonton, young boys at the modern Orthodox Ramaz Academy in Manhattan, founded in 1937, went bareheaded or donned inconspicuous caps on the street but wore their *yarmulkes* in Jewish settings.[33]

Weilerstein's stories took the reader through the cycle of Jewish holidays. But her purpose was not so much to model holiday observances as Jewish values. More often than not, the Jewish values she stressed were humanistic and universal. Perched on his father's Talmud, K'tonton recites his *shiur*, or lesson: "*Tzaar baale hayyim de oraita.* Causing pain to living creatures is forbidden by the Torah." He saved the sparrows from a big black cat on Shabbat Shirah, visited the sick on Purim, and rescued a calf that was separated from its mother on Shavuot eve. K'tonton also scrupulously observed particularistic ritual commandments and celebrated Jewish holidays and customs with gusto. An old woman in the synagogue gallery summed things up when she called K'tonton "a wonder child. Even when he runs away, where does he run to? The synagogue!"[34]

But in emphasizing the universal as well as the particular, Weilerstein was suggesting to her readers that there was nothing about being a good Jew that would stand in the way of their being good Americans. In one story she even found rabbinic sanction for the peculiarly American penchant for prizing the practical over the abstract or abstruse (and for American Jews' similar privileging of *tachlis* [the practical and purposeful] over traditional Jewish learning). K'tonton's father instructs him, "Don't you remember what the Rabbis say, 'Not learning but doing is the chief thing'? I'd rather have you show tender mercy to God's creatures than be the greatest scholar in the world."[35]

In the introduction to *The Best of K'tonton* (1980), Francine Klagsbrun commented on "K'tonton's special combination of mischief and morality, of Jewish observance and universal values," which "reaffirm[s] the things we believe in most strongly."[36] Weilerstein, for her part, asserted that "K'tonton is unique only in his size and his precocity. His dreams and ambitions, the festivals he celebrates, the ceremonials he delights in, are shared in varying degree by Jewish children everywhere."[37] K'tonton provided an ideal model of cultural integration. He was identifiably American in the language that he spoke and the clothes that he wore, yet remained immersed and literate in Jewish culture and traditions. Moreover, his penchant for mischief and troublemaking encouraged readers to identify with him. Weilerstein succeeded in avoiding the "syrupy didacticism" that plagued so many earlier works of Jewish children's fiction.

Weilerstein continued to provide affirmatively Jewish models of cultural integration in such books as *What the Moon Brought* (Jewish Publication Society, 1942) and *Molly and the Sabbath Queen* (Behrman House, 1949). However, by the 1950s, younger American Jews were feeling increasingly secure Jewishly and more inclined to take for granted their American identity. In part, the shift in attitude was generational. Second and third generation youngsters had been socialized in the public schools and on the city streets with little or no direct memory of the immigrant experience. But a variety of socioeconomic factors also influenced the environment, including the decline of antisemitism, the elimination of quotas at many universities, the postwar religious revival, and the rapid ascension of Jews into the ranks of the middle and upper middle classes. As Jews set down roots in the suburbs they increasingly adopted the ethos of their neighbors, which presupposed church (or synagogue) membership and (at least occasional) attendance. Their tendency to conform was reinforced by the rise of television and the political atmosphere engendered by the Cold War.

Integral to the new atmosphere was an improvement in Jewish-Christian relations. The wartime mood emboldened an emerging "intergroup relations" movement spearheaded by a variety of religious, civil rights, defense and welfare organizations, and unions. By the postwar period, their ranks included Jewish organizations like the Anti-Defamation League, the American Jewish Committee, and the American Jewish Congress. Liberal rabbis increasingly placed social justice and interfaith dialogue at the heart of their rabbinates, while publishing houses and denominational commissions of Jewish education published textbooks and other materials designed to promote brotherhood, tolerance, and religious coexistence.[38]

The new social climate was reflected in Weilerstein's book *Dick: the Horse That Kept the Sabbath* (Bloch, 1955), a largely autobiographical story of a turn-of-the-century urban Jewish family that sends its lame horse to live with gentile friends on a country farm rather than having it euthanized. *Dick* culminated a stylistic transition for Weilerstein away from the Bank Street technique to a narrative-centered approach. According to some reviewers, it also signified a departure from the more transparently educational tone of her earlier books, an observation to which Weilerstein would take exception. "The autobiographical factor prevents this work from being as 'pure' in Jewish educational value as her previous books," argued Deborah Karp. "Hearing that Dick helped take beer bottles to a brewery or that Papa belonged to the Odd Fellows does not particularly add to Jewish appreciations."[39] Yet as Karp herself admitted, the book showcased a variety of Jewish teachings, particularly, the importance of compassion for animals. When Papa returns from work he declines to eat until after the horse is fed. Following the biblical injunction, Papa also refuses to allow Dick to work on the Sabbath. When Dick breaks his leg, the veterinarian suggests shooting the horse, pointing out that he could no longer be useful to the family. But Papa responds indignantly: "He'll be of use to himself."

Arguably, the greatest Jewish act of kindness comes at the story's end when the family sends Dick to live out his final days on the country farm, where the dirt roads would be easier on his leg and he could spend the Sabbath in the pasture rather than a stable. Significantly, however, non-Jews are also shown performing acts of loving-kindness. The non-Jewish Cole family not only takes in Dick, but also respects the "Jewish" horse's Sabbath.

> "Mr. Cole doesn't keep Shabbos," Rebekah reminded her [sister]. "He keeps Sunday."
>
> But do you know what Mr. Cole said when he came to fetch Dick the next week? He said, "Don't worry about Dick's Sabbath. Dick will rest on the seventh day as he always has."
>
> Then to show them that he knew about their Sabbath, Mr. Cole recited from the Bible. . . . After this the family felt sure that all would go well with Dick. And it did.[40]

The non-Jewish Cole family is presented sympathetically as exemplifying homespun American values. Mr. Cole is a wounded Civil War veteran who proudly marches in Decoration Day parades; Mrs. Cole makes homemade taffy for the children in her large country kitchen. The couple attends church every Sunday. Most important, perhaps, they respect the traditions and culture of their Jewish friends. The relationship between the Coles and the Jewish family is warm and intimate. Weilerstein evinced strong sympathy for interfaith initiatives. Growing up, she saw that her parents maintained social as well as business contacts with non-Jews and worked side by side with non-Jews on a variety of political causes.

Despite the centrality of Sabbath observance to the story, the Jewish values that Weilerstein stressed were overwhelmingly universalistic. Her earlier books also modeled Jewish humanistic values, like giving *tzedakah*, visiting the sick and even the prohibition of inflicting cruelty to animals, which underpins the *Dick* story, but they were presented within the context of particularistic ritual and ceremonial observances associated with the Jewish holidays. In *Dick*, even the particularistic was spun as universal:

> "Supper's on the table," Mama would call as they passed the kitchen door.
>
> "Coming," Papa would answer, "as soon as I feed Dick."
>
> "Can't Dick wait?" Mama would ask. "The soup will get cold, but the hay won't."
>
> This went on day after day, until one day Papa strode through the

kitchen into the middle room, opened the curtained bookcase door, and drew out a big book with Hebrew letters. It was a book of the Talmud.

"Do you know what it says in here?" Papa asked Mama. "It says 'It is forbidden for a man to eat until he has fed his animals.'"

Then Papa hurried back to the barn where Dick and Davy were waiting.

"Books people need!" Papa grumbled, as he tossed down a forkful of hay. "Their own sense should tell them."

He turned to Dick.

"I can get my own food, but you *can't* get your own food. Right, Dick?"

Dick nodded his head and took a mouthful of hay.

"Then should *you* wait for your supper, or should I wait?" Papa asked.

Dick lifted his head with hay still sticking out of the corners of his mouth, and poked his nose against Papa.

"Dick's answering you, Papa. He says *you* should wait," Davy cried excitedly.

"Of course," Papa said. "Dick knows without books. Dick's got horse sense."[41]

Here, Weilerstein was instructing her readers that Judaism's ethical code was as much a product of common sense as divine directive. As such, Jewish values could be equated with American or human values. Gentiles (at least in America) were essentially decent people and should be embraced as neighbors. It is unclear whether Weilerstein was implicitly going one step further and rejecting the belief in Jews as a chosen people. Her husband Reuben considered himself to be a Kaplan disciple, but it is uncertain whether either endorsed this particular tenet of Kaplan's theology. But even if she accepted chosenness, it is apparent that she did not equate it with superiority.

Ten and a Kid: *Romancing the Shtetl*

One of the more interesting aspects of *Dick* is its Rochester setting. In this respect it served as inadvertent counternarrative to Sydney Taylor's popular 1951 *All of-a-Kind Family*, which more than any other children's book contributed to the sacralization of the Lower East Side in the collective American Jewish memory as *the* authentic turn-of-the-century American Jewish "cultural homeland."[42] Weilerstein, to be sure, was tapping into the same nostalgic appetite that Taylor had whetted. Weilerstein offered her readers a somewhat more established family whose relationship to its American surroundings was less studied and more instinctive than Taylor's. But the two families were similar in other important respects: they lived richly textured

Jewish lives largely untouched by the specters of antisemitism and assimilation. Both books glorified what they presented as a simpler, more wholesome time.

The historian Steven Zipperstein noted that whereas urban Jews living in ethnic neighborhoods were able to take community for granted, suburban Jews were largely preoccupied with community building. This in turn encouraged a heightened consciousness about identity and assimilation, and a sacralization of emblems of a past gone by. Part of the allure of the Lower East Side was its continued accessibility to tourists and local suburbanites. As one scholar explained, "It had within it just enough residue of the past, just enough markers of times gone by to seem authentic. It even still had some Jews, many of whom sold pickles, bread, kosher meat and Jewish books."[43]

The romance with the past soon extended to eastern Europe as well. Mark Zborowski and Elizabeth Herzog's 1952 anthropological study *Life Is with People* did much to enshrine the image of the shtetl in the American Jewish imagination, along with works like Abraham Joshua Heschel's 1950 *The Earth Is the Lord's*, and Irving Howe and Eliezer Greenberg's popular 1954 anthology *A Treasury of Yiddish Stories*. What Philip Roth aptly described as "shtetl kitsch" went mainstream in 1964 when *Fiddler on the Roof* opened on Broadway.[44]

Suburban American Jews' increasing fascination with their immigrant origins was understood at the time as paradigmatic of Marcus Hansen's theory about immigrant cultural tension: "What the son wishes to forget, the grandson wishes to remember."[45] More recent studies have to some extent continued to view the creation of a "memory culture" around the Lower East Side and the shtetl in generational terms. "The more comfortable and acculturated Jews became in America, the more at ease they were in discussing where they had come from, the 'authentic' culture of the eastern European shtetl associated with their grandparents, and the early years of their families' experiences in America," wrote Hasia Diner. Historians have also recognized the profound impact of the destruction of European Jewry on the American Jewish community's relation to its past. The recognition in the postwar years that theirs had become the single largest Jewish community in the world, saddled with the responsibility to keep Judaism alive, spurred a new interest in American Jewish history and memory and lent urgency to preservation efforts, like the rescue of tens of thousands of books and archival materials that had been housed at the Yiddish Institute for Jewish Research in Vilna, and the establishment of the American Jewish Archives in Cincinnati. Postwar Jews elevated the biblical injunction *zakhor* (remember) to a Jewish imperative. For many, the Holocaust became *the* interpretive lens through which they conjured up the past. Regrettably, as Zipperstein points out, the result was often "a past flattened into something relentlessly grim or (incredible as the juxtaposition may seem) insipid and sweet."[46]

Sensing, perhaps, that the timing was right, Weilerstein set out in the late 1950s to write a book based on the stories her mother told her about growing up in a small Lithuanian shtetl. Her efforts produced a volume that she counted among her favorites, *Ten and a Kid*, which was published in 1961 by Doubleday.[47] While acknowledging her own creative license, Weilerstein considered the book an act of remembrance:

> *Ten and a Kid* had its beginning when I was a little girl with curls. Having tangles combed out is not usually a pleasant experience. But my mother had a way with curls. She gave each one a name, usually the name of someone out of her childhood in Lithuania, and told a story about it. She had the gift of vivid speech. Through her stories, the world of her childhood came alive for me — so alive that the people in her little town went on living in my imagination, growing, changing, increasing, as living people do, until — more than sixty years later, after the stories had gone through many incarnations and had been told and retold first to my children, later to my grandchildren — they finally got into a book.[48]

Unlike her previous books, which targeted the nursery school and kindergarten set, these stories were geared to an elementary school, primarily female, audience, the same demographic that avidly consumed Sydney Taylor's volumes. Whether Weilerstein consciously patterned her book after Taylor's is unknown. Clearly, however, the commercial success of *All-of-a-Kind Family* helped to convince Doubleday and Jewish publishing houses like JPS that the market for Jewish-themed juvenile fiction extended beyond holiday stories.[49]

Illustrator Janina Domanska's drawing of the large family joyfully dancing the horah with their pet goat, which adorns the book's dust jacket, suggests a tale dripping in sweet sentimentalism. Indeed, the stories sometimes veer in that direction. Predictably, the family is dirt poor yet their house is overflowing with Jewish values and Yiddishkeit. Weilerstein also manages to convey the pathos of shtetl life with a soft touch. She at once observes and subtly undermines the cruelest implications of the shtetl's rigid class system. The mean existence of the have-nots is consistently leavened by acts of loving-kindness from those who are better off, and, perhaps, miracles from God. But the story never descends into unadulterated schmaltz due to Weilerstein's gifts as a storyteller, her humor and wit, and her ultimate regard for practicality and common sense. Even in this most mystical of Weilerstein's books, the miracles are of the everyday variety, never straining the reader's credulity.

One aspect of the book that stands out today, but which drew little attention from reviewers at the time, is its protofeminist message. Inquisitive eight-year-old Reizel, the most developed of the family's eight children, is determined to educate herself despite her family's meager circumstances and conventional attitudes about gender roles. In one story, she surreptitiously becomes a regular attendee of a weekday all-male class in the House of Study and eventually teaches herself how to read Hebrew. In another, she convinces her parents and her little brother's Hebrew teacher to let her attend *heder* (school), which was traditionally restricted to boys. Reizel's enthusiasm extends to the fulfillment of *mitzvot* (commandments) that are incumbent only on men. She becomes enamored of the Holy Maiden of Ludmir, who reputedly donned *tallis* (prayer shawl) and *tefillin* (phylacteries) and decides that the women of her family should voluntarily take on the commandment of eating in the *sukkah*, the booth that male Jews traditionally ate and slept in during the fall harvest holiday of Sukkoth.

Weilerstein implicitly contrasted Reizel's ambitions with the habitual concerns of her momme, which revolved primarily around putting food on the table and marrying off her daughters. But if Weilerstein characterized Reizel's actions as unconventional, she did not paint them as subversive. She carefully noted that the Maiden of Ludmir was praised for her piety not excoriated for her avant-garde behavior. Moreover, the mitzvah that Reizel ultimately adopted was widely observed by contemporary American Jewish women. But Weilerstein knew full well that the wider principle that she was touting had broad and potentially radical implications including the ordination of women. She based Reizel on her suffragette mother. "The law says a man is required to put on *tefillin*. It does not say that a woman is not permitted. A woman is excused. But if the Maid of Ludimir did not want to be excused, if she preferred to take on the commandment, what was to prevent her?" Weilerstein rhetorically asked.[50]

If Weilerstein ever imagined herself as a rabbi, she never told her family. But in her later years she adapted easily to the changing role of women in the synagogue. Daughter Debbie also remembers her mother as a maverick, less punctilious than her husband and in-laws in her observance of Jewish law. Weilerstein took a relaxed approach to *kashrut* observance that was fairly typical of the era and eagerly accepted the Rabbinical Assembly's 1955 decision to permit the use of electricity on the Sabbath despite her husband's misgivings, yet she was zealous in her fealty to pet causes. Her love of nature, which was cultivated at a young age by her father, evolved in later years into a strong support for conservationism and other environmental causes. She gave expression to these convictions in her 1976 volume, *K'tonton on an Island in the Sea*, which was illustrated by Michael Berenstain. At the same time, she became the driving force behind the establishment of a children's nature center in Atlantic City, and at eighty-three launched a successful campaign to revitalize the Atlantic City Environmental Museum. *K'tonton on an Island in the Sea* was set on one of the many islands in the Atlantic City coastal area and Berenstain, a Philadelphia native, lovingly evoked the local flora and fauna from a Lilliputian's perspective.[51]

Weilerstein's other long-standing commitment, fostered by her pioneering "Hadassah lady" mother and reinforced by her connections with the Women's League and her husband's attachment to Mordecai Kaplan, was to Zionism. Thinkers like Kaplan and philosopher Horace Kallen espoused a Zionism that was consonant with democracy and liberalism. For the first generation, Zionist lodges, societies, and youth groups became vehicles of Americanization, advancing American adjustment through their educational, social and welfare activities. Moreover, Zionism became a central component of the Jewish Theological Seminary's ideology. Conservative leaders recognized that "Zionism, which contained the peoplehood element in its most pristine form, offered an opportunity to bridge the gulf between the ethnic and religious components of Judaism," and were among the most steadfast proponents of cultural and political Zionism on the American scene.[52] Weilerstein encouraged identification with the Zionist project in her earliest books. In *The Adventures of K'tonton*, for example, our hero wants Hanukkah *gelt* (coins) so that he can fill his blue and white JNF *tzedakah* (charity) box. "See my Palestine box—the blue one with the white star. I'm going to fill it to the very top. Clinkety, clink, away the pennies will go to Palestine! They're to buy land, you know—for the Jewish farmers, the *Halutzim*. You ought to get a big piece of land with a whole box full of money." In another story, K'tonton asks a bird to bring his New Year's greetings to an almond tree in Palestine that was planted in honor of his birth.

As Jews became more acculturated, Zionism was promoted as a means of maintaining ethnic cohesion. This became especially true on the postwar suburban frontier and in communities like Miami and Los Angeles, where by the 1960s support for Israel became a primary expression of Jewish identity.[53] American Jews performed their attachments in a variety of ways, including giving philanthropy, buying Israel Bonds, learning Israeli folk dances, teaching their kids Israeli songs, and decorating their homes with made-in-Israel Judaica, prints, wall hangings and other objects. As air travel became more affordable, they also began visiting the country in increasing numbers. The Weilersteins made the trip in 1955, and their visit became the basis for *K'tonton in Israel*, which was published by the Women's League in 1964. Weilerstein later explained: "I didn't mean to write a book, but wherever I went I saw K'tonton."[54]

Parents who grew up with the thumbling were delighted to have a new book of stories to share with their children. It had been almost three decades since the publication of the original volume. But what stands out about the book years later is how accurately it captured American Jews' growing romance with Israel prior to the June 1967 Six-Day War. The book succeeded in vividly conjuring up the Israel of the American Jewish imagination. As with

Ten and a Kid, the tone is conveyed in the image on the book's dust jacket, which is Lawrence of Arabia meets the Jewish National Fund. Illustrator Elizabeth Safian pictures K'tonton sitting on a sunflower under a palm tree with a *kova tembel* (sunhat) on his head and a knapsack on his back, gazing at an Israeli village nestled among the dunes in an expansive vista of flowing sands, camels, and Bedouin tents.

Weilerstein gives her readers the Israel they want and expect: an old-new land existing in harmonious balance, where Bedouin hospitality evokes the open tent of the biblical patriarch Abraham while kibbutzniks make the desert bloom. Her primary interests are the historical sites of the ancient Israelites and the modern achievements of the "new Jews." Weilerstein's Israel is airbrushed of its impoverished immigrant development towns — but not of its immigrants, who are exhibited as poster-children for the county's diversity. Nor does she dwell on the bustle of city life in Tel Aviv. Indeed, Weilerstein's approach is epitomized by her treatment of Haifa, which merits attention in the book only as the ancient setting for the biblical stories of the prophet Elijah and the modern-day home of the Technion, Israel's premier scientific institute. Just as Elijah worked wonders atop Mount Carmel in ancient times, she wrote, so too, were modern miracles being performed by Israeli scientists on the mountain today.[55]

Weilerstein invites her readers to experience Israel vicariously through K'tonton's adventures. In some stories, K'tonton effectively becomes a stand-in for Joe American Jewish tourist, intent on finding the tree that his JNF (Jewish National Fund) pennies helped to plant or trying to discern Lot's wife (whom God purportedly turned into a pillar of salt) from among the jagged peaks overlooking the Dead Sea. More often than not, however, Weilerstein imagines that K'tonton's size enables him to experience Israel in ways American Jewish tourists only wished they could. The barbed wire fence bisecting pre-June 1967 Jerusalem hardly impedes K'tonton, who manages to visit the Western Wall and Rachel's Tomb — both in Jordanian territory. In another story he inadvertently discovers a parchment scroll from the days of the second-century general Simon Bar Kokhba in a Judean cave; while in a third, scientists at a top-secret Negev facility send K'tonton into the earth's orbit aboard a supposedly unmanned Israeli rocket ship.

Weilerstein's skill at channeling American Jewish perceptions of Israel finds no better expression than in her representation of Arabs. She was careful to distinguish between Israeli Arabs and those K'tonton encounters in Jordanian-held territory. The former were "friendly Arabs," while the latter were often hostile. In the dusty Negev town of Beersheba, which Weilerstein like other Americans compared to the Wild West, the kibbutzniks and the Arabs were akin to "cowboys" and "Indians." She was quick to romanticize the Negev Bedouin as authentic bearers of biblical nomadic culture, "like Abraham in the Bible." When a young Bedouin Arab offers K'tonton desert hospitality, K'tonton asks the boy if he is the patriarch Isaac. Upon discovering that the boy's name is Selim, K'tonton muses: "He couldn't be kinder to a stranger if he really were Abraham's son."[56]

Like many American Jews, Weilerstein sensed the hand of divine providence in Israel's victory in 1948. "Five armies came with guns, and tanks, and grenades, and airplanes with bombs. . . . But with God's help the few can win against the many. The Jews fought hard for their land, and Israel and Jerusalem were saved . . . except the old part of Jerusalem behind the walls."[57] She provides her readers with little understanding of the underlying causes of the Arab-Israeli conflict and even less appreciation for the perspective of the Palestinian Arabs. To the extent that she engages in political contextualization, the Jewish claim on Israel is presented as a matter of fairness, a core American value (albeit rather simplistically defined). When K'tonton overhears an Arab tour guide in East Jerusalem complaining to his group that his family was evicted from their home in the West Jerusalem Qatamon neighborhood, the thumbling recalls that his friend Shimshon's family resides in Qatamon, conceivably in this very Arab's house:

> K'tonton knew that Shimshon's grandmother used to live in the Old City near the western wall. But the war came and Arab soldiers blew up her house, so she had to find a new place to live.
>
> K'tonton felt he had to explain: "Sir," he said, raising his voice so high, so that the man might hear. "Shimshon's grandmother didn't want to go to your house. She wanted to stay in her own house. She too, is sad, — for her house, and because she cannot pray at the wall of the Holy Temple."[58]

The Arab becomes so incensed that he threatens to "wipe [K'tonton] off the earth." But though the Arabs Weilerstein imagines in East Jerusalem reinforce violent and primitive stereotypes, she does not evince fear or unbridled enmity for Palestinian Arabs. Indeed the Arab children K'tonton sees in Bethlehem "laughing and chattering" seem no different than Israeli children, except that they speak Arabic rather than Hebrew. "K'tonton wished he could speak to them. They didn't look like enemies. He remembered that Arabs were Children of Ishmael, Father Abraham's son." Weilerstein follows up on this thought a few pages later. A note K'tonton surreptitiously plants between the Western Wall's massive Herodian stones reads: "Please, God, let the Children of Israel and the Children of Ishmael be friends. For the sake of Abraham our Father, speedily in our day."[59] In short, Weilerstein manages to reinforce American Jewish perceptions of Arabs both as warlike enemies and noble savages — modern-day Bible characters — while expressing an abiding, arguably naive belief in the possibility of Arab Jewish coexistence. Of course, Weilerstein was writing in a pre-1967 environment, before the ascension of Yasir Arafat and the Palestine Liberation Organization and the radicalization of the population in the West Bank and Gaza under Israeli occupation.

K'tonton in the Circus: *Bounded and Unbounded*

In the late 1970s, Sadie Rose Weilerstein entered the twilight of her career as a writer. Often deriving inspiration from the trees that grew outside the window of her independent living facility apartment in Rockville, Maryland, she continued to write stories and poems until she was incapacitated by partial blindness and frailty. But even in her final book, which was, appropriately enough, a collection of K'tonton stories titled *K'tonton in the Circus* (Jewish Publication Society, 1981), she remained an astute student of the American Jewish experience. The book's plot was classic K'tonton: the pocket-size hero is beguiled by his own curiosity and credulity to join a circus when he mistakes a clown on a white horse for the prophet Elijah. Its theme had an equally familiar ring to it: retaining one's Jewish loyalty while remaining a full-fledged citizen of the larger (non-Jewish) world.

Yet, while the continuities between *K'tonton in the Circus* and Weilerstein's previous volumes were manifest, Weilerstein once again updated her message to reflect the contemporary zeitgeist. Indeed, there is more than a passing similarity between K'tonton's predicament and that of Joel Fleischman, the New York Jewish doctor who establishes a practice in the utterly *goyische* Alaskan town of Cicely, in the popular television series *Northern Exposure* (1990–95). Just as that roughly contemporaneous "fish out of water" program cleverly upended the not-so-secret Jewish belief in *goyische kop* (non-Jewish inferiority) and brushed aside perennial Jewish fears of latent antisemitism, so too did Weilerstein's book present a gentile America populated by warm and sympathetic individuals who were curious but respectful of K'tonton's faith and traditions.

It could be argued with some justification that a circus troupe comprised of outsiders and misfits like the Fat Lady and the Human Skeleton was particularly sensitized to the plight of the other. But like the eccentric population of fictional Cicely, Alaska, the circus in all its human diversity could also be understood as a metaphor for multicultural America. In Weilerstein's story, Clarence the clown presented K'tonton with a makeshift Hanukkah lamp, while Lillibelle, a daughter of one of the circus hands, offered up a box of candles left over from her previous birthday. Meanwhile, the flapjack man eagerly fried up potato pancakes including tiny ones made in a special doll-size pan especially for K'tonton. The only impediment to his new friends' full participation in the festivities was their inability to correctly pronounce the holiday's name. "Some called it Tshanukkah or Kanukkah. But everybody got the 'Happy' right," Weilerstein wrote. She added that K'tonton was so excited that he momentarily forgot that his friends did not speak Hebrew.[60] Thus

Weilerstein symbolically erased, albeit fleetingly, the boundary between Jew and gentile.

Thank goodness, although K'tonton grew older and taller over the years, he remained safely prepubescent. Even so, it is clear from K'tonton's interactions with his circus friends that Weilerstein envisioned the performance of American Jewish identity in part as a negotiation of inherent tensions between American pluralism and Jewish particularism. To be sure, K'tonton's celebration of Hanukkah in 1981 was a far cry from the 1930s stories where Jewish holidays were celebrated only in the company of other Jews. Nevertheless, unlike the creators and writers of *Northern Exposure*, Weilerstein retained the category of purity and pollution as a facet of Jewish ethno-religious identity even as she assiduously strove to explore and exploit the permeability of Jewish-gentile boundaries. For example, while the thought of K'tonton violating Jewish dietary laws was unimaginable, she portrayed K'tonton adapting to his new surroundings, finding a way to eat alongside his friends, but on separate miniature-size dishes. K'tonton gladly ate the cook's home-baked bread, which was made with vegetable shortening, baked potatoes, hardboiled eggs, as well cold food like salad and tuna fish. Weilerstein wrote that "Daisy [the Fat Lady] was glad her diet wasn't like K'tonton's. 'But it's his religion,' she explained to the others. 'We have to help him.'"[61]

K'tonton's interactions with non-Jews in Weilerstein's final book were not unlike those of the Jewish and non-Jewish families in *Dick: The Horse That Kept the Sabbath*. Yet they pushed the ecumenical envelope beyond the level of mutual respect. K'tonton's circus friends did not merely show consideration for K'tonton's religious differences; they actively celebrated with him. Her exploration of this issue was somewhat blunted because she sidestepped the real December dilemma faced by many American Jews: how to approach Christmas. Would K'tonton have been able to show a similar appreciation for his friends' holiday and celebrate with them? One wonders whether Weilerstein deliberately chose for K'tonton to be reunited with his family before Christmas so as to avoid grappling with the predicament.

Conclusion

Writing about author Sydney Taylor's *All-of-a-Kind Family* series, June Cummins observed that the books "validate[d]" Jewish identity and traditions while simultaneously promoting American acculturation and assimilation. Taylor's books were as much about "becoming American" as they were about "being Jewish." Taylor, she remarked, depicted an "assimilative process that works, ultimately, to pull her characters slowly away from their traditional roots. . . . Accurately reflecting the experience of the majority of second-generation immigrant Jews, Taylor widens the world of her characters, expanding their horizons, but at the same time turning their attention towards

American values and away from Jewish values."[62] For Sadie Rose Weilerstein, too, the integration process of second generation American Jews serves as an unspoken contextual backdrop for many of her stories. But unlike Taylor, Weilerstein refused to view Americanization as necessarily a zero sum game. Well into the postwar era, her books were countercultural because they sought to subvert the predominant melting pot ethos, substituting instead a view that was more consonant with cultural pluralism, as articulated by the philosopher Horace Kallen. America, he famously opined, should be likened to a symphony; each ethnic group played its own instrument creating a harmonic and distinctly American sound.[63]

Even in the 1970s and 1980s, when the ethos of multiculturalism seemed to have prevailed over that of the melting pot, Weilerstein refused to peddle a facile, symbolic ethnicity in her books. She allowed that environmental factors profoundly affected the ways in which American Jewishness evolved over time. But she rejected the notion that evolution implied attenuation and dilution. Consider, for example, the evolution of K'tonton's celebration of Hanukkah. In the original *Outlook* magazine Hanukkah story, K'tonton took a ride on a runaway *trendel* (top) and lamented that he had not received any Hanukkah *gelt* to place in his blue and white JNF *tzedakah* box for the *halutzim* (pioneers) in Palestine. In *K'tonton in the Circus*, K'tonton played *dreidel* with Sylvia the Seal, and his celebration of Hanukkah incorporated the American tradition of gift-giving associated with Christmas. On an anthropological level, the Zionization and Americanization of Hanukkah, indeed the elevation of this minor Jewish holiday into the second most widely observed festival on the Jewish calendar, represented a textbook example of acculturation and the "invention of tradition." But none of this, Weilerstein reminds us, detracts from its current authenticity.[64]

Clearly, Weilerstein was often writing for a narrower, more tradition-minded audience than Taylor. While Taylor's adventures of Momma's girls found an eager audience among elementary-age children in Jewishly identified families, she was also an early crossover success. Her books were published by Follett and were designed to be equally accessible for Jewish and gentile youngsters. Indeed, as Cummins recounts, when Taylor's first volume was in prepublication, her editor at Follett was forever fretting about the book's potential marketability. Her repeated appeals led Taylor to insert a Fourth of July celebration that was not in the book's original draft as well as play up a subplot involving the book's two most prominent non-Jewish characters. Similar pressure may have also influenced Taylor's decision to significantly pare down the use of Yiddish and Hebrew words in her books. Thus, *challe* became "white bread," and *Shabbos* became "the Sabbath."[65] Weilerstein, on the contrary, recognizing language as a fundamental component of religio-ethnicity, liberally peppered her volumes with Yiddish and Hebrew nouns and aphorisms. Then again, only one of her volumes was published by a non-Jewish press. Her books were initially marketed to the Jewish mothers (and grandmothers) who read *Outlook* magazine and joined Hadassah; they became fixtures in Jewish bookstores and postwar synagogue gift shops as opposed to the children's section of the local bookseller.

In *The Adventures of K'tonton* and other early volumes, Weilerstein offered interwar readers and their children models of how to be Jewish in America. A product of the gilded Jewish ghettos of interwar Brooklyn, K'tonton was an archetype of American Jewish integration designed by a *rebbetzin-cum-children's* author concerned about Jewish survival and integration in an environment of assiduous acculturation. As postwar American Jewish children increasingly took their bifurcated identity for granted, Weilerstein responded. Increasingly she used her stories to shape and enrich her readers' Jewish identification by contributing to the memory culture of the Jewish past and nurturing a connection with the modern state of Israel. Anticipating the rise of eco-Judaism she also sought to deepen American Jews' spiritual connection with their natural environments. Throughout her writing career Weilerstein implicitly acknowledged that integration remained an ongoing project, that American Jews were still in the process of *becoming*. Weilerstein's books provide a valuable and often fascinating lens through which to chart the evolution of American Jewish identity in the twentieth century.

NOTES

1. Rochelle Saidel, "Children's Author Still Delights at Age 91," *Detroit Jewish News*, August 16, 1985. Weilerstein made almost identical remarks during a 1981 interview with Martin Bookspan on the radio program *The Eternal Light*. See, "A Conversation with Sadie Rose Weilerstein," *The Eternal Light*, program no. 1440, NBC Radio Network, June 14, 1981. Produced under the auspices of the Jewish Theological Seminary of America.

2. Deborah Weilerstein, interview with the author, June 8, 2004.

3. Helen Mintz Belitsky, "K'tonton's Mother Recalls Her Boy: Sadie Rose Weilerstein at 98," *Washington Jewish Week*, November 26, 1992.

4. Sadie Rose Weilerstein, *The Adventures of K'tonton: A Little Jewish Tom Thumb* (New York: League Press, 1935), 9.

5. Saidel, "Children's Author Still Delights."

6. Jeffrey M. Green, "Hereby Hangs a Tale," *Jerusalem Post Magazine*, June 10, 1983.

7. Judith Sloan Deutsch, "Author Sadie Rose Weilerstein at 90: Her Focus Is the Future," *Washington Jewish Week*, July 26, 1984, 3; Belitsky, "K'tonton's Mother Recalls Her Boy"; "Sadie Rose Weilerstein, Author," *Washington Post*, June 24, 1993; obituary press release, June 23, 1993, in possession of the author; dedication program for the Sadie Rose Weilerstein Children's Corner of the Isaac Franck Jewish Public Library, Board of Jewish Education of Greater Washington, Sunday April 24, 1994, in possession of the author.

8. Deborah Weilerstein, interview with the author, June 8, 2004.

9. Deutsch, "Author Sadie Rose Weilerstein at 90," 3.

10. Sadie Rose Weilerstein, typescript, recollections on the occasion of Rochester Ha-

dassah's seventy-fifth anniversary, 1989, revised, January 28, 1992. Copy in possession of the author.

11. Ibid.

12. Ibid.

13. Henrietta Szold to Carmel Finkelstein, February 9, 1936. Copy in possession of the author.

14. Sadie Rose Weilerstein, "Trees through the Years," ca. 1978. A poem shared with the author by Deborah Weilerstein.

15. Belitsky, "K'tonton's Mother Recalls Her Boy."

16. Ibid.

17. Bloch Publishing undated publicity material for *What Danny Did*. In possession of the author.

18. Rochelle Saidel, "K'tonton's 'Mother' Is Still Writing at 90," *Philadelphia Jewish Exponent*, October 5, 1984.

19. Shuly Rubin Schwartz, *The Rabbi's Wife: The Rebbetzin in American Jewish Life* (New York: New York University Press, 2006), 219, 73.

20. Saidel, "K'tonton's 'Mother' Is Still Writing." For examples of similar statements about how she began her writing career "by accident," see Belitsky, "K'tonton's Mother Recalls Her Boy," and Deutsch, "Author Sadie Rose Weilerstein at 90."

21. *Something about the Author*, s.v. "Weilerstein, Sadie Rose," 249–50.

22. Weilerstein, "Trees through the Years"; Belitsky, "K'tonton's Mother Recalls Her Boy"; Deutsch, "Author Sadie Rose Weilerstein at 90."

23. Belitsky, "K'tonton's Mother Recalls Her Boy"; Deutsch, "Author Sadie Rose Weilerstein at 90"; "A Conversation with Sadie Rose Weilerstein," *Eternal Light*, radio program.

24. Belitsky, "K'tonton's Mother Recalls Her Boy."

25. Deborah Weilerstein, interview with the author; Belitsky, "K'tonton's Mother Recalls Her Boy."

26. "Sadie Rose Weilerstein: K'tonton's Creator Still at Work," *Moment*, October 1990.

27. See Francine Klagsbrun's introduction to *The Best of K'tonton* (Philadelphia: Jewish Publication Society, 1980), 9–12, and Jonathan Sarna, "From K'tonton to the Torah," *Moment* (October 1990), 46–47. Sarna's dating of the first K'tonton story to 1920 is a misprint.

28. Sarna, "From K'tonton to the Torah," 46; Weilerstein is quoted in Jonathan Sarna, *The Americanization of Jewish Culture, 1888–1988* (Philadelphia: Jewish Publication Society, 1989), 171.

29. Weilerstein, *Adventures of K'tonton*, 9.

30. While in *The Adventures of K'tonton* Weilerstein never explicitly states that K'tonton lives in Brooklyn, she does so in a later volume, *K'tonton in the Circus* (Philadelphia: Jewish Publication Society, 1981), 4.

31. In later years Sadie Weilerstein identified K'tonton's neighborhood as a heavily Jewish section in Brooklyn, New York. Deborah Weilerstein interview with the author.

32. See Beth Wenger, *New York Jews and the Great Depression: Uncertain Promise* (New Haven: Yale University Press, 1996), 80–102.

33. Jeffrey Gurock, "The Ramaz Version of American Orthodoxy," in *Ramaz: School, Community, Scholarship, and Orthodoxy*, ed. Gurock (Hoboken, N.J.: KTAV, 1989), 56.

34. Weilerstein, *K'tonton*, 26, 32–35, 55, 90–95.

35. Ibid., 70.

36. Klagsbrun, introduction, in Weilerstein, *The Best of K'tonton*, 11.

37. Weilerstein, *Adventures of K'tonton*, 9.

38. Svonkin, *Jews against Prejudice*, 17. See Svonkin's volume for an in-depth study of the propagandistic, educational, legal, and social action initiatives of the ADL, AJC, and American Jewish Congress. On the impact of intergroup relations and the interfaith movement on American Jewish textbooks see Jonathan Krasner, "Representations of Self and Other in American Jewish History and Social Studies Schoolbooks: An Exploration of the Changing Shape of American Jewish Identity" (PhD diss., Brandeis University, 2001), 409–29.

39. Deborah Karp, "Workhorse Six Days a Week," *Jewish Welfare Board Circle*, November 1955.

40. Sadie Rose Weilerstein, *Dick, the Horse That Kept the Sabbath* (New York: Bloch, 1955), 39–40.

41. Ibid., 6–8.

42. Hasia Diner, *Lower East Side Memories: A Jewish Place in America* (Princeton, N.J.: Princeton University Press, 2000), 31. See Diner's discussion of *All-of-a-Kind Family*, 59–65. See also June Cummins, "Becoming an 'All-of-a-Kind' American: Sydney Taylor and Strategies of Assimilation," *Lion and the Unicorn* 27 (September 2003): 324–43.

43. Steven Zipperstein, *Imagining Russian Jewry: Memory, History, Identity* (Seattle: University of Washington Press, 1999), 37; Diner, *Lower East Side Memories*, 171.

44. The story behind the writing of *Life Is with People* and its controversial coauthor Zborowski is told in Barbara Kirshenblatt-Gimblett's introduction to the 1995 edition. See Mark Zborowski and Elizabeth Herzog, *Life Is with People: The Culture of the Shtetl* (New York: Schocken, 1995).

45. Hansen's "The Problem of the Third Generation Immigrant," which was originally published by the Augustana Historical Society was reprinted with a foreword by Oscar Handlin in *Commentary* magazine in November 1952. It was also popularized and explicitly applied to the Jews in Will Herberg's *Protestant-Catholic-Jew* (Garden City, N.Y.: Doubleday, 1955), esp. 30–31, 186–87. Indeed, Herberg dedicated his book "to the Third Generation upon whose 'return' so much of the future of religion in America depends."

46. Diner, *Lower East Side Memories*, 170; Arthur Goren, "The 'Golden Decade': 1945–1955," reprinted in *The Politics and Public Culture of American Jews* (Bloomington: Indiana University Press, 1999), 197–98; Zipperstein, *Imagining Russian Jewry*, 13.

47. The book was subsequently republished by the Jewish Publication Society. As in the musical *Fiddler on the Roof* the term "shtetl" never actually appears in the book.

48. *Something about the Author*, 250.

49. Apparently, Doubleday's appetite for Jewish-themed juvenile literature was limited. After *Ten and a Kid* was published, Weilerstein's editor invited her to submit other book manuscripts to Doubleday but cautioned that they should not be overtly Jewish. Belitsky, "K'tonton's Mother Recalls Her Boy," 47; JPS did not hire a separate children's book editor until the late 1970s, but it began to avidly experiment with various juvenile and young adult genres in the mid-1950s. See Sarna, *JPS*, 226–27, 288–89.

50. Sadie Rose Weilerstein, *Ten and a Kid* (Garden City, N.Y.: Doubleday, 1961), 130. Ludimer is a Yiddishized pronunciation of Ludmir.

51. Deborah Weilerstein, interview with the author, June 8, 2004.

52. Ben Halpern, "The Americanization of Zionism, 1880–1930," *American Jewish*

History (September 1979): 17–22; Henry Feingold, *A Time for Searching: Entering the Mainstream, 1920–1945* (Baltimore: Johns Hopkins University Press, 1992), 105, 161.

53. Deborah Dash Moore sees evidence of this trend in the mid to late 1940s as American Jews galvanized on behalf of the *Yishuv* and, later, the fledgling State of Israel. But she rightly underlines the importance of both the book (1958) and film version (1960) of Leon Uris's *Exodus* in making Israel into "a frontier myth, a staple of American Jewish popular culture." Deborah Dash Moore, *To the Golden Cities: Pursuing the American Jewish Dream in Miami and L.A.* (New York: Macmillan, 1994), 227–61, quote on 243.

54. Jeffrey Shandler and Beth Wenger, "'The Site of Paradise': The Holy Land in American Jewish Imagination," in *Encounters with the "Holy Land": Place, Past, and Future in American Jewish Culture*, ed. Shandler and Wenger (Hanover, N.H.: National Museum of American Jewish History and University Press of New England, 1997), 11–37; Joellyn Wallen Zollman, "The Selling of Israel: Ideology and Material Culture in the American Synagogue Gift Shop," "Shopping for the Future: A History of the American Synagogue Gift Shop" (PhD diss., Brandeis University, 2002); "Sadie Rose Weilerstein: K'tonton's Creator Still at Work," *Moment*, October 1990, 61.

55. Sadie Rose Weilerstein, *K'tonton in Israel* (New York: National Women's League of Conservative Judaism, 1964), 113–14.

56. Ibid., 145.

57. Ibid., 51.

58. Ibid., 68.

59. Ibid., 59, 73.

60. Weilerstein, *K'tonton in the Circus*, 61–68; quote on 67.

61. Ibid., 22–23.

62. Cummins, "Becoming an 'All-of-a-Kind' American," 324–25.

63. On Kallen's cultural pluralism see, for example, Daniel Greene, "A Chosen People in a Pluralist Nation: Horace Kallen and the Jewish-American Experience," *Religion and American Culture* 16 (2006): 161–94; William Toll, "Horace M. Kallen: Pluralism and American Jewish Identity," *American Jewish History* 85 (1997): 57–74; and Sidney Ratner, "Horace M. Kallen and Cultural Pluralism," *Modern Judaism* 4 (1984): 185–200.

64. The concept of invented tradition is borrowed from Eric Hobsbawm. See his introduction in *The Invention of Tradition*, ed. Hobsbawm and Terence Ranger (Cambridge: Cambridge University Press, 1983), 1–14. On the modern invention of Christmas see John Gillis, *A World of Their Own Making: Myth, Ritual, and the Quest for Family Values* (Cambridge, Mass.: Harvard University Press, 1996), 98–104. On the evolution of Hanukkah see Jenna Weissman Joselit, "'Merry Chanuka': The Changing Holiday Practices of American Jews, 1880–1950," in *The Uses of Tradition: Jewish Continuity in the Modern Era*, ed. Jack Wertheimer (New York: Jewish Theological Seminary of America, 1992), 303–25.

65. Cummins, "Becoming an 'All-of-a-Kind' American," 333–37.

7 : "Three Cheers for Anna!"
Anna G. Sherman, Adult Jewish Educator

1897?–1980

Anna G. Sherman.
Courtesy of Varda S. Lev

M y interest in Anna Grossman Sherman began with a casual conversation. Her daughter, Varda Lev, asked if I knew that her mother had taught Hebrew at the Jewish Theological Seminary (JTS) for nearly forty years. I didn't, but I was intrigued. I was a graduate of the Seminary College of Jewish Studies (now List College), a faculty member, and a woman. Why didn't I recognize this name? I scoured the published histories of the institution for a mention of Anna Sherman but found nothing (Cardin and Silverman, 1987; Wertheimer, 1997). Several months later, at the JTS commencement exercises, I noticed that the program included the Anna Grossman Sherman Prize in Hebrew "established in her memory by family and friends; awarded annually to a student who has shown excellence in the study of Hebrew language and literature." Surely anyone who devoted so many years to an institution deserved more recognition than an eponymous award, last in a list of more than a hundred prizes. I was determined to discover as much as I could about Mrs. Sherman (as she was known at that time) and her pedagogy, not only to satisfy my curiosity as to why she is missing from the narrative of JTS, but also to learn more about adult Jewish education, a field that is belatedly attracting the attention of researchers in Jewish education.

In my initial forays, I discovered that Sherman was a beloved teacher in the Israel Friedlaender Classes (IFC), a division of the Teachers Institute of the Jewish Theological Seminary. On the twenty-fifth anniversary of the establishment of the JTS extension division, Sherman received a letter of commendation from Louis M. Levitsky, the director of the Seminary School of Jewish Studies, as the IFC had become known. "I would like you to know that your personal contribution in the service that you rendered as a member of our faculty has been the largest single asset which the school possesses" (Levitsky, 1945). Sylvia Ettenberg, a faculty colleague in the 1950s and 1960s, corroborates Levitsky's assessment, referring to her as the "mainstay of the Extension department" (Ettenberg, 2001). Today, when large numbers of Jewish adults are enrolling in programs like Me'ah, the Florence Melton Adult Mini-School, and other synagogue and communal adult education initiatives, with Torah study taking place in corporate boardrooms and lawyers' offices, researchers in adult Jewish education might be able to learn from an expert practitioner in an earlier era. In analyzing Sherman's pedagogy, I have found that it prefigured the best practices in adult education, Jewish and general, today.

I was privileged to interview two of Anna Grossman Sherman's children, Varda Sherman Lev and A. (Ari) Joshua Sherman. (Joshua's twin brother, Ori, died in 1988.) I also interviewed Sylvia Ettenberg, a younger colleague of

Mrs. Sherman, and Lucille Ross, one of Sherman's students from the fifties. Joshua Sherman provided me with another even more informative source. He shared with me an invaluable cache of papers, articles, and notes his mother had compiled on the subject of Jewish education and the Hebrew language. In the Ratner Archives of JTS, I found another cache of materials: correspondence of the registrar of the IFC, Israel Chipkin, which contained materials related to Anna Grossman Sherman and her students, as well as materials from the other JTS extension schools in which Sherman taught.

Beginnings

Anna Grossman was born in either 1897 or 1898. Varda suspects that it might have been even earlier. According to her daughter, Anna was evasive about her age; she may not have known the exact date because of the chaotic way records were kept or she may have been self-conscious because her husband was considerably younger than she (Lev, 2000). Both Varda and Sherman's son Joshua began their interviews the same way, noting the need to pay attention to context, to Anna Grossman's birthplace. Anna's story begins at Kastina, now known as Be'er Tuvia, with the Zionist/Hebraist dreams of her father, Shlomo Grossman.

Kastina was at one time the southernmost settlement of the *Hovevei Tzion* (lovers of Zion), the Zionist pioneers committed to rejuvenation of the land of Israel and the Hebrew language. The colony was established in 1887 by Jews from Bessarabia and supported by Baron Rothschild's Palestine Jewish Colonization Association. Shlomo Grossman arrived there in 1889. An orphan by the time he was eleven, Shlomo was a brilliant student who resented having to live off the charity of his fellow townspeople, folk who could barely sustain themselves. After wandering through the Carpathian Mountains, earning his way by giving bar mitzvah lessons and helping the farmers he met, and fulfilling his obligatory army service, he acquired a wife, Sarah Weinstein, Imbued with the Zionist ideal, Shlomo decided to leave Europe where there was no future for Jewish life. Varda muses:

> How this particular spot was chosen, God only knows. It was a complete failure almost from the start. It was unproductive. The cattle died. The crops failed. The Bedouins stole almost everything. The Turks wanted baksheesh at every turn. All my mother remembered of her mother was a woman weeping at the window. . . . Sarah was eighteen when he [Shlomo] took her away from her family, and she never saw them again. (Lev, 2000)

Joshua augments his sister's description of the harshness of the conditions and his grandfather's ideological purity. He recalls his mother telling him that within a very short time, most of the members of the settlement either returned to Europe or died of the various illnesses that beset the settlers in the *yishuv* (settlement). Joshua tells the story of his grandfather standing up to the emissary of the baron who offered to subsidize the settlement to alleviate the hardship of the settlers. Shlomo Grossman, ever the idealist, believed that Jews had to work with their hands, that they had to remake their destiny and their language (A. J. Sherman, 2001).

Weakened by hard labor and battling congestive heart failure, Shlomo was unable to continue *z'khut hakibush* (the privilege of conquering the land) (Spiegel, 1930, 408). In 1905 or 1906, he reluctantly moved to New York with his family, Sarah, and the three children who had survived the rigors of Kastina: Shoshana, Ovadiah, and Hanna (Anna). Like Eliezer Ben-Yehuda (the creator of modern Hebrew), Shlomo Grossman insisted on speaking to his children only in Hebrew. Sarah barely spoke the language; she and her husband communicated in Yiddish. Shortly after their arrival in New York, the penniless family suffered a tragic loss. Shoshana contracted scarlet fever, measles, or pneumonia, and died, unable to communicate in English or Yiddish to her caregivers in the hospital. Although Shlomo firmly believed in the A. D. Gordon philosophy of the dignity of labor, his health prevented him from sustaining his family with factory work. He worked as a Hebrew teacher and bar mitzvah tutor. The family was nearly penniless.

Hanna, now known as Anna, attended Julia Richman High School. At fourteen, she got her first job teaching Hebrew. According to her daughter, "She put her hair up, said she was sixteen, and went straight from high school to the Downtown Talmud Torah." Her children recall very little about her life as a high school student; Joshua reflects that the Jewish Theological Seminary was the only educational institution of which she spoke (A. J. Sherman, 2001).

Anna Grossman Sherman studied at the Teachers Institute (TI) of JTS during those heady years when Mordecai Kaplan and his colleagues were changing the shape of American Jewish education. Studying from 1912 to 1916, when the TI was changing from a part-time program to a serious institution committed to teacher education (Kaufman, 1997, 586), she must have been exposed to the teaching of the Benderly boys. By 1915, Berkson, Chipkin, and Honor were teaching on the faculty, espousing *Ivrit b'Ivrit* (teaching Hebrew in Hebrew), as a living language.

While Hebrew was not a primary concern for the Rabbinical School, it was for the TI. Mintz (1997) claims that "the price paid for relative autonomy in matters of culture and curriculum cast the Teachers Institute into the role of poor relation to the Rabbinical School" (102). I suggest that diminished status produced curricular autonomy and not the reverse. The incorporation documents of JTS, dated March 9, 1902, indicate the institution's priorities: "for the education and training of Jewish rabbis and teachers" (Kaufman, 1997, 569). Its second-class status was further institutionalized by the gender of its student body, attracting as it did "ladies who seem to be a very intelligent class and drawn from all sections of the city" (571) unlike the all-male Rabbinical School. "Intelligent ladies" like Anna Grossman Sherman thrived on the benign neglect accorded to the TI by the leadership of JTS; this inattention gave Kaplan the freedom to follow his agenda, one that shaped Sherman's philosophy and pedagogy.

Sherman received her diploma in 1916, winning an award for the outstanding graduation essay. Both of her children recall that she had the distinction of being the first woman to study Talmud at the TI. Varda points out, "Her father taught her Talmud the way you would a son because Ovadiah [her brother] wouldn't study with him. [Shlomo] sat with her, and she studied from the time she was very small because she was very smart, and he took great pride in her" (Lev, 2000).

Cobbling together a career of teaching in various Hebrew schools, she helped to support the family with her meager earnings. She taught Hebrew at the YWHA in Harlem, where she was recruited as a private teacher for Mrs. Felix (Frieda Schiff) Warburg. Joshua Sherman recalls that the director was asked for a bright and attractive young woman to teach Mrs. Warburg. Sherman fit the bill, and thus they began a lifelong association. Joshua recalls hearing stories about how his mother would be fetched in a car and driven up to Harlem where the Warburgs were living in the magnificent building now the home of the Jewish Museum. Anna told her children that Mrs. Warburg was invariably well prepared for her lessons. The children recall meeting Mrs. Warburg on her frequent trips to Palestine while Anna and her children were living there (1932–36); both Varda and Joshua are convinced that it was Frieda Schiff Warburg's association with her tutor that kept the Warburgs as anchored as they were to Jewish tradition (A. J. Sherman, 2001).

In 1923, Sherman was asked to teach Hebrew in the Extension Division as a special instructor. She was one of four women on the faculty, three out of four of whom were teaching Hebrew. The majority of their students, like those enrolled in the Teachers Institute, were women. In 1922, the Extension Division was named the Israel Friedlaender Classes after the JTS professor whose life was tragically cut short while doing relief work in Russia. The original purpose of the classes when they were instituted in 1919 was as follows:

> The Extension Department of the Teachers Institute has been established as a result of the growing interest in Jewish Studies on the part of Jewish youth, and the increasing demand for trained workers in the field of Jewish service. The courses in this department afford an opportunity for acquiring a general Jewish education. Special professional courses have been organized for those who wish to prepare themselves for Jewish club work and teaching in Jewish Sunday Schools. (JTS Register, 1923–24, 56)

Sherman taught in the IFC throughout the twenties, taking postgraduate courses at the TI and studying at Teachers College (although to her great sorrow, she never obtained a degree). At this time, she was a stunning, slim redhead, and according to Varda, pressured by her father to get married before he died. She did marry, someone with great *yihus* (stature), the nephew of Ahad Ha'am. The nephew was also named Asher Ginsburg. A scholar in his own right, he shared Sherman's interest in Hebrew grammar and Hebrew literature. Sherman suffered a series of tragic reversals. Within a year, she had lost a husband, a child, and both parents. Heartbroken, she cashed in her savings of six thousand dollars to finance her return to Palestine.[1]

The Anglo-American community in Palestine extended itself to the attractive young woman with a passion for Hebrew. She quickly earned one of the coveted invitations to Lord Samuel's Shabbat afternoon teas in his Jerusalem home. Varda speculates, "Her story was so dramatic that, guess what? Back in Jerusalem, which had a very small English-speaking community, people had heard of her story. This beautiful young Hebrew teacher who had had these terrible tragedies befall her. . . . People talked about it" (Lev, 2000). The young widow had come to Jerusalem to study with a noted grammarian and had no interest in remarrying.

But at one of the Jerusalem get-togethers, she met an idealistic young dentist who had sold his practice in the Bronx, looking for an opportunity to express his Zionism and his interest in preventive dentistry, and perhaps to escape an overbearing family. At a conference in Paris, he had met an older dentist who told him about an unusual opportunity, to take charge of a dental clinic in Jerusalem, newly donated by the Strauss family.[2] Earl Mayo Sherman fell madly in love with Anna Grossman and pursued her to Tiberias and Egypt in the hopes of making her his wife. Eventually she set aside her academic plans and her reservations about remarriage and their difference in age. (Despite his gray hair, he was younger than she.) She yielded to his persistence, charm, and kindness. On a hike in what is now the Sinai desert, she noticed the attention Earl paid to a fellow hiker who was lame. "He kept hanging back so that she wouldn't feel alone although he was young and energetic and could have [moved faster], but he was so concerned about her and helped her. . . . My mother couldn't get over that — his kindness." Within three months, on *erev* Hanukkah 1931, they were married, and within three years, Anna Grossman went from a childless widow to "an overwhelmed mother with three babies" (Varda, referring to her birth in 1932 and that of her twin brothers in 1934 [Lev, 2000]).

The rigors of postwar Palestine and frail health took their toll on Sherman. As a result of having contracted scarlet fever as a child, she suffered from chronic kidney disease, exacerbated by two pregnancies in quick succession. The local doctors suggested that she return to the United States for surgery. She alerted the registrar of the IFC classes of her availability to resume teaching during the summer of 1936, including pictures of her growing family. Israel Chipkin made no promises: "My happiness [at seeing Anna's family photographs] is mingled with some sense of sorrow that you are forced to leave the country for some reason, and especially for reason of health. . . . As for classes here, I am sorry that I cannot make any definite promise. There may be one class for women which does not pay very much" (IFC, Chipkin to Anna Sherman, July 29, 1936). With only the barest promise of sustenance, Sherman left for the United States with Varda; her husband reluctantly straightened his affairs and followed with the twins.

During the thirties, the Extension Department included both Jewish professionals and those who wished to study *Torah l'shma* (learning, for its own sake). A division of the IFC was named the Women's Institute, consisting of morning classes sponsored by the Women's League of the United Synagogue, Hadassah, Ivriah, and the New York section of the National Council of Jewish Women. (This is the division in which Anna would teach the one class Chipkin promised her in their summer 1936 correspondence.)[3] The courses offered included Hebrew, Jewish History, Bible, Post-biblical Literature, Customs and Ceremonies, Jewish Music, Jewish Community Life, and Parent-Child Relations (JTS Register, 1937–38, 63). Mordecai Kaplan (1939) describes the students attracted to the Israel Friedlaender Classes and Women's Institute, the sort of people who studied with Anna Grossman Sherman after her return from Palestine:

> The 225 or more students who have been attending these classes during each of the last few years are young persons over eighteen, and mostly in the twenties. They are usually graduates of secondary schools, are either attending college, or are college graduates, and are engaged in some profession, or have an extended experience in business or in communal work. They may not know Hebrew, but they expect matured and scientific method in the teaching of the Bible or of Jewish History, and when they study Hebrew they make relatively rapid progress. Because the Friedlaender Classes have maintained a high academic standard, in addition to being stimulating and inspiring, they have not only attracted many young people but have also served as a stimulus to the establishment of adult study groups in New York and other cities. (134)

Anna must have had another acute episode of recurring renal disease, making an operation unavoidable. She was operated on in April 1937 at Mount Sinai Hospital, a short distance from the Warburg mansion. Mrs. Warburg, who had maintained a correspondence with her former tutor and visited her in Palestine, looked after Anna. She insisted on moving her from a ward to a private room and paying for a private nurse. According to Varda, Mrs. Warburg probably saved her mother's life. Sherman had begun to hemorrhage, and had there not been a private nurse looking after her, her complications might have gone unnoticed. (Varda remembers a steady stream of her mother's former students coming to the apartment to help during her convalescence, like "Esther Frank who came every single Sunday for a year" [Lev, 2000].) Mrs. Warburg also gave Earl Sherman an interest-free loan, enabling him to buy a dental practice in New York, a tribute to the affection that she and so many of Mrs. Sherman's students—competent, successful women in their own realms—felt for the teacher who introduced them to the Hebrew language and Hebrew literature.

Between 1942 and 1944, the IFC became the Seminary School of Jewish Studies. Anna Grossman Sherman taught at this school or at the Women's Institute throughout the forties and fifties, with brief periods during which she was on leave (no doubt because of the poor health that plagued her all her life). In the JTS Register that covers the years 1960 to 1964, her name appears at the same rank of instructor, with the words "on leave of absence." This is the last time her name appears on the faculty roster.

Anna Sherman's Pedagogy

Modern Hebrew, as Alan Mintz (1997) notes in his history of Hebrew at the Jewish Theological Seminary, was never a passion for Solomon Schechter or Cyrus Adler. It was for Mordecai Kaplan. And in the benign neglect the early presidents afforded the Teachers Institute in favor of the rabbinical school, Kaplan created a school with Hebrew at its core, an ideal environment for a Hebraist like Anna Grossman to study and for Anna Grossman Sherman to teach.[4] Kaplan brought Benderly's pedagogic vision in its programmatic particulars to the TI: *Ivrit b'Ivrit*, using clubs outside the classroom, creating programs related to the holidays that included music and dance, to the students of the Teachers Institute (Scult, 1993). Kaplan also supported Benderly on the provision of play space for children's recreation and on speaking Hebrew throughout the day, in the classroom and on the playground (Scult, 1993, 120).

Sherman, like Kaplan, subscribed to the ideology of Ahad Ha'am and the role of Hebrew as a catalyst for cultural change, wholeheartedly embracing his views that Hebrew language was the key to cultural literacy and renewal. In his article "Hebrew: A Language of Identity," Gilead Moragh (2000) acknowledges the contributions of Benedict Anderson to his thinking. In his book *Imagined Communities*, Anderson (1991) posits it is language that is the primary binding force of all imagined communities. Anna's classes and her club meetings took place on the Upper West Side of Manhattan, not in *Eretz Yisrael*, but as a talented teacher, she used language to evoke what Alfred Schutz (1962) called "the imagining self" in her students, encouraging them to create an alternate world. This is what Anderson meant by an "imaginary community," transporting the learner to the place that Schutz calls "a finite province of meaning" (230).

JEWISH CULTURAL LITERACY

Sherman was a true Reconstructionist, a member of Kaplan's congregation at the Society for the Advancement of Judaism. She insisted that her daughter celebrate a bat mitzvah in that congregation. She subscribed to her mentor's views of Judaism as a civilization and the role of Hebrew to provide both the access and the glue for that civilization. Kaplan shared his views on the place of Hebrew for the educated Jew in an article in the *Menorah Journal*: "The Hebrew language would be cultivated not only for synagogue responses, but as the medium of expression for a regenerated Israel and as the tangible evidence in the Diaspora of the collective mind of the Jewish people" (Scult, 1993, 315). Like Kaplan, Sherman appreciated the role of ritual in Jewish cultural literacy and in shaping Jewish identity in America. Her understanding of reflects her mentor's functionalist point of view.

> *Kashrut* was not instituted for health reasons alone. The laws of *Kashrut* reflect the innermost nature of the Jewish character. They stem from the Jew's respect for life; from his repugnance for the unnecessary shedding of blood, from his desire to lift himself above the animal drives in man. He does not deny them or attempt to subjugate them, as does the Christian, but he does try to hallow them. The Jew attaches religious significance to the commonplace in life; to his everyday acts, hence our manifold blessings for various occasions. (A. G. Sherman, 1960)

Sherman and Kaplan wrote articles for the spring 1956 issue of *Adult Jewish Education*. Both stressed lifelong learning and the need for Jews to live in two cultures. Both warned that the survival of American Jewry would depend on knowledge of Jewish history and culture. Both offered a grand vision for adult Jewish education. Kaplan delineated a comprehensive course of study that would include religious, ethical, and Jewish culture. "Talmud Torah, or adult Jewish education, cannot confine itself to what has been narrowly regarded as Jewish subject matter. It must include all areas of human thought that have a bearing on human life" (Kaplan, 1956, 3–4). Like Kaplan, Sherman's vision of a well-educated Jew included religious and ethical literacy, Zionism, and Jewish peoplehood. She simply could not imagine

> the possibility of raising a Jewish child without providing him with a knowledge of his people's history and culture. I feel that the parent who denies his child a Jewish education robs him of a vital source of comfort and strength throughout his life. . . . A home in which the Sabbath and the *yamim tovim* [holidays] are observed esthetically and with dignity is bound to make a deep and memorable impression upon the children.

However, knowledge alone of things Jewish is not enough. I may know every last *din* governing Jewish living but if I do not practice it, it is useless. On the other hand the Jew who observes all the minutiae of Jewish ritual but washes his hands clean of any responsibility towards either *Medinat Yisrael* or *k'lal Yisrael* is also not practicing Judaism. (A. G. Sherman, n.d.*a*)

Like her hero, Mordecai Kaplan, Sherman embraced the principle of moderation and balance expressed in Kohelet: *Tov asher te'ehoz bazeh v'gam mizeh* (It is best that you grasp the one without letting go of the other [Ecclesiastes 7:18]).

Sherman was horrified that Jews well educated by American secular standards were abysmally ignorant of Jewish civilization. Her goal was to awaken her students to the unknown treasures they had inherited. Joshua Sherman observes that in his mother's era Jewish identity included religious observance, commitment to Jewish culture, and an embrace of the best of secular culture. In this golden age, when Sherman and others like her tried to create an "imagined community," these Hebraist-Zionists were not just preaching religious observance; they were living it. He notes that the family observed *kashrut* and the *hagim* (Jewish holidays) without self-congratulation, ethnocentrism, or smugness. He recalls that although his parents were Zionists, there was no idolatry of the land. Noting that although his mother's greatest satisfaction was directing people to the magnificent tradition to which they were heirs, her son claims that it would never occur to Anna to tell them they must eat *kasher* or strictly observe the Sabbath (A. J. Sherman, 2001).

The research literature on adult Jewish education contains a chorus of voices on what the goals of the enterprise should be: history, self-discovery, or transformation (Bernstein-Nahor, 2000). Anna Sherman's cultural literacy approach included all three: her learners were expected to see themselves as part of a glorious past, present, and future, all which were personally enriching. She hoped to reach their hearts and minds; she was not didactic about their behavior.

Remembering a Consummate Teacher

I was able to interview one of Anna Sherman's students from the early fifties, Lucille J. Ross, now a pediatrician, who shared her inestimable recollections with me.

I had the privilege of studying Hebrew at the Seminary evening classes with Mrs. Sherman for about half a year before I went to work in Israel. My father had taught me the Hebrew consonants and a few of the vowels in previous years. But I never had time to study more. Mrs. Sherman managed in the half year of her teaching to get me to the point where I could somehow get along with patients and their mothers in the clinics where I worked [in Ramat Ha'Sharon, in the outskirts of Herzliya, and a Herziliya neighborhood called Neve Amal]. How did she do it? She was a very interesting teacher, very interested in her students, gentle, and encouraging — and a "congenital teacher." Ari once described her method as "devoted, passionate teaching." Her actual tricks of the trade I don't recall. But I do recall her writing *yod-vav-nun*, differing only in the lengths of the letters, next to each other, on the blackboard. To this day, I remember how amazed I was at the word *Yavan* [Greece]. Forty-eight years ago, at this season, I was introduced to *Tu B'Shvat* [Arbor Day] and carobs. I'd never seen one. I went to a *shuk* [a market] on the Lower East Side of Manhattan, near where I was working. I found carob pods in, I think, an Italian store. I took some to Mrs. Sherman's home so that she could show them to her classes the next day. . . . *B'kitzur* [in short] — I loved Mrs. Sherman. (Ross, email correspondence, February 15, 2001)

I met Lucille Ross in Jerusalem in the summer of 2001. She fleshed out her observations of Mrs. Sherman's teaching and added a new insight: "If she never got a penny, she still would have taught." Ross was apologetic for not remembering more; her reflections help to flesh out Anna Sherman's philosophy of teaching, and augmented by the artifacts and interviews, creates a richer portrait of an exceedingly good teacher. Ross depicts a woman who felt that her teaching was a calling, a teacher who was passionate about her subject and cared about her students.

Excellence in Teaching

Excellence in teaching is a combination of subject matter mastery, knowledge of pedagogy, and what contemporary educators call pedagogic content knowledge, knowing what students will find difficult, designing the right questions, providing crisp, clear examples and designing activities to turn inert facts into long-lasting learning. Excellent teaching invariably combines the affective domain with the cognitive.

VOCATION

David Hansen (1995) and Parker Palmer (1997, 1999) have helped educators understand the role of vocation in teaching. Palmer (1997) refers to Frederick Buechner, who defines vocation as "the place where your deep gladness meets the world's deep need" (30). Vocation is about finding one's truest self while trying to change the world. Anna Grossman Sherman taught for reasons of the heart — her love of Hebrew language and her belief that she could help Jews survive as Jews in the United States. Varda describes the time her mother devoted to her subject. "Her lessons that she prepared were . . . meticulous.

She'd spend hours with lesson plans . . . hours correcting the papers of her students, hours sitting at home with her red pencil, every *dagesh* (dot) every little mistake was thought about. It was a sacred calling for her" (Lev, 2000). It was a calling, and as Ross so astutely understood, it was done out of love, not as a way of earning a living.

I discovered a touching exchange in the correspondence of Israel Chipkin, the registrar of the TI and its extension division, the IFC. In April 1937, Sherman could no longer stave off the surgery for which she had returned to the United States. Chipkin wrote to the JTS treasurer, Arthur Oppenheimer, to ask his advice. He needed to pay a substitute for Mrs. Sherman eighty dollars, which he didn't have in his budget. "One way of solving the problem is to use the funds of the regular teacher to pay the substitute. I happen to know, however, that Mrs. Sherman is badly in need, and would certainly need her funds at this time" (Chipkin, 1937a). Oppenheimer passed the buck, suggesting that Chipkin discuss the situation with Dr. Finkelstein, who approved Chipkin's plan.

On May 14, 1937, Earl M. Sherman responded to the receipt of a check to Anna in the sum of seventy-five dollars, which she refused to accept, despite her precarious finances and ill health, insisting that it go toward her substitute's salary. Her husband concluded, "It seems to me that her forced absence from work at this time has affected her emotionally, perhaps as much as the necessity of the operation she underwent" (IFC, Dr. Sherman to Israel Chipkin, May 14, 1937). The registrar insisted that Dr. Sherman must prevail upon his wife to take the money. "This check is for her work in the Women's Classes, and is lower than I hoped it would be. Please tell her, therefore, to accept it with no compunction of conscience. She has earned it even before she became ill" (Chipkin, 1937b).

Evidently, Sherman took the money, albeit reluctantly, as one can surmise from a letter written *erev* Rosh Hashana expressing her regrets about not teaching a full complement of courses during the coming year:

> I shall be glad to continue my work with the Women's Classes of the Institute of Jewish Studies but should like to take a year's leave from the Friedlaender classes. [Although] I should not care to be burdened with a regular programme of evening teaching, I shall nevertheless be very happy to co-operate with you if ever you find yourself in need of some additional assistance such as help with registration, substituting for absent teachers, leading the Raanana (a Hebrew-speaking student club), or any other task. It will be only a small recompense for your kind consideration last year and it will give me pleasure to keep in touch with the classes that way." (A. G. Sherman, 1937)

Ross was correct: it was never about the money. In her eulogy for Israel Chipkin, Anna Sherman remembered, "There were periods in the early years of the Friedlaender Classes when some teachers served without pay and during the Depression years, the entire faculty willingly accepted a 50% cut in salaries" (A. G. Sherman, 1955). As Blacker suggests in *Dying to Teach* (1997), Anna Sherman taught for a set of metaphysical rewards, to live on in one's students by giving them something of herself, her love of Hebrew and Jewish culture, while achieving a kind of immortality through the relational enterprise of teaching.

PASSION

In "Eros and Education," Joseph Schwab (1978) describes the process of successful teaching. If the teacher can connect to her students, she creates not only a bond between them, but to the content matter that is so central to that teacher's selfhood. In describing their mother's teaching, both of Sherman's children use language that evokes energy and libido. Varda says that Sherman would come home late at night from her evening classes, her face glowing "as if she had been with a lover" (Lev, 2000). Joshua states that although he never observed her teaching, he recalls that his mother's students were uniformly enthusiastic about her energy and her varied instructional strategies like singing and play production. Like his sister, Joshua remembers his mother's excitement when she returned home on cold winter evenings from meeting with her class. He remembers her "glow" and notes more than fifty years after the fact, she had a very keen sense of what would excite people and what would engage them (A. J. Sherman, 2001).

The affection expressed by Ross was evident in Anna Sherman's students throughout her career at JTS. In suggesting her availability to teach during the 1936–37 year, Chipkin extends the following accolade: "Miss Grossman [*sic*] has just arrived from Palestine where she has been on leave from our Classes for several years. As you know, she has been one of our very popular Hebrew teachers" (Chipkin, 1936c).

In the Ratner Archives I unearthed a collection of parodies written by the students in the Harlem Branch of the IFC as part of a 1929 Hanukkah celebration. These students were primarily college-age students, or young people in their twenties, preparing for positions as Sunday School teachers, informal Jewish educators, or other Jewish communal professionals. The IFC had yet to do serious outreach to the more mature single women professionals like Ross who would later become the mainstay of the Women's Institute, women for whom Jewish education was an avocational endeavor rather than a professional pursuit. The youth of the students explains some of the giddy, childish tone of these parodies, but there is something more. These students, like Ross, adore their teacher. The following ditty, sung to the tune of "Mary Had a Little Lamb," was created by the Harlem Branch of the IFC as part of a Hanukkah celebration:

Anna had a little class,
As dumb as dumb can be.
And everywhere that Anna went,
That class was sure to be.
Three cheers for Anna,
Three cheers for the class,
Three cheers for the little girls
Whose other name was Rah, rah, rah!
Rah, rah, rah! Rah, rah, rah,
Harlem, Harlem, Harlem! (IFC, 1929)

The source of this affection might have been Anna's glamour and elegance. (Ross remembers her still-attractive teacher pouring tea during the study break afforded to the students in the Rabbinical School and TI during the fifties.) But I believe it was Schwabian: their returning the passion she had for her them and for her subject. One of the parodies in the 1929 collection deals with the registrar's attempt to cancel one of Anna's classes and her determination to hold onto it. Playing on Anna's Hebrew name, the students represent their teacher as being a modern-day Hannah, the heroine of Maccabees II, and themselves as her sons facing a gruesome end (the cancellation of their class, no doubt an effort to ease some of the strain on the JTS budget).

Parody on Sons of Hannah

Seven are in the class of Anna,
We will not stop for words or kicks,
But *Mar* Chipkin was very angry—
Then there were six.
Six are now the pupils of Anna,
We thank our teacher we're still alive
But *Mar* Chipkin was very angry,
Then there were five.
Five are now the pupils of Anna
Once we did have more,
But *Mar* Chipkin was very angry,
Then we had four.
Four are now the pupils of Anna
Forever true we'll be!
But *Mar* Chipkin was very angry—
Then we had three!
Three are now the pupils of Anna,
Leave IFC we'll never do!
But *Mar* Chipkin was very angry,
Then there were two.

Two are now the pupils of Anna,
Only we are left alone,
But *Mar* Chipkin was very angry
Now there was one!
Six brave students of IFC
Who war for Harlem and heaven,
Fight *Mar* Chipkin, save Anna's class,
And now again we're seven. (IFC, 1929)

These students wrote their own lighthearted commentary on the centrality of Jewish education in Jewish life. The Hellenized Syrians denied the Maccabees the opportunity to study; their response was to take arms and risk death for what they held dear. Emboldened by the threat of the cancellation of their class, these women opted for "martyrdom" by pressuring Chipkin, not only because a transfer would be inconvenient, but also because the loss of Anna was the equivalent of "death." The students gave the Hanukkah legend a happy ending: Unlike Hannah who sacrificed her seven sons for the Jewish cause, these six students fought back and were victorious, reunited with their beloved teacher.

CONNECTIVITY

Feminist pedagogy underscores connectivity, an emphasis on building relationships, a commitment to diverse instructional methodologies, and the need to transform a classroom into a community (Maher and Tetrault, 2001). Like the feminist pedagogy of the early eighties, Sherman's teaching also relied on consciousness-raising; unlike the feminists of a later era, her concern was not to reclaim consciousness of gender, but of culture. Anna Sherman wrote for the journal *Adult Jewish Education* on the impact of Hebrew on adults who study it; she emphasized the importance of relationship: "in retrieving lost souls and bringing them closer to Judaism and to Hebrew culture" (A. G. Sherman, 1956, 20). This is a theme she returns to in her discussion of *kashrut*: "The Jew of today who observes *kashrut* is establishing one more tie with the faith of his people" (A. G. Sherman, 1960). Embedded in her students' parody are the echoes of Sherman's own pedagogy of relatedness: the community of learners, in league with their teacher, who have transcended the obstacles that faced them, superimposed against the larger Jewish story of survival.

Sherman let her students know she cared about them, even when many years and miles separated them. In the minutes of the November 10, 1935, meeting of the IFC Alumnae Association, Rose R. Rosenberg notes, "There were ice cream and cake and Palestine letters from Anna Sherman, better known as Anna Grossman" (IFC). Her correspondence with Ross was nearly twenty years long, interrupted only by the onset of Sherman's congestive heart failure, which would eventually end her life.

Jane Vella (1994) suggests twelve principles that characterize successful adult education. All of them were present in Sherman's pedagogy.

1. Needs assessment: Learners' participation in deciding what is to be learned
2. Safety of the environment and the process
3. A sound relationship between teacher and learner for learning and development
4. Careful attention to sequence of content and reinforcement
5. Praxis: action with reflection or learning by doing
6. Respect for learners as subjects of their own learning
7. Cognitive, affective, and psychomotor aspects
8. Immediacy of the learning
9. Clear roles and role development
10. Teamwork: using small groups
11. Engagement of the learners in what they are learning
12. Accountability: Students must be able to demonstrate what they have learned.

From the accounts of Ross and the interviews with Varda Lev and Joshua Sherman, there is ample evidence of Anna Sherman meeting these criteria. The pediatrician who states unequivocally, "Mrs. Sherman was the best teacher I ever had" is someone who, by her own admission, barely knew how to read Hebrew when she entered the class as a medical school graduate. In less able hands, she might have resented being treated as a raw beginner. A carefully designed, experiential pedagogy in Hebrew immersion brought her from barely recognizing the Hebrew alphabet to readiness to make aliyah. But few of Sherman's students came with such an agenda. Anna's reflections support Vella's principle of the adult educator's need for praxis and the recognition of the diversity of her students.

Among the students whom I have taught, Jewish and non-Jewish, white and colored, I have often been astonished by the variety of reasons for their coming. A schoolteacher who spent her youth caring for an invalid mother is on the verge of a breakdown when the mother dies. She comes to a Hebrew class not only to learn the language but above all to fill an emotional void by drawing closer to her own people. A brilliant young scientist, a Catholic who holds a doctorate in chemistry, tells me that he has read the Psalms in English and Latin, and is it not time that he got to the original! Every once in a while, one meets a young person whose parents had thrown their Jewish heritage overboard many years ago, but who, through some experience or other, develops a desire to know something about his people. A number of white and colored ministers come. Many a young *rebbitzin* [*sic*] has sat in class. The establishment of the State of Israel has aroused the interest of many in the Hebrew language. (A. G. Sherman, 1956, 20)

Like other effective adult educators, Anna knew how to make her teaching relevant and to sequence her students' learning. Rather than introducing grammatical rules, Joshua recalls that his mother preferred to start a class immediately with greetings and introductions and very simple but real conversation, making Hebrew a living language as well as a key for unlocking ancient texts (A. J. Sherman). She brought Benderly and Kaplan's pedagogy to adult Jewish education. Anna Sherman also displayed a wide range of teaching approaches, involving all of the senses in classic Deweyan style. The Raanana Club would be praised today as an ideal arena to showcase multiple intelligences (Gardner, 1983). Varda recalls being drafted to play the piano when her mother used music in her lesson. Students took responsibility for their learning, creating their own agendas for their extracurricular activities, modeling what educators forty or fifty years later would call "a community of learners" (Shulman, 1998). Varda remembers her mother using her artistic skills to draw on the blackboard, to appeal to visual learners.

The criterion of serving as a role model for one's students was one that Anna Sherman was also able to accomplish. In an undated draft of a speech she was to give on objectives in Jewish education, Sherman captures the power of a teacher to change his or her students without didacticism. This is the attribute of teacher as an agent of change or what Henry Giroux (1988) calls being a "transformative intellectual": "When I taught adult students, I was pleased to hear from some of them that more than the Hebrew they learned from me, they had learned a new way of life — a Jewish way of life. Frankly I was not conscious that I was teaching anything beyond the curriculum I was expected to cover. Apparently enthusiasm is contagious and example can wield a wide influence" (A. G. Sherman, n.d.*a*).

By honoring her learners as competent adults, by respecting their diversity, by making Hebrew relevant to their needs, by using diverse strategies to engage them in the enterprise of learning, and by becoming a role model for them in a nonthreatening, nondoctrinaire manner, Anna Sherman displayed all the qualities that Vella uses to characterize outstanding adult educators.

Anna Sherman's Role in the JTS Narrative

In trying to understand why Anna Sherman's contributions were not included in the official histories of JTS, there are a cluster of factors to consider: who Anna was, what she taught, and whom she taught. These categories suggest issues of gender, advanced degrees, the role of Hebrew language at JTS, and adult vs. professional education. These factors also play a role in why many of the women in this anthology have been overlooked.

It is tempting to read Anna Sherman's story as yet another example of the tyranny of the glass ceiling, keeping women in their place, pouring tea while the men with whom Anna Grossman began her career, people like Abraham Halkin and Hillel Bavli, rise higher and higher in the academic hierarchy, leaving her at the bottom of the JTS academic register. That may well be the case, as David Kaufman suggests regarding Sylvia Ettenberg, who was passed over as dean of the Teachers Institute and drew a lesser salary than others with similar responsibilities, "a clear case of gender discrimination (another subject which must await future study)" (Kaufman, 1997, 628). As Harvey Goldberg notes in his history of the faculty, Anna's colleagues (often neighbors and patients of her husband) called themselves "the boys" (Goldberg, 1997, 395). Anna was not in the club.

It is important to acknowledge that Anna was a product of her time, using male pronouns to represent all teachers and students, male or female, just as she uses the term "colored" to refer to the African American community. Both of her children spoke of her concern for her male colleagues who, when their salaries were cut during the Depression, had the responsibility of supporting their families. In reviewing the financial reports of the IFC, I noted no difference between Anna's salary and those of her male colleagues. In 1930–31, she was the only woman on the faculty, and like her full-time male colleagues, earned one thousand dollars. This salary was cut in half in 1936–37, most of which was restored when money became available (IFC, 1931; 1937). It is, however, important to note that the salaries of those who taught in the Women's Institute, whether male or female, were less than for teaching in the other Extension Schools of JTS.

Even though Anna was not "one of the boys," she socialized with them. They were her guests for frequent Shabbat and holiday dinners. This was not a self-conscious attempt to create a salon like Rahel Varnhagen in eighteenth-century Berlin or to emulate the *maskilot* (enlightened women) like Chava Shapiro who were the "salon Jewesses" of eastern Europe (Balin, 2000). The context for sharing ideas was a home celebration of Jewish ritual, beginning with chicken soup and ending with a cake purchased at a neighborhood bakery. Varda recalls the meals as being unimaginative, "boiled chicken so that we could have the soup, but then in an attempt to make the chicken look as if it had been roasted, [my mother] would put ketchup over it and put it in the oven" (Lev, 2000). Food was secondary to the discussion of Hebrew poetry and prose. Varda points out that her mother had little in common with the faculty wives. After one of these meals, Anna confided to her daughter, "Oh, you know so and so is *so* simple. I mean it's just amazing to me. Her husband is so brilliant" (Lev, 2000).

Joshua Sherman refers to his mother as a feminist before her time, noting that she always believed in the independence of women. Hebrew was Anna Grossman Sherman's "room of her own." He muses that one of the attractions of Hebrew teaching, however badly it was paid, and it was deplorably paid, was that it was her terrain, independent of that of her husband (A. J. Sherman, 2001). Neither child recalls either anger or resentment by their mother. She was a woman, and her choices were limited.

Although Anna surely had "the right stuff," she did not have the right degrees. The fact that she had no earned degree besides the diploma from the Teachers Institute impeded her rise in the faculty. Both Varda and Joshua speak of Anna Grossman Sherman's sorrow at not completing her degree at Teachers College. Enumerating the possible reasons why she failed to complete the degree, Joshua includes the lack of a mentor in her life, her chronic illness, and the responsibilities of taking care of her home, husband, and children. These issues still confront women in academia today. Women like Temima Gezari and Tzipora Jochsberger who did obtain master's degrees might never reach the higher echelons of teaching in the Rabbinical School, but at least they could teach in the Teachers Institute. Anna could not.

The importance of degrees was tied to the Seminary's self-perception. It was not going to be Schechter's yeshivah, but an academic institution with as many of the trappings of academia as it could muster. Schorsch (1994) notes that the nineteenth-century scholars who created the Wissenschaft des Judentums were trying to remake the history, literature, and institutions of Judaism in Western categories. If the scholars of the Wissenschaft refashioned the content and mode of Jewish education, they were surely hoping to refashion the faculty entrusted with the transmission of that education as well. Credentials and curriculum were inseparable. Although *b'kiyut* (mastery) might be enough to teach in a yeshivah, *b'kiyut* without advanced degrees would not provide entry to the upper echelons of the faculty of JTS as envisioned by Schechter's successors. Israel Friedlaender was a find, hired to teach at JTS during Cyrus Adler's tenure because Friedlaender had the cachet of university training (Shargel, 1985). If advanced degrees were to be the passport to legitimacy at the Jewish Theological Seminary, Anna's personal and familial responsibilities kept her at the bottom of the academic hierarchy.

The place of Hebrew at JTS is also connected to gender and advanced degrees. Even today, the department is largely female, untenured, and without advanced degrees. The Hebrew department is referred to as a service department, a kind of *shamash* (servant), a means to provide students with the tools needed by the other academic disciplines under the broad umbrella of Jewish studies. In his discussion of Hebrew literature in America, Mintz (1993) notes that "like the Wissenschaft des Judentums a century earlier, Jewish studies rejected Hebrew as the language of Jewish scholarship and made history and philosophy the regnant disciplines" (45). The role of Hebrew at JTS, despite Kaplan's unconditional embrace of the language, was ambiguous.

Commenting on Cohen and Greenstein's essay "The State of Jewish Studies," Morahg observes that in what the authors construe as Jewish studies,

Hebrew is not included (1993, 191.) Neither for that matter is Jewish education. Committed as she was to the teaching of Hebrew, Anna Sherman cast her professional lot into two disciplines of dubious merit in the JTS curriculum, or with what Michael Apple would label "low status knowledge" (Apple, 1991).

Being female, lacking the right credentials, and making her life's work the transmission of a subject area of disputed merit meant that Anna Sherman could not gain access to teaching in the high status schools of JTS, the all-male Rabbinical School, and the lesser light, the largely female Teachers Institute. The priorities of the institution were clear in its incorporation on March 9, 1902; it existed "for the education and training of Jewish rabbis and teachers." The first order of business was to create a cadre of Jewish professionals for the impoverished Jewish community in America. Adult education at JTS grew haphazardly as an offshoot of the Teachers Institute. As the school sought to reshape its image as a serious academic institution, Sherman's teaching moved farther and farther away from the epicenter of the Teachers Institute, which offered a diploma (and eventually a degree) to those who completed a four-year course of study. She began teaching in the Israel Friedlaender Classes, which provided a diploma for those interested in "teaching in Sunday Schools, conducting clubs, or supervising extension activities in Jewish institutions" (JTS Register, 1933–34, 36). The IFC classes, including its later iteration, the Seminary School of Jewish Studies, while not offering a degree, did grant a certificate of graduation upon the completion of three years of study. By the time she ended her career, Sherman was primarily associated with the Women's Institute of Jewish Studies, a nondegree, noncertificate-bearing program. The 1937–38 Register describes its more marginal status, which manifested itself in the lower wages for its faculty:

> Associated with the Israel Friedlaender Classes is the Women's Institute of Jewish Studies. This institute consists of special classes for women, which meet on Monday and Wednesday mornings. They are sponsored by four local women's organizations: Women's League of the United Synagogue, Hadassah, Ivriah, and the New York Section of the National Council of Jewish Women. These classes provide a three year course for those who wish to train for leadership in Jewish women's organizations, or to pursue Jewish studies generally. (63)

In a letter to Dinin, the JTS registrar, Israel Chipkin questions the wisdom of grouping all the faculty members together, regardless of schools. Although he says that he is happy to have the faculty of the Women's Institute listed, he notes that it "raises certain questions. I am wondering whether there are not certain implications in this listing which introduces certain undesirable situations" (Chipkin, 1937c). Would the "implications" include a diminution of the academic status of JTS?

As Grant et al. (2004) note, since the mid-eighties there has been a burst of programs in adult Jewish education, not only in the United States, but also in Europe and Israel. In their volume, they note the motivations of the learners in the Florence Melton Adult Mini-School (FMAMS): The need to become more informed, the search for a Jewish learning community, the quest for rigorous intellectual engagement, and a structured learning plan (Grant et al, 47–55.) Like Sherman's learners decades ago, most of the learners in the FMAMS were women who studied part-time. Graduates often become "Jewish learning junkies" who continue to look for more educational experiences (Cohen and Davidson, 2001; cited in Grant et al., 2004, 68). Hungry for making meaning, building connections, and, for some, enriching practice, alumni of FMAMS and other intensive practices have turned to "postgraduate" programs. Anna's students enriched their studies with their volunteer activities, like Hadassah; their volunteerism was enriched by their increased Jewish literacy. As was true in Sherman's day, adult Jewish education is an appealing solution for what ails the American Jewish community. For many, blessed with gifted teachers, it can be "a journey of the heart and mind," a truly transformative experience.

When Anna Grossman Sherman recalled one of her teachers, she quoted his response to questions regarding the paucity of his scholarly output. He said, "And who is to say if inscriptions imprinted upon the hearts of students may not prove more enduring than those inscribed in books?" (A. G. Sherman, n.d.*b*). Who indeed? The same might be said of Anna herself, a transformative adult Jewish educator. "Three cheers for Anna!"

NOTES

1. The date of this return is unclear. Varda remembers hearing that it was just before the stock market crash in 1929. However, Anna Grossman is listed as a member of the faculty and is celebrated in songs prepared by her students during Hanukkah 1929. She also appears as a member of the faculty in 1930–31.

2. In 1918, Hadassah had formed the American Zionist Medical Unit (AZMU) comprised of doctors, nurses, dentists, and sanitary workers to combat the wretched health conditions of postwar Palestine among the Jewish and Arab communities. Once again, Hadassah plays a significant role in the lives of the women profiled in this volume.

3. In a letter to Kaplan, dated October 22, 1936, Chipkin notifies him of a change in the teaching staff of the IFC. Anna's longtime friend Leah Klepper could not continue as an instructor, making additional teaching time available for the financially strapped Anna.

4. The Teachers Institute was so autonomous that Kaplan agreed to a rental contract for the school without authorization from the JTS board and without Cyrus Adler's knowledge (Robinson, 1997, 122).

REFERENCES

Anderson, Benedict. 1991. *Imagined Communities: Reflections on the Origin and Spread of Nationalism*. New York: Verso.

Apple, M. W. 1991. *Ideology and Curriculum*. New York: Routledge.

Balin, C. B. 2000. *To Reveal Our Hearts: Jewish Women Writers in Tsarist Russia*. Cincinnati: Hebrew Union College Press.

Bernstein-Nahar, A. 2000. The new learning in adult Jewish education: "Modern Judaism" out of its biblical and philosophical sources. *Journal of Jewish Education* 65(3) (Fall–Winter): 33–40.

Blacker, D. J. 1997. *Dying to Teach: The Educator's Search for Immortality*. New York: Teachers College Press.

Cardin, N. B., and D. W. Silverman, eds. 1987. *The Seminary at One Hundred. Reflections on the Jewish Theological Seminary and the Conservative Movement*. New York: Rabbinical Assembly and the Jewish Theological Seminary of America.

Chipkin, I. 1936a. Report. IFC Correspondence. Ratner Center.

———. 1936b. Letter to A. G. Sherman, July 29. Ratner Center.

———. 1936c. Letter to A. G. Sherman, October 22. Ratner Center.

———. 1937a. Letter to A. Oppenheimer, April 20. Ratner Center.

———. 1937b. Letter to E. M. Sherman, May 17. Ratner Center.

———. 1937c. Letter to S. Dinin, July 29. Ratner Center.

Cohen, S. M., & A. Davidson. 2001. *Adult Jewish Learning in America: Current Patterns and Prospects for Growth*. New York: Florence G. Heller/Jewish Community Centers of America Research Center.

Ettenberg, S. 2001. Audiotaped interview, February 15.

Gardner, H. 1983. *Frames of Mind*. New York: Basic Books.

Giroux, H. A. 1988. *Teachers as Intellectuals: Toward a Critical Pedagogy of Learning*. Granby, Mass.: Bergin and Garvey.

Goldberg, H. E. 1997. Becoming history: Perspectives on the seminary faculty at mid-century. In *Tradition Renewed: A History of the Jewish Theological Seminary*, ed. J. Wertheimer, 355–437. Vol. 1. New York; JTSA.

Grant, L. D, D. T. Schuster, M. Woocher, and S. M. Cohen. 2004. *A Journey of the Heart and Mind: Transformative Jewish Learning in Adulthood*. New York: JTSA.

Hansen, D. T. 1995. *The Call to Teach*. New York: Teachers College Press.

IFC (Israel Friedlaender Classes). 1923–64. Registrar's correspondence, Ratner Archives, JTSA Registers.

JTSA Register. 1923–24.

———. 1933–34.

———. 1937–38

———. 1960–64.

Kaplan, M. M. 1939. *The Teachers Institute and Its Affiliated Departments in the Jewish Theological Seminary of America*. Semicentennial volume, ed. Cyrus Adler. New York: JTS.

———. 1956. Talmud Torah as adult Jewish education. *Adult Jewish Education* (Spring): 3–6.

Kaufman, D. 1997. Jewish education as a civilization: A history of the Teachers Institute. In *Tradition Renewed: A History of the Jewish Theological Seminary*, ed. J. Wertheimer, 567–621. Vol. 1. New York: JTSA.

Lev, V. S. 2000. Audiotaped interviews, June 9, 19, and 27.

Levitsky, L. 1945. Letter to A. G. Sherman, June 18. IFC Correspondence. Ratner Center.

Maher, F. A., and M. K. Tetrault. 2001. *The Feminist Classroom*. Lanham, Md.: Rowman and Littlefield.

Mintz, A. 1993. A sanctuary in the wilderness: The beginnings of the Hebrew movement in America in *Hatoren*. In *Hebrew in America*, ed. A. Mintz, 29–67. Detroit: Wayne State University.

———. 1997. The divided fate of Hebrew and Hebrew culture at the seminary. In *Tradition Renewed: A History of the Jewish Theological Seminary*, ed. J. Wertheimer, 83–107. Vol. 1. New York: JTSA.

Morahg, G. 1993. Language is not enough. In *Hebrew in America: Perspectives and Prospectives*, ed. A. Mintz, 187–208. Detroit: Wayne State University Press.

———. 2000. Hebrew: A language of identity. *Journal of Jewish Education* 65(3) (Fall–Winter): 9–16.

Palmer, P. J. 1997. *The Courage to Teach*. San Francisco: Jossey-Bass.

———. 1999. *Let Your Life Speak: Listening for the Voice of Vocation*. San Francisco: Jossey-Bass.

Robinson, I. 1997. Cyrus Adler: President of the Jewish Theological Seminary, 1915–1940. In *Tradition Renewed: A History of the Jewish Theological Seminary*, ed. J. Wertheimer, 105–59. Vol. 1. New York: JTSA.

Ross, L. 2001. Interview in Jerusalem, August 17.

Schorsch, I. 1994. *From Text to Context*. Waltham, Mass.: Brandeis University Press.

Schutz, A. 1962. *Collected Papers*. Vol. 1. The Hague: Martinus Nijhoff.

Schwab, J. J. 1978. Eros and education. In *Science, Curriculum, and Liberal Education*, ed. I. Westbury and N. J. Wilkof, 105–32. Chicago: University of Chicago Press.

Scult, M. 1993. *Judaism Faces the Twentieth Century: A Biography of Mordecai M. Kaplan*. Detroit: Wayne State University.

———. 2001. *Communings of the Spirit: The Journals of Mordecai M. Kaplan, 1913–1934*. Detroit: Wayne State University.

Shargel, B. R. 1985. *Practical Dreamer: Israel Friedlaender and the Shaping of American Judaism*. New York: KTAV.

Sherman, A. G. n.d.*a*. Objectives in Jewish education. Manuscript.

———. n.d.*b*. Untitled address at the graduation of the Teachers Institute. Manuscript.

———. 1937. Letter to I. Chipkin, *Erev* Rosh Hashanah. IFC Correspondence. Ratner Center.

———. 1955. Untitled eulogy for Israel Chipkin. Manuscript.

———. 1956. Why adults study Hebrew. *Adult Jewish Education* (Spring): 20–22.

———. 1960. Jewish identity. Speech or article commissioned for the National Women's League of the United Synagogue of America. December.

———. 1962. Professor Hillel Bavli: An appreciation. Typescript. January 14.

Sherman, A. J. 2001. Audiotaped interview, March 27.

Sherman, E. M. 1937. Letter to I. Chipkin, May 14. IFC Correspondence. Ratner Center.

Shulman, L. S. 1998. Communities of learners, communities of teachers. *Jewish Education News* (Spring): 32–35.

Spiegel, S. 1930. *Hebrew Reborn*. New York: Macmillan.

Vella, J. 1994. *Learning to Listen, Learning to Teach: The Power of Dialogue in Teaching Adults*. San Francisco: Jossey-Bass.

Wertheimer, J., ed. 1997. *Tradition Renewed: A History of the Jewish Theological Seminary*. New York: Jewish Theological Seminary.

8 : Temima Gezari

An Art Education Pioneer

1905–2009

Temima Gezari, 1976.
Photo by S. J. Leicher; courtesy of Daniel Gezari

As a professionally trained Jewish educator and artist, Temima Gezari laid the foundation for teaching Jewish studies through the arts and for art education in Jewish schools. Gezari studied in a Benderly school as a young girl, experiencing the synthesis of Jewish and progressive education firsthand. Alexander Dushkin, a Benderly boy, and Mordecai Kaplan encouraged her efforts to promote the use of art in Jewish education. A "born teacher," she paved the way for the profusion of today's arts-infused Jewish educational programs (T. Gezari, 2002c, 19).

Using the methodology of Lawrence-Lightfoot and Davis (1997), I paint a verbal portrait of Gezari, whose contributions to Jewish education span eighty years. For my research, I interviewed Gezari, her family, her students, and her colleagues at the Jewish Theological Seminary (JTS) and at the Bureau of Jewish Education of New York. In addition I used archival materials, read her books, articles, papers, the bulletins of the Jewish Education Committee, and *Brush and Color*, the journal she created, wrote for, and edited.

Student of Art and Judaism

Temima Gezari, née Fruma Nimtzowitz, was born on December 27, 1905, in Pinsk, Russia. She came to the United States with her mother when she was nine months old to reunite with her father who had left Europe to look for a better life in the New World. She lived with her parents, sister, and brother in the back of her father's hardware store on Pitkin Avenue in Brownsville, New York.

Her first grade teacher, Ms. McKenny, singled her out as a gifted artist and sent a note of praise about her drawing skills to her parents. Her father, a devoted family man, recognized her talent and took her every day on the subway from Brooklyn to Manhattan for art classes, a gesture that impressed her greatly (T. Gezari, 2002c, 36; D. Gezari, 1985). In 1912, Gezari enrolled herself in a Jewish school, Prep School for Girls No. 3, a Benderly model school. Her father was more interested in her progress and accomplishments in the arts than in her Jewish education (T. Gezari, 2002c, 42).

In Benderly's schools boys and girls were educated according to new principles of the "natural method" of teaching the Hebrew language, *Ivrit b'Ivrit* (teaching Hebrew by speaking only Hebrew), reading the stories of the Bible, and learning about Jewish rituals and holidays through art, music, and dance. The elementary programs focused on Jewish music, dramatics, biblical history, holidays, and some Hebrew, and the high school programs were geared toward preparing the next generation of Jewish educators (Winter, 1966).

Gezari loved the teachers at the school—"young women, idealistic and enthusiastic" (T. Gezari, 2002c, 43). She was fascinated by the Bible stories she learned and enjoyed social activities, especially the frequent picnics. She often commented on how much she appreciated the lively spirit and the interesting way Judaism was introduced in the school. Gezari continued her Jewish education during high school and eventually taught art at the same school (T. Gezari, 2002c, 43). Throughout her high school years, She took art classes with Beulah Stevenson, a social realist painter. Social realism focused specifically on social issues and the hardships of everyday life; urban American artists of the Depression era found it appropriate for their drawings and paintings. The encounter with this style made a lasting impact on Gezari, who had a strong social conscience and was seeking a form of art that lent itself to depicting social issues.

Becoming a Jewish Teacher

Upon her graduation from high school in 1921, Gezari, passionate about Judaism, enrolled in the Teachers Institute (TI) of the Jewish Theological Seminary of America during an exciting time in which the arts were being introduced into the curriculum. Mordecai Kaplan, who would become a significant mentor for Gezari, infused the TI with the philosophy he delineated in *Judaism as a Civilization* (1934), his magnum opus. In this book he defines Judaism as a civilization, characterized by beliefs and practices and by language, culture, literature, ethics, art, history, social organization, symbols, and customs. Kaplan promoted the notion of a synagogue center, which offered prayer services, but also study programs, drama, dance, song, sports, and exercise. He believed that the solution to Jewish education "required a basic reorientation toward Jewish life, a veritable 'reconstruction of Judaism'" (Kaufman, 1997, 580). Kaufman posits that the new Teachers Institute at JTS, with its innovative curriculum and alternative Jewish culture, was Kaplan's first experiment in what would later be known as Reconstructionism.

From its inception, the TI curriculum had four major sections: Hebrew (*Ivrit b'Ivrit*), Bible, history, and pedagogy. In addition, Kaplan introduced the arts into the curriculum. "This was due, once again, to the consistent influence of Benderly, and was derived from modern educational theorists such as Pestalozzi [1746–1827, a Swiss educator whose theory of education was based on the importance of a pedagogical method that corresponds to the natural order of individual development and of concrete experiences] and Dewey." The emphasis on the arts also stems from Kaplan's belief that "the intellectual and spiritual emphases of traditional Jewish culture were to be augmented by the material and the aesthetic" (Kaufman, 1997, 598). Hebrew and the arts were considered the soul and the heart of the school, and Kaplan's teaching of the Bible and biblical interpretation were its mind.

To implement his convictions, Kaplan invited a specialized faculty to teach the arts. Kaufman (1997) describes the various art classes that were offered at the TI: "The first arts class to be introduced to the teachers' college was in music, historically the most Jewish of the arts" (698). Samuel Goldfarb was invited to teach a class titled Jewish Music and Methods of Teaching Jewish Songs. Judith Kaplan, Mordecai Kaplan's daughter, and later on, Tzipora Jochsberger, taught music in the school. Reuben Leaf taught graphic arts from 1929 to 1935. Ari Kutai arrived in 1929 to teach elocution and dramatics, and folk dance was added to the curriculum. Hillel Bavli, one of the professors at the TI, commented on the warm and friendly atmosphere at the institute (599). Indeed the Teachers Institute was distinguished by its community feeling and acceptance. The student body was made up of the entire range of Jewish affiliations: Orthodox, Reform, secularists, Zionists, Bundists, and so on (601). Gezari describes what Kaplan's philosophy meant to her. "[He] ushered forth a philosophy that changed our ideas of Judaism. It was no longer limited to religion. It was civilization with [a] long history, a land, a language, a culture, and, of course, a religion, which would develop with the passage of time in which I could find my place without difficulty" (Gezari, 2002a, 8).

Although she was not always a stellar student (Minutes, July 1924), in her final examination in her education practicum, Gezari received the highest grade in the class (Practicum in Jewish Education, 1926). She maintains that Kaplan could see beyond grades, that he recognized her special talent and creativity and encouraged her to become a teacher (T. Gezari, 2005). In interviews and numerous speeches, Gezari describes Kaplan with admiration: an imposing man, tall, with penetrating, deep blue eyes. She often mentioned that due to his recognition of her talents in the arts, her love of teaching, and her passion for Judaism, she was given a unique opportunity to enter the world of Jewish education.

> You do not make it [in] the world of men unless you are strong. I had to be strong. I knew who I was. I knew where I was going. This is the world of art, and I am an artist. And I am doing wonderful things, and I am saying wonderful things. I speak my mind. That is why I made it. And of all people, Mordecai Kaplan! How come that he picked me? How come that he picked me from all the students? He had a great intuition, and he had admiration for creative people. All my teachers thought that I was unusual because I was an artist. It was the art that made me what I am. (T. Gezari, 2005)

Gezari's artistic and educational careers developed concurrently. Upon her graduation from the Teachers Institute in 1925 (T. Gezari, 2002b), Kaplan hired her to teach in his school at the Society for Advancement of Judaism and empowered her to integrate art into the school's curriculum. Eventually, with his support, Gezari designed her own curriculum using the arts as a teaching method for all subjects (T. Gezari, 2002b, 34).

Teacher of Jewish Teachers: Joining the Faculty of the Teachers Institute

In 1935 Gezari returned from a long visit to Israel, and once again it was Kaplan who opened a window of opportunity for her. This time he invited her to teach art at the Teachers Institute (T. Gezari, 2001a, 52). This was a unique opportunity for the young artist, allowing her to amalgamate her passion for Judaism and Israel, her love of art, and her innate desire to teach and educate. It was also an extraordinary opportunity for a woman. Sylvia Ettenberg, a 1937 TI graduate, underscores the fact that at this time there were only a few women on the faculty of JTS (Ettenberg, 2005). This pluralistic school provided the perfect environment for Gezari. Her title at the Teachers Institute was "special instructor in arts and crafts at the Teachers Institute" (Register, 1936, 32). She taught four sections of a two-credit class, Arts and Crafts in the Hebrew School, which met twice a week. The aims of the course were "to train the prospective teacher in the use of drawing and design as aids to the teaching process and to correlate arts and crafts with the various subjects of the Hebrew School curriculum" (Register, 1936, 32). Gezari's tenure at JTS spanned forty-two years, ending only with her retirement in 1977.

Sylvia Ettenberg reminisces, "Temima was teaching arts and crafts and her course was a required course at the Teachers institute. She taught art, and Judith Kaplan taught music. They were not full-time faculty; they were adjunct faculty. The whole idea was that you are going to be teacher and you are going to do crafts with your students" (Ettenberg, 2005). Ettenberg explains that Gezari's role was more than just introducing the students to various materials such as clay and wood in order to teach art skills and to create holiday projects. She also nurtured her young students and enhanced their general education.

Temima was invited because it was decided that teachers needed to know how to work with the arts in the classroom. You have to understand that in the early days people came from neighborhoods and communities where they did not have experiences with museums and with art. Dr. Kaplan felt that educators need to have experience with art and should receive art education. When I was a student, she took me to museums. She insisted that we go to museums, and she went with us. She took our education seriously. I remember her saying that "my job is to open you up as a flower," and she repeated this saying over and over again. That was her goal. (Ettenberg, 2005)

Director of an Art Department:
The Bureau of Jewish Education

In 1940 Alexander Dushkin, who wrote his dissertation on Dewey and Jewish education, invited Gezari to head the department of art at what was then called the Jewish Education Committee of New York and was later renamed the Bureau of Jewish Education (BJE). Dushkin, an idealist, was influenced by Dewey's commitment to democracy. He wanted Jewish education to be considered an integral part of general education, offered to everyone, and not an institution detached from American mainstream education (Kronish, 1982). When he invited Gezari to head the art department, it served over 150 congregational schools that met after public school hours all over the metropolitan area.

Gezari realized that most teachers did not have a solid background in the arts and various media such as clay, woodworking, papier-mâché, plaster of Paris, and so on. Accordingly, she saw her role as the head of the department as fostering the teaching of basic art skills to all the teachers. She was also interested in demonstrating how art could enhance Jewish studies. Gezari wrote in her news column, "It was most important to establish some workshops where they [Hebrew school teachers] could become acquainted with [techniques of making art]. . . . The art workshops came as an oasis to a wanderer in the desert" (T. Gezari, 1948, 5). Consequently Gezari instituted teachers' workshops, holiday craft and art festivals, and annual international art exhibitions for children and teachers on Israeli and Jewish themes. Some of these were A Three-Dimensional Tour of Israel; From Adam to Prophet; From Swords to Plowshares; and exhibitions based on the children's books *The World of Peretz: Life in Eastern Europe* and *A Walk through the Streets of Jerusalem* (T. Gezari, 1966, 4). Sometimes the teachers requested a specialized in-service art education course. For example, in 1961, the teachers asked her to "broaden their knowledge of both the Persian and Egyptian periods in connection with their preparation for Purim and Passover" (T. Gezari, 1961, 9). Gezari conducted this workshop at the Jewish Museum.

Miryom Kass, a TI student in 1962, has powerful memories of Gezari's classes. She remembers a workshop about Purim where she learned how to make a *ra'ashan* (a noise-maker for Purim) decorated with Persian decorations, but her favorite memory was from a unit on chalk painting based on the Song of Songs. "For the series of pastels on the Song of Songs we had to draw with a chalk in one continuous line. [Gezari] wanted to free our hands and our head from hesitations about drawing. I still have things that I made with her. I was very proud of them, and I used them when I taught Talmud Torah." Miryom describes Gezari as a very passionate and colorful woman. "It is more than forty years ago, and I still remember it as if it was yesterday. She instilled us with something that could not be duplicated. She was more than a teacher. She made us excited about Judaism through the art" (Kass, 2005).

Gezari retired from the Bureau of Jewish Education in 2002 when she was ninety-seven, but she did not stop advocating for the arts. She stayed busy making art, exhibiting, and writing her memoirs.

Always an Artist

Looking for new experiences to expand her horizons as an artist, Gezari pursued unusual adventures in travel. In 1931, she bought a car and drove with two female friends to New Mexico to study at the Taos School of Art. Throughout her life she continued to travel extensively around the globe, alone and with her husband, explore different cultures, and present papers about art and education. Along the way, Gezari met people who inspired her art and recognized her special talent. One of these artists was Diego Rivera (1886–1957), a Mexican social realist painter who concerned himself primarily with the physical process of human development and the effects of technological progress. For him, murals, with their public accessibility, were the perfect canvas on which to tackle the grand themes of the history and future of humanity. A lifelong Marxist, Rivera saw the mural as an antidote to the elite walls of galleries and museums. Both his original painting style and the force of his ideas remain major influences on American painting.

In 1933, while painting a mural at Rockefeller Center, Rivera let Gezari observe him paint and taught her the art of mural and fresco making (T. Gezari, 2002b). She was fascinated by his stories about his murals "based on the history of the Mexican people, showing them their proud heritage, hoping to awaken in them pride and dignity, and raise them from the depths of despair and hopelessness" (T. Gezari, 2002b, 23). Inspired by this philosophical approach to mural painting, she used murals to express herself as an artist. Additionally, she used it extensively while teaching as a form of communal art that enhances ethnic identity and Jewish peoplehood.

Following the meeting with Rivera, Gezari went again to New Mexico. From there she proceeded to Israel, where she was deeply inspired by the sights, sounds, and smells of the land, and immersed herself in the Israeli way of life for a year. Upon her return from Israel, it was again Kaplan, her mentor, who helped her with a major breakthrough as an artist. Kaplan, a disciple of Ahad Ha'am, believed that Jewish continuity could be achieved by creative efforts, especially in the arts (Scult, 2001). True to his convictions, in 1935 Kaplan commissioned Gezari, who was a member of the Reconstructionist synagogue and a friend of the family, to paint a mural for his synagogue, the Society for the Advancement of Judaism (SAJ), at 15 West Eighty-sixth Street in Manhattan (T. Gezari, 2002b, 34).

The mural was the outcome of Kaplan's strong desire to bring visual art to the synagogue and his belief that there is "something unprecedented in the very idea of having a mural in a synagogue" (Kaplan, 1935). In spite of a stormy exchange with the synagogue board members, who, according to Kaplan, objected to the mural, the SAJ leaders eventually agreed to his plan: a mural by "Miss Temima Nimtzowitz as a memorial to Israel Unterberg" (Kaplan, 1935). Israel Unterberg, together with Louis Brush, funded the Teachers Institute building at 3080 Broadway that is the current home of the Jewish Theological Seminary. Unterberg was also one of the founders of the Society for Advancement of Judaism.

Receiving this commission was an important milestone in Gezari's professional life as an artist as well as a landmark in the Jewish approach to synagogue art. She considered this mural to be a natural continuation of the long tradition of murals, mosaics, and other wall and floor decorations in synagogues that was interrupted by an extremist interpretation of the second commandment (T. Gezari, 1935). Following in the footsteps of Kaplan, Gezari argued that with the transformation of the synagogue to a community center, the decorations on its walls should also undergo a change, drawing on Jewish life, not just nature and abstract designs. "The variety of subject matter at the disposal of the artist is infinite" (T. Gezari, 1935, 7). The mural was painted in the social realist style that she had learned while studying with Beulah Stevenson and assisting Diego Rivera in Rockefeller Center in 1933. Titled *Palestine's Past, Present, and Future,* the mural expressed her love of Israel and her idealistic view of the country as a place where everyone can live in harmony.

> One panel dealt with the ancient architecture, Hasidim praying, Hasidim dancing, young children in the old "*heder*" set up, money lenders, and many colorful types of characters walking through the narrow, arched cobblestone streets of Jerusalem. Another panel dealt with the new land, new architecture, students at the Hebrew University, scientists, researchers, the Haifa Technion, youths marching, and workers involved in construction. (T. Gezari, 2002a)

One of the members of SAJ described the mural as "a departure from the norm in synagogue decoration." He suggested that the message of the mural was pluralism in Israel, "being able to see the Hasidim and being able to smell the oranges" (Zuckerbraun, 2005). In 2005, for the seventieth anniversary of the installation of the mural, the SAJ congregation honored Gezari and the mural, restored, was rehung on the walls of the social hall of SAJ.

Mural painting allowed Gezari to make art a communal experience, accessible to all, not just to a few chosen students or artists. She continued to paint in that style for many years. A vivid example of a communal mural in the social-realism style is the one she created with her students for the synagogue at Camp Cejwin in 1935. The mural, 20 by 8 feet, focuses on the ancient *bik-*

kurim (first fruits) procession, the agriculture aspect of Shavuot (Pentecost) as described in the Bible and the Mishnah. Gezari depicted the children singing, carrying their baskets of fruits on their way to the old Technion (an institute of higher learning founded in 1924 and dedicated to technology and sciences) to be sold for the benefit of Keren Kayemet (the Jewish National Fund). The mural is now at the Yemin Orde Youth Village in Israel (Ettenberg, 2005).

The murals at SAJ and Yemin Orde are only two examples of Gezari's love of murals and community projects. In a letter to Ayala Gordon, a former student who later on became the director of the Children's Wing at the Israel Museum in Jerusalem, Gezari stressed the art of murals as an important community project that could lead to ethnic pride, peace, and harmony. She argued that mural painting offered "the opportunity of developing relationships that lead to cooperative living and an understanding of one another" (T. Gezari, 1964). Indeed, she was a pluralist in her approach to Judaism (Silberstein, 2005). This inclusive approach helped her in her work at the Teachers Institute at JTS and at the BJE where she worked with diverse religious denominations and teachers from a range of educational venues, such as camps, day schools, and congregational schools. For her, art was the language that could bridge differences among Jews and among the people in the world.

A Mother

Many of Gezari's paintings and sculptures depict her parents, grandparents, and other family members. For her, family life and motherhood were a natural extension of her life. In 1936, after the completion of the synagogue mural, she went back to Israel, met Zvi Gezari and was married in 1938. Her children were born in New York in 1942 and 1944.

Gezari's commitment to art did not deter her from integrating motherhood with her work nor did it diminish her creative output. She readily made some adjustments once her children were born. In interviews Gezari described motherhood as a privilege. "It is important that the female artist never forget that she has the most marvelous role to fulfill — that of a mother. My experience with my two children is one that I will never give up" (Stocks, 1976). During her child-rearing years, she took up sculpting and rented a studio at the Arts League in New York City. She felt that it was easier to leave a sculpture unfinished than a painting (T. Gezari, 2005). In her artwork, Gezari uses images of motherhood. In her mosaic *Woman of Valor* Gezari depicts a woman with three heads and four hands: each hand is performing some feminine duty, such as holding a baby, stirring the pot, sweeping the floor (T. Gezari, 2001b, 27).

Despite his mother's adventurous life as a young artist, Gezari's son Daniel remembers a surprisingly conventional childhood with family trips, lively dinners, and many holiday parties. "It is very interesting that she was a very traditional type of a mother. She was a very good mother. If I imagine an artist today, I imagine someone very cool, sophisticated, a person who is a little mysterious. Mama was not at all like this. She was very much of an old-fashioned mother, old-fashioned girl. And she was very loving and active, a hardworking mother" (D. Gezari, 2005). Daniel recalls a favorite picture of family life, an oil painting, *Traveling to Rocky Point*, the Gezari weekend home on Long Island (D. Gezari, 1985, 53). In the painting, Gezari depicts herself sitting next to her husband, Zvi, while he drives the family car, the two boys smiling in the back seat. In the mirror one can see the city's bridges and Manhattan skyscrapers in the distance while the car moves toward the farms and fields of rural Rocky Point.

A Feminist?

Commenting on his mother's experiences that were atypical for Jewish women of her time, Daniel tries to reconcile the differences in his description of her as an old-fashioned woman and mother, an adventurous artist, and an accomplished Jewish educator at the TI and BJE. He describes his mother, in her youth, as an unusual, free-spirited, and daring woman.

> She was the first liberated woman. What I mean is that she did things that were so unique. She was truly liberated, and it came from the inside. It had nothing to do with politics; she did not need to work on her self-esteem or go to yoga and free herself from expectations and restrictions of society. She did not care about what other people thought or said. She had her own agenda, her tremendous spirit and her own dreams and plans. She just operated completely freely, and she did what she wanted to do. It really did not matter to her. I am not even sure that she was aware what society had in mind for women to do during the twenties and thirties. I am not sure that she was aware of what the traditional role should be. She was just completely motivated, enthusiastic. A very idealistic woman. She had a big blind spot for what a woman had to do or should have been or could not do. (D. Gezari 2005)

When asked about her views on feminism, Gezari identifies art as the driving force in her life and her career. Her gender, she claims, never posed any insurmountable challenges. "I do not belong to a feminist group. I was always liberated. I was liberated at an early age when I discovered that I was an artist" (Stocks, 1976, 31). It is this combination of power, independence, warmth, and spontaneity that made her unique. While fulfilling all of women's traditional roles as a mother, a wife, and a hostess in her famous Hanukkah parties and Friday dinners, Gezari was highly determined and ambitious about her career as an educator and as an artist.

According to her friends, Gezari displayed at home the same creative and innovative educational methods she used in her work. Her close friend Harriet Zion recalls a visit to the Gezari family. "She raised her children in a creative way. They would do the most unusual things. We came to visit them one evening, and Daniel was sewing a pair of suede pants for himself. My children were mesmerized. For Dan it was normal, but my children never saw something like [that] before" (Zion, 2006). She was a creative person and respected the individuality of her children. Long before Gardner (1983) introduced the theory of multiple intelligences, Gezari intuitively understood that children express themselves in many ways. At home and at work she allowed them to be creative and explore new areas. She realized that people could excel in many different ways. Both her son Daniel and his daughter are astrophysicists. Her younger son, Walter, is an innovative engineer.

An Author

In addition to her teaching position at the Teachers' Institute, running the art department at the BJE, illustrating children's books, and exhibiting her own art in local galleries and synagogues, Gezari was an author. Her first book, *The Jewish Kindergarten*, which she wrote with Deborah Pessin, received a warm welcome. The reviewer, Libbie Braverman (1945), explained that the greatness of the book was its focus on children receiving their first impression about Judaism in a positive manner through the arts. "[The book] is an important advance in both methods and approach, for it represents a decided departure from the formal traditional procedures current in too many religious schools today. It raises the level of the educational approach in the entire primary department" (56).

In 1956 Gezari and the art department of the Jewish Education Committee published the first issue of *Brush and Color*, which appeared annually until 1997. The journal served as a platform for exchanging views on different art topics. In it, Gezari highlights the importance of art "to help Jews to transcend ideological differences through shared emotional experiences communicated by the skill of the artist" (T. Gezari, 1956, 5). From the first issue, Gezari, made clear that the mission of art department was in concert with Dushkin's vision for the JEC: to be inclusive of all Jewish schools: day schools, Yiddish Schools, and congregational schools (Krasner, 2005). The goal was not to develop artists, but to appreciate the Jewish cultural heritage and to facilitate "integration of art with the curriculum in all the schools regardless of their ideology that spanned the spectrum of Orthodox, Conservative, Reform, Yiddish, and secular Israeli schools" (T. Gezari, 1966, 2). Depending on the school, art was taught as extracurricular classes or integrated with the general studies, as it was in the Yeshiva of Crown Heights (Potter, 1986, 6).

The aims Gezari articulated were consonant with Dewey's belief about art as a powerful force of expression (Dewey, 1934/1980) and highlighted the need to nurture and mentor teachers, a continuation of her career at the TI. Her goals were:

> To further the introduction and development of art as a force for creative living
>
> To foster art as a basic medium for the growth and development of our children
>
> To set up standards for effective art teaching
>
> To improve conditions so that the art teachers will be able to develop to their maximum potential. (T. Gezari, 1963, 2)

These goals are broadly stated, addressing the issues of art education in general. However, the vehicle for their implementation was always a universalized Jewish theme. This approach allowed her to open the door for all her constituents and gave them the freedom to integrate the arts in ways that were acceptable to and comfortable for them.

Brush and Color introduced the topic for an annual children's exhibition, explained the subcategories of the theme, specified instructions for the art, and described the submission process. It included ideas and suggestions for projects, stories from art teachers who studied with Gezari and participated in the annual exhibitions, and letters from teachers around the tristate area commenting on the previous exhibition. Gezari always included an editorial, a section called "Broadening Our Horizons," with a book review; reviews of new art exhibits; suggestions for further reading in journals, magazines, and books on art education; and an educational essay she wrote. The annual often featured Gezari's talks at INSEA (the International Society for Education through the Arts) conferences. It included essays by prominent figures in the art world in general such as Cecil Roth (1899–1970), the Jewish historian, educator, and author of *Jewish Art* (1961), and Viktor Lowenfeld (1903–60), a professor of art education at Pennsylvania State University who helped define and develop the field of art education in the United States. There was a special section for letters from art educators from around the world who kept in touch with Gezari.

Gezari was proudest of *Footprints and New Worlds: Experiences in Art with Child and Adult* (1957) published by the Reconstructionist Foundation. It was again Kaplan who encouraged Gezari to articulate her philosophy of religion and art education, to document her ideas about art and Jewish education, and write a textbook for teachers. In the introduction, she defends the integration of art and Jewish religion and maintains that one can be deeply Jewish and still be a humanist. She identifies the principles of her teaching methods and explores their implementation with many examples, such as teaching Shabbat, building *sukkot*, and offering descriptions of teaching units for children and adults.

In subsequent years, Gezari published numerous articles and papers, short biographical books, an album of her major works; she also illustrated children's books such as *Hillel's Happy Holidays* (1939), by Mamie Gamoran. As an educator, Gezari understood the power of the written word in promoting her vision of art education and that by publishing books and journal articles she was creating a formal field of Jewish art education.

A Philosophy of Art

When Gezari studied art as a child, it was mostly taught as a discrete subject and was based on modeling, coloring books, and color by numbers (T. Gezari, 1957, 2002c). In 1936, in an editorial about the curriculum of the Hebrew school, Rabbi Kohn states, "Most Jewish schools operate with curricula that are based on tradition rather then on the educational needs of the modern child . . . and with correspondingly unsatisfactory methods" (Shindelman, 1936, 24). Gezari had different ideas about art education. Harriet Zion stresses that what was important for Gezari was the individual. She wanted her student teachers to honor the child's creative mind and imagination, to respect their freedom of expression (Zion, 2005). Hyman Campeas vividly remembers his first encounter with Gezari and how she scolded him for modeling for his students rather than letting them create their own paintings.

> I was just discharged from the Navy, and I took a teaching job at the Forest Hills Jewish Center. Of course I had no idea about what it meant to be a Jewish educator. We were preparing for one of the exhibitions that Gezari organized. She came to inspect the artwork and told me, "Hyman, I see a 'campenious' in every single painting." (Campeas, 2006)

In 1967 the Jewish Education Committee published *Art in Our Classrooms*, which compiled many of the writings of the art teachers who participated in Gezari's art workshops. The introduction to the book outlines Gezari's most cherished principles of art education, stressing the students' creative ability, rejecting the use of precut, predrawn patterns, modeling of shapes, and allowing each child to experiment with the material.

It is not clear whether Gezari was familiar with Dewey's ideas about education in general and art education in particular, but she must have soaked up Dewey's principles while a student in Benderly's Prep School for Girls. Zealously, she objected to exclusive text teaching and advocated for learning by doing, since it facilitated understanding, expression, and recall. Like Dewey, she challenged teachers to create projects that would be interesting to the students and relevant to their lives (Dewey, 1902/1990). Gezari used to say, "Children may not remember what they read, but they remember what they did" (Zion, 2005). She knew that any content, whether history, literature, or the Hebrew language, could be taught through the arts. The teacher needed to be sensitive to children's needs, attracting the student to Jewish content through the right questions and recognizing students' achievements in the arts as legitimate expressions of knowledge. Creating and drawing stories of the Bible improves learning, she argued. Like Dewey (1938) who explored the importance of experience and relevance to the child's life in his classic work *Experience and Education*, Gezari insisted that art does not take away from text study; rather it enriches it.

Like contemporary art educator Karen Gallas (1995) who encourages teachers to listen to the narratives behind children's art, Gezari argued that through paintings and drawings, teachers could hear the hidden stories children tell. "And if the child paints the sky pink or the grass pink, does that mean that he thinks all grass is pink? No, he likes that color, and he likes where he put it" (Sofer, 1985, 59). Chana Silberstein, who worked with Gezari at the Bureau of Jewish Education, corroborates her lifelong focus on creativity and respect for the child (T. Gezari, 2001c). "Temima used to say to the teachers, 'They are creative human beings; just let them create, and then let them talk and write about what they drew.' She was truly ahead of her time" (Silberstein, 2005). Gezari acknowledged learning differences and argued that with enough encouragement and a positive atmosphere, teachers could help students learn.

> Every child needs the right climate for learning and creating. There is no telling how far he will go. He reaches his potential and then, because of understanding and encouragement, he grows beyond his potential. In the realm of the spirit there is no ceiling. One goes from growth to growth, ever refueling oneself through one's own creative energy. (T. Gezari, 1971)

Lifsa Schachter, who studied with Gezari in 1950, describes similar experiences as a student in Gezari's art class:

> It was just before Hanukkah. I stepped into the class, a new class. Temima handed all of us pieces of clay but did not give any instruction. I was playing with the clay, studying the texture, the possibilities of shapes. Everyone around me was busy making *hanukkiyot* [candleholders] for the approaching holiday. I felt a little embarrassed to be left behind. As I was looking around, Temima approached me and complimented me that I was not rushing to produce, [that] I was taking my time. She was so happy that I wanted to study the clay before rushing to make something. She was not at all a product-oriented teacher. She really wanted the art to come out of our hearts and our souls. It was not the end product that was important, but the process of creation. (Schachter, 2005)

Gezari insisted that there was a tight link between being an artist and an art educator. A practicing artist, Gezari continued to sculpt, draw, paint, and exhibit in many galleries and synagogues. She believed that one cannot teach art without being an artist, and at the same time, one cannot be an artist without sharing one's art with the world.

> I feel very strongly that art teachers must never stop being artists. They must continually work in their art media for personal growth and development in creative way. We urge teachers constantly to spend a good proportion of their time painting. . . . I, too, cannot be useful as an art educator unless I continually improve myself as an artist. (T. Gezari, 2001a, 84)

The Lincoln Center Institute, founded to meet the needs of public schools, was created in 1978 under the leadership of the noted educator, Maxine Greene (Holzer and Noppe-Brandon, 2005). The institute offers experiential professional development for teachers by in the use of art, including dance, music, theater, visual arts, and architecture. Many years before the birth of the institute, Gezari argued that studying the arts made teachers more creative and expressive and taught them how to better reach and understand their students. Intuitively, Gezari understood that in order to teach through the arts, teachers should experience making art.

Children's Art Exhibitions

In 1940 Gezari began to mount art exhibitions. There were children's exhibitions, teachers' exhibitions, international exhibitions, and traveling exhibitions. In addition, there were three exhibits titled Special People—Special Gifts, which were dedicated to teaching children with special needs (John, 1997). Children's exhibitions—in museums and on Jewish themes—were a new and unheard of concept at the time. The Metropolitan Museum Children's Wing opened in 2007. The first Met family program that involved children painting occurred in 1974 (Metropolitan Museum Education Department, personal communication, May 1, 2006). Gezari was always ahead of her time.

Gezari educated Jewish teachers not only about art, but also about pedagogy and Judaism. She understood the impact of exhibiting student work on the artists' self-esteem and that group work could energize students, teachers, and schools. Before "exhibition of mastery" became one of the buzzwords of constructivist education, Gezari realized that content knowledge could be demonstrated through painting, sculpture, and model building.

The Children's Art Committee, headed by Gezari, developed the guidelines to educate students and teachers about thematic art units (Drake, 2004), a term that had not yet become fashionable. The themes were always connected to Judaism or to Israel. Titles included the "American Jewish Calendar," "We Open the Bible," and "From Adam to Prophets." Preparing for the Focus on

Israel exhibition, Gezari outlined areas of learning for the teachers: geography and topography of Israel; modes of transportation in Israel, such as El-Al or Zim (ships); models of major cities, villages, and kibbutzim; and important sites of religious observance. Gezari elaborated on how to teach each particular theme, how to introduce it to the students, and how to create a discussion around the issues (or core concepts, as we refer to them today).

Gezari's approach, combining the universal with the particular, drawing upon the diversity of Jewish culture and texts can be seen in the suggestions for teachers for the "Try a Little Kindness!" exhibition. Gezari explained that the topic, although found in the Talmud was not just a Jewish value but a universal value. The theme might be extended to popular American culture, such as the song "Give a Helping Hand." She suggested that teachers use biblical stories as well, such as Rebecca giving Abraham's servant and his camels water, Ruth showing concern for her mother-in-law, or the *Halahmah anya* passage in the Passover *seder* that invites all the hungry to come and eat. She recommended teaching about the mitzvah of *bikur holim* (visiting the sick), consoling mourners, or planting trees for the next generation. She also included the state of Israel's involvement with helping the emerging nations of Africa. Gezari provided a list of foundations to which students could donate money to help the poor, such as ORT (Organization for Rehabilitation through Training) and Keren Ami. Additionally, Gezari promoted world knowledge and humanistic values by referring to current events, such as hunger in Biafra.

Gezari was always looking for exciting artistic materials for her yearly exhibitions, and she varied the specifications for submission. Often she asked for three-dimensional submissions such as wood and bronze sculptures, and mosaics, in addition to more conventional two-dimensional paintings. Being true to her ideal that teachers need to keep learning and growing, she challenged them as well as their students and exposed them to new materials, The 1966 exhibition "For Everything There Is a Season" was built around Ecclesiastes 3:1. For this exhibition, Gezari planned a wall consisting of a series of 3-foot by 3-foot squares made of various metals, such as copper, aluminum, brass, and nickel. She suggested embossing, piercing, or etching the metals. For the annual exhibition in 1967, the holiday theme "Let There Be Light" was to be executed as mobiles and stabiles. They could be made from plastic, glass, or other transparent materials that played with light.

Participation in the children's exhibitions was not limited to students in the United States. During 1947 there were submissions from Canada, Mexico, China, and Palestine (T. Gezari, 1947, 7). The exhibitions took place in various locations. In 1947 the exhibition appeared at the Museum of the City of New York; from 1948 to 1963, exhibitions were held at the Jewish Museum in New York, where Gezari also opened the city's first "Please Touch" gallery (T. Gezari, 1951). During the first years, the exhibitions traveled. The

1948 exhibition "Life in Our Community" traveled to Florida and Colorado. Stephen S. Kayser, a curator at the Jewish Museum, wrote to Gezari, "I want very much to thank you for the opportunity of having this large international exhibition of children's art here" (quoted in T. Gezari, 1948, 7). He was referring to the many visitors that the show brought to the museum. This point of view changed fifteen years later, when the Jewish Museum decided that children's art had no place in a "real" museum. At some point the directors Allan Solomon and Sam Hunter decided that having a children's wing and having children's art hung side by side with that of great artists diminished the importance of the Jewish Museum (T. Gezari, 1968, 17).

Recounting a similar event, Ettenberg explains that being ignorant of the process of making art decreases the value of the art product in the eyes of the observer. "Judah Goldin, who was the dean of the TI from 1952–58 and a graduate of the Teachers Institute himself, once said to me, 'Why are these pictures and cutouts pasted on the windows?' I said, 'It is from the art class.' He said, 'Get them down; this is not a children's gallery'" (Ettenberg, 2005).

The permanent home for the Gezari exhibitions became the BJE of New York. She continued to mount exhibitions until her retirement in 2002. Miryom Kass remembers the art exhibitions vividly:

> This woman turned the building of the Board of Jewish Education on Fifty-eighth Street to an art gallery every year. All the schools participated. It was a different theme every year, and it gave you ideas to discuss, things to teach to children in a way that children could relate to. And then they drew pictures, and we sent them to her and she would put them up. It was not professional art, but she treated it as if it was professional. She did a fantastic job. (Kass, 2005)

Art and Democracy

How did Gezari organize the exhibitions? To emphasize her commitment to art as an educational tool and as a method to connect students to Jewish studies, she established a democratic way of exhibiting children's art. There were no competitions and juries. Compliance with the guidelines in terms of skills, content, and medium was enough to merit exhibition.

Gezari objected passionately to competitions and saw no educational value in them. The only form of healthy competition, according to her, was "competition within the self." Her distaste for competition was consistent with her philosophy that "art belongs to all and not only to the few. Contests may offer incentives, but they do not bring about great artists. We should not concentrate on the few and neglect the others" (T. Gezari, 1981, 14). It was not the end product that was important, but the process as it unfolded in creation and expression. Hadassah Rubel, one of Gezari's students, described the art projects she did in class as "democratic ventures." She notes that the children understood and accepted differences in artistic talent and ability, "but they tried to encourage one another for the good of the project at hand" (cited in T. Gezari, 1967, 77).

Was Gezari's philosophy about competition influenced by her studies at the Prep School for Girls? Samson Benderly was also interested in eradicating competition as an impetus to learning. At Camp Achvah, he staged performances in which every single child was active and played a part, thus emphasizing that drama and acting are learning situations rather than performances that require auditions for roles (Winter, 1966, 137). Like Benderly, Gezari rejected the notion that "the triumph of one depends on the failure of the other." She argued, "Wherever you find a contest, there also you will find a poor or mediocre teacher, or a principal without principles, or a commercial enterprise looking for a free advertising" (T. Gezari, 1970, 7).

Gezari objected vehemently to any form of competition, not only for children, but also for adults, including herself. "I am not a competitive artist. I am not interested in being better than anybody else. The person I compete with is myself" (T. Gezari, 1981, 14). She was continuously cautioning parents and teachers against competition and the desire to obtain prizes and awards. She explained that children have a natural tendency to express themselves through art, and the opportunity to participate in exhibitions with other children, sometimes from all over the world, was motivation enough to create artwork on a high level.

A Legacy

What is Gezari's legacy for Jewish educators today? During her tenure as a teacher at JTS and the director of the art department at the BJE, Gezari championed a model of educational innovation, creating the field of art education in Jewish education. She argued for child-centered education, sensitivity to creative expression, the nurturing of imagination, and differentiated learning. Even though she was a passionate advocate for demonstration of mastery and loved creating art exhibitions, she emphasized above all the value of the process of making art. In her teaching she always stressed the teaching of skills and the integration of art and Jewish studies. Most of these terms and concepts are now central to contemporary educational thought. But before these terms became common, Gezari incorporated them into her progressive pedagogy and taught them to Jewish teachers and teachers-to-be. Gezari's goal of using the arts to explore Jewish texts, values, and holidays eventually took hold in synagogue schools, camps, informal education, and some day schools. However, Gezari might have been critical of some of the current practitioners, who emphasize the product and not the process. She believed in a twofold process, first a mastery of the art form and then its application to Jewish texts. Administrators and educators who subscribe to Gezari's sophisticated vision do not revert to product-based art projects (Backen-roth, 2005).

According to Kronish (1982), much lip service was paid to the influence of Dewey and progressive education on Jewish education. He claims that educators might have used Dewey's language, but they failed to make the bridge from theory to practice. "Dewey's impact upon Jewish education was more superficial or external than previously assumed" (189). However, Gezari, like many of the women who worked with Benderly and Kaplan, worked directly with teachers and was more likely to implement Dewey's principles of education that she had imbibed from Benderly, Kaplan, and Dushkin.

Gezari changed teachers' practices by showing them how to integrate art into content teaching and by creating venues for encouraging students' creativity and expression. According to Chana Silberstein, "Temima never quoted Dewey in her numerous papers and books; however, she spoke his language. She talked about art with a 'small a'" (Silberstein, 2005). (Dewey contrasted art with a "small a" to art with a "capital A," the former being art by everyone and the latter being high art exclusive to museum and art critiques.)

What happened to Gezari's life's work once she retired? Who replaced her? Silberstein explains that there was a change in the way things were being done at the BJE even during the last few years of Gezari's employment. With the relocation of the bureau to Fifty-eighth Street, Gezari no longer had the proper space for workshops and exhibitions. In addition, the process of decentralizing art services, which started back in 1958, and bringing teachers' art workshops to the suburbs continued on a larger scale (Silberstein, 2005). Indeed, from 1958 on, Gezari traveled to the individual schools in places such as Westchester, Long Island, and Brooklyn to give art workshops (T. Gezari, 1958, 5). Silberstein elaborates:

> We changed the model of art education. We do not do direct service any more. We do not do exhibitions any more; we are trying to train people who will coach other teachers. At the time we changed direction it was already hard for Temima to run around from borough to borough and give lectures to teachers. It is a different service delivery model. Temima moved with us to the new building two years ago but there was no place to mount exhibitions anymore. We gave her an office but she was very restricted in what she could do. . . .
>
> Gezari was a visionary, and she was able to infect many people with her passion for the arts and teaching Judaism through the arts. She was electric and in perpetual motion. She was a walking history. She took great pride in her work and in her students' work. She had a council that met twice a year, but she was a one-person show. (Silberstein, 2005)

Was she a one-person show? Gezari's focus on the process of making art and on learning through art was not understood by some of her supervisors.

Schiff, the Irving L. Stone Distinguished Professor of Education at the Azrieli Graduate School at Yeshiva University, and Gezari's supervisor for twenty years at the BJE, acknowledges her contributions to the field of Jewish education. He echoes Silberstein's views and suggests that Gezari was a singular voice with unusual perseverance to work toward and achieve her goals. "She always had a clear vision of what she wanted to do, teach, paint, exhibit; she had total focus. She never gave up" (Schiff, 2006). Schiff acknowledges her contributions to the field of Jewish education. He argues that there was a disagreement among educators about the importance of the arts. Even though the 1947 enrollment report in congregational school stated that adding experimental arts courses to the Jewish school curriculum created anticipation for robust enrollment in the schools (Shindelman, 1947, 24), using the arts did not become a routine practice in Jewish schools at that time. Rabbi George Ende, an educational consultant on Hebrew teaching for high school students at the Bureau of Jewish Education, remarked, "While it is true that there is a growing tendency to leave room for the arts in the schedule of the class, too few schools have felt the need for making use of them in the teaching of what is regarded as the basic curriculum. This is largely responsible for the idea that the arts are frills, or at least a minor subject" (T. Gezari, 1949, 16).

Schiff emphasizes the positive influence of the art exhibitions and the teaching of art to the teachers and to their students. Disagreeing with Ende, he notes that schools would point to their art programs as an indicator of the quality of the school. He claims that schools were eager to hire an art teacher, to produce good art, and to participate in the exhibitions (Schiff, 2006).

Though Gezari might have been a "one-person show" at the BJE, she produced disciples who were influenced by her wisdom and her passion for child-centered and experiential education. Sylvia Hershkowitz, the director of Yeshiva University Museum since the 1970s, recalls that her father, himself a student of Benderly and Kaplan, urged her to take classes with Gezari at the BJE in 1944. Hershkowitz says that when the museum moved to its present location on Sixteenth Street in 2002, she staged a Gezari retrospective exhibition (Hershkowitz, 2006). In creating the Yeshiva University Museum, Hershkowitz, in classic Gezari fashion, emphasized its educational potential, using Jewish objects as teaching tools in the hands of museum educators.

Gezari felt that her contribution to Jewish art education was alive. In her numerous publications and conversations with me and other interviewers she often repeated, "Because of art, thousands of Jewish adults will remember their early impressionable years in Jewish schools with warmth and joy" (T. Gezari, 1983b, 36; 2001c, 6). Indeed, many of her students remember her fondly and emphasize her passion and love of teaching and nurturing.

To those who study the profusion of Jewish educational initiatives such as arts-based schools and camps (Backenroth, 2005), Avoda Arts (a nonprofit educational organization that uses art and culture as entry points into Jewish learning), and the growth of arts *batei midrash* (programs that involve both Judaica scholars and arts educators), it is clear that Gezari's legacy is indeed alive. Whether they studied with Gezari herself or with her students, the arts educators who implement these programs surely believe in her vision and add to her legacy.

REFERENCES

Backenroth, O. A. 2005. Weaving the arts into Jewish education. *Journal of Jewish Education* 70(3): 50–60.

Braverman, L. L. 1945. The Jewish kindergarten. *Jewish Education* 16(3): 56–57.

Campeas, H. 2006. Telephone interview, May 15.

Dewey, J. 1902/1990. *The Child and the Curriculum.* Chicago: University of Chicago Press.

———. 1934/1980. *Art as Experience.* New York: Perigee Books.

———. 1938. *Experience and Education.* New York: Collier Books.

Drake, S. 2004. *Integrated Curriculum*: Alexandria, Va.: ASCD.

Ende, G. 1949. The arts in the school curriculum. *Bulletin of the Jewish Education Committee of New York* 8: 16. Box 1, 301, 2, 21, Collection of the American Historical Society, New York.

Ettenberg, S. 2005. Interview, May 6.

Gallas, K. 1995. Arts as epistemology. *Harvard Educational Review* 24 (special issue on arts as education): 19–32.

Gamoran, M. 1939. *Hillel's Happy Holidays.* Cincinnati: Union of American Hebrew Congregations.

Gardner, H. 1983. *Frames of Mind: The Theory of Multiple Intelligences.* New York: Basic Books.

Gezari, D. 1985. *Temima Gezari.* Rocky Point, N.Y.: Studio Workshop Press.

———. 2005. Interview, July 7.

Gezari, T. 1935. Mural decorations in synagogues. *Reconstructionist* 1(10): 6–12.

———. 1947. Art for creative learning. *Jewish Education Committee Bulletin for Principals and Teachers*, 5. Box 1, 301, 2, 21, Collection of the American Jewish Historical Society, New York.

———. 1948. International exhibits. *Jewish Education Committee Bulletin for Principals and Teachers*, 7. Box 1, 307, 2, 21, Collection of the American Jewish Historical Society, New York.

———. 1951. Adventure in the Jewish museum. *Jewish Education Committee Bulletin for Principals and Teachers.* Box 1, 301, 2, 22, Collection of the American Jewish Historical Society, New York.

———. 1956. Your grandmother doesn't speak English? *Brush and Color* 1: 5–6.

———. 1957. *Footprints and New Worlds: Experiences in Art with Child and Adult.* New York: Reconstructionist Press.

———. 1958. *Jewish Education Committee Bulletin for Principals and Teachers*, 5. Box 1, 307, 27, Collection of the American Historical Society, New York.

———. 1961. Editorial. *Jewish Education Committee Bulletin for Principals and Teachers*, 9. Box 2, 301, 28, Collection of the American Historical Society, New York.

———. 1963. Editorial. *Brush and Color* 7: 2.

———. 1964. Excerpt from a letter. *Brush and Color* 8: 3.

———. 1966. An outline of the department of art education and its influence on the Jewish community, 1940–1965. *Brush and Color* 10: 4–5.

———, ed. 1967. *Art in the Classroom*. New York: Jewish Education Committee.

———. 1968. Editorial. *Brush and Color* 12: 17.

———. 1970. Editorial. *Brush and Color* 14: 7.

———. 1971. Editorial. *Brush and Color* 15: 11.

———. 1981. Editorial. *Brush and Color* 20: 14.

———. 1983a. Exhibition guidelines. *Brush and Color* 28: 18.

———. 1983b. The role of art in my life and in Jewish education. *Jewish Education* 51(3): 31–36.

———. 2001a. *Art and Education*. Rocky Point, N.Y.: Studio Workshop Press.

———. 2001b. *Now That I'm Ninety-five*. Rocky Point, N.Y.: Studio Workshop Press.

———. 2001c. The role of art in Jewish education in the last sixty years. Paper presented at the Jewish Theological Seminary Graduation.

———. 2002a. Dr. Mordecai M. Kaplan. *Jewish Theological Seminary Alumni Magazine*, 8–22.

———. 2002b. *I Remember*. Rocky Point, N.Y.: Studio Workshop Press.

———. 2002c. *Mama, Papa, and Me*. Rocky Point, N.Y.: Studio Workshop Press.

———. 2005. Telephone interview, May 12.

———. 2005. Public lecture, May 15. SAJ, New York.

Hershkowitz, S. 2006. Interview, October 23.

Holzer, M. F., and S. Noppe-Brandon, eds. 2005. *Community in the Making*. New York: Teachers College Press.

John, W. H. 1997. Learning about the world through art at the BJE. *Brush and Color* 34: 1–3.

Kaplan, M. 1934. *Judaism as a Civilization*. New York: Schocken Books.

———. 1935. Kaplan diary. Personal collection of Mel Scult.

Kass, M. 2005. Interview, August 8.

Kaufman, D. 1997. Jewish education as a civilization. In *Tradition Renewed: A History of the Jewish Theological Seminary*, ed. J. Wertheimer, 567–621. Vol. 1. New York: Jewish Theological Seminary of America.

Krasner, J. 2005. *Jewish Education* and American Jewish education, Part 1. *Journal of Jewish Education* 71(2): 121–77.

Kronish, R. 1982. John Dewey's influence on Jewish educators: The case of Alexander M. Dushkin. *Teachers College Record* 83(3): 420–33.

Lawrence-Lightfoot, S., and J. H. Davis. 1997. *The Art and Science of Portraiture*. San Francisco: Jossey-Bass.

Minutes. 1924. Students' Progress. Teachers Institute, Jewish Theological Seminary, New York.

Paine, R. 2006. Telephone interview, May 1. New York.

Poster. 1950. Jewish Education Committee. Box 1, 307, 1, 4. Collection of the American Jewish Historical Society, New York.

Potter, R. 1986. Art at the Yeshiva of Crown Heights. *Brush and Color* 1: 6.

Practicum in Jewish Education. 1926. Grades. Teachers Institute, the Jewish Theological Seminary, New York.

Register. 1936. Teachers Institute. New York: Jewish Theological Seminary.

Registration. 1956–57. Teachers Courses in Jewish Education. Box 1, 307, 1, 4. Collection of the American Jewish Historical Society, New York.

Schachter, L. 2005. Telephone interview, May 9.

Schiff, A. 2006. Telephone interview, August 2.

Shindelman, A. 1936. Curriculum of the Hebrew Week Day School; Reconstruction of the course of study. *Jewish Education Committee Bulletin for Principals and Teachers*, 24. Box 1, 307, 1, 8. Collection of the American Jewish Historical Society, New York.

———. 1947. Children's art exhibit praised by educators. *Jewish Education Committee Bulletin for Principals and Teachers*, 24. Box 1, 307, 2, 20. Collection of the American Jewish Historical Society, New York.

Scult, M., ed. 2001. *Communings of the Spirit: The Journals of Mordecai M. Kaplan.* Vol. 1. Detroit: Wayne State University Press.

Silberstein, C. 2005. Interview, September 20. New York.

Sofer, T. 1985. On purple cows and pink skies. *Jewish Education* 53(4): 57–60.

Stocks, J. 1976. Interview with Temima Gezari. *Brush and Color* 17 (February): 31–32.

Winter, N. H. 1966. *Jewish Education in a Pluralistic Society: Samson Benderly and Jewish Education in the United States.* New York: New York University Press.

Zion, H. 2005. Telephone interview, December 6. New York.

Zuckerbraun, M. 2005. Telephone interview, December 6. New York.

9 : Hava N'halela

Tzipora Jochsberger and Her Vision
for the Hebrew Arts School

1920–

Tzipora Jochsberger, circa 1960.
Photograph by Editta Sherman; courtesy of Tzipora Jochsberger

here has been a veritable explosion of interest in the arts and their place in American Jewish educational life. Jewish educational reformers are embracing the arts, once dismissed as a frill in an already-too-full-curriculum, as a tool to motivate, inform, and make meaning for students. It is not only that Jewish education is following, as it usually does, in the wake of general education, which is finally heeding the insistent voices of advocates like Maxine Greene and Elliot Eisner for aesthetic education. Jewish educators, like their counterparts in general education, are concerned about the ephemeral nature of "fragile learning." They are beginning to seek solutions in the work of Howard Gardner (1983) and his theory of multiple intelligences, or that of Eric Jensen (1998, 2001), who champions the findings of brain researchers to fuel curricular and instructional reform. Both of these theorists maintain that the arts promote learning that lasts. They are only two voices in the chorus encouraging the arts in schools, secular and Jewish, as an alternative to rote learning. The arts provide a catalyst for creativity, an opportunity for discovery rather than coverage and for rewarding process as well as product. This interest in the arts is not confined to liberal Jewish circles; Rabbi Chaim Brovender, *rosh yeshivah* (dean) of Yeshivat HaMivtar in Efrat, has recently endorsed the serious study of fine arts in Orthodox schools. He contends that the arts are surely not a *bitul Torah* (a waste of time that might be better spent in the study of Torah); the arts can serve as a gateway to *ahavat Hashem* (love of God) (Handelman and Saks, 2003).

The power of the arts in evoking a religious or cultural imagination is not a phenomenon only for schoolchildren. It forms the premise of Avoda, a program bringing Jewish college students to the arts, and has inspired what the National Foundation for Jewish Culture calls a Jewish cultural renaissance for adults as well (Siegel, 2002). The last time the arts appeared so prominently in discussions of Jewish educational reform was during the golden age of Jewish education, in the profusion of programs and projects inspired by Samson Benderly and Mordecai Kaplan. Jochsberger's school, which she founded in 1952 and directed until 1986, was the embodiment of the synthesis of the Hebraist-Zionist ideal and progressive education, the vision of the women captured in this album of pioneers. Like them, Jochsberger saw herself as offering an alternative to the vapid lives of American Jews, appealing to their imaginations through music. Jochsberger's view of Jewish cultural literacy was a broad one, extending well beyond classic texts and ritual competence to all aspects of Jewish civilization, modeling the worldview of Mordecai Kaplan.

In this chapter I analyze the original vision of the school, built upon interviews with Jochsberger, her supporters and former students; Jochsberger's accounts both published and unpublished; her publications; and archival documents from the early years of the school housed in the library of the Kaufman Center. I explore how a European-born Israeli, one whose parents were murdered in the Holocaust, understood the value of the Hebraist-Zionist ideal for American Jews and how she came to be a progressive educator.

A Biography

Hilde Jochsberger was born in 1920 in southern Germany, in the small town of Leutershausen.[1] Leutershausen, with a population of 2,000, was home to ten Jewish families. She became aware of antisemitism as early as the age of six, when she was excluded from a communal May festival in her town. The children with whom she grew up threw stones at her and referred to Jews as "the lowest of the low" (Jochsberger, 2003). Against this cacophony, there was always the music. Jochsberger (2003a) recalls these early sounds: "There was a dance hall in the village with dances held every Sunday night, and a brass band played. It was the first music I ever heard. I would stand by [my] window and listen to the music before going off to sleep. There was also a church in the town with an organ. I would stand behind the church to listen to the music. These were the first musical sounds I heard." Jochsberger's piano was the first one in the village. She studied from the age of eight with an excellent teacher her mother found in the nearby town of Ansbach.

One profile of Tzipora Jochsberger is titled "Saved by the Music" (Furstenberg, 1996). The descriptor is neither empty metaphor nor hyperbole. Jochsberger reflects on the course of her adolescent life:

> My parents promised my grandfather that they would send me to a better place to study. At ten I went to Heilbronn, [a town in Wuerttemberg] to the Realschule, where I studied until I was thirteen. I knew no one and stayed with my aunt. I would come back home with a Wuerttemberg accent. The Jewish girls in the school would accompany me to the station and take me back and forth [from home]. After I turned thirteen, the Nazis wouldn't let Jews study in their schools anymore [1933–34]. I organized the Jewish girls and we put on plays. I can't remember what they were. We did this at the house of my aunt. We charged admission and sent the money to a Jewish orphanage. (Jochsberger, 2003a)

A classmate was going to study at the Jewish Teachers Seminary (JTS) in Wuerzburg, and Jochsberger went along. There her teachers nurtured her love of music and her commitment to Jewish observance, the latter a novelty for Tzipora whose parents were not Shabbat observers. A meeting with Emil Hauser, the director of the Palestine Academy of Music, in 1938, led to an entrance exam and then a place in his school. This saved her life.

Too proud to ask for a scholarship, Jochsie paid for her tuition by working as a maid and taking on music students. She recalls, laughing, "Here a student, there a student; soon I had enough to exist!" (2003a). Jochsberger graduated from the academy in 1942. From 1942 to 1947, she was instructor of music at the Arab Teachers College in Jerusalem, run by the British government. In 1946, she was asked by the British to design a music curriculum for all the Arab schools. The basis for this curriculum was a genre that she would return to again and again: folk music.

From 1944 to 1947, Jochsberger taught piano and recorder, and directed the children's choir at her alma mater. It was there she developed a method of teaching music through Hebrew folk songs, using an authentic Israeli instrument, the *halil* (recorder). She extended the curricular approach she piloted in the Arab school project to her own people; it was based on a belief in the power of folk music to encapsulate a people's memories, aspirations, and values.

In 1945, Jochsberger learned what had happened to her parents during the war.

> When the Nazis broke into our house in 1938, my parents had to hide in an attic. At 5:00 A.M. they were told that they had to sell their estate and leave. They moved to Nuernberg. In 1942, they were sent to Terezin. In 1944, at the end of September, my father was sent to Auschwitz. In October, my mother was sent to Auschwitz. I heard about an uncle who had left Terezin and came to America. I went to New York to learn about my parents' last years. I took a course at the Juilliard Summer School with Bernice Frost.[2] (2003a)

The birth of the Hebrew Arts School was a response to the deaths of the millions who died because they were Jews but whose lives had never been enriched by Judaism. Jochsberger realized that American Jews were living similarly impoverished lives. How could they be introduced to the beauty of Jewish culture?

> The best way to do this is to sing. But people didn't know Hebrew. I was the first instructor to get the recorder accepted for study at the Conservatory. The recorder is good instrument to get started with — you can learn the basics of music in preparation for a real instrument. In the United States, people didn't know Hebrew. Hebrew melodies do something to your heart. Something that will wake up your soul. All music does this. But in playing Israeli folk songs, something inside will be moved. (2003a)

A chance meeting with Shulamith Halkin, the wife of Abraham Halkin, a professor of Jewish history at the Jewish Theological Seminary, led to an appointment with Hayim Greenberg, the head of the Department of Education and Culture for the Jewish Agency. By this time, Jochsberger had become one of the founders and directors of the New Jerusalem Conservatory and Academy of Music, later renamed the Jerusalem Academy of Music and Dance. In 1950, with the money Jochsberger had been saving to resettle her parents, she came to the United States.

It was Moshe Davis, Mordecai Kaplan's successor as dean of the Teachers Institute, who helped connect Jochsberger to the Hebraist community in New York. Davis had been the chief ideologue of Hanoar Haivri while a student at JTS during the thirties. Hanoar Haivri, sponsored by its parent group, the Histadrut Ivrit, created a series of impressive ventures to expand the boundaries of Hebrew culture: a theater group, *Pargod*; an orchestra, *Synfonietta*; a literary journal, *Niv*; and a series of meetings and conferences that brought together American-born students of teacher education programs across the United States (Leaf, 1989). In 1941, Davis was in charge of the Hebrew Arts Foundation of the Histadrut Ivrit, and a Hebrew Arts School suggested another avenue to achieve the objectives of the idealistic Noar Ivri. Jochsberger (1957) quotes Davis in her master's thesis: "The Hebrew Arts Committee, born in America, believes in the possibility of creative survival in the Diaspora. Through its work, a small but significant contribution may be made to the translation of this belief into a realistic program" (Jochsberger, 1957). This group had already achieved one significant translation, the establishment of Camp Massad. The support of the Hebrew Arts School and its role in launching Jochsberger's vision would become a second.

Davis and his circle greeted Jochsberger warmly. In 1951, she became a music counselor at Camp Ramah in Wisconsin, hired by Sylvia Ettenberg, a longtime friend of Davis and his wife, Lottie, a member of Noar Ha'Ivri, a graduate of the Teachers Institute, and an influential voice on the board. A full half century later, one of Jochsberger's campers from that era recalls her impact:

> Our music counselor Tzipora, patient Tzipora, was coaxing out melodies for an original musical from those of us who had the *chutzpah* to think we could write an original musical. I was one of those teenagers. I am indebted to you, after all these many years, for persevering back then. Sitting at that old upright in the Beit Am, night after night when our minds were blank, you acted as if our possibilities were endless. Your faith made me, for one, heady with my own potential. (Klaff, 2003)

Ettenberg (2003) thought that the *halil* project was perfect for camp. "Playing the *halil* was a terrific idea because it gave every child a chance to learn to play an instrument." Other members of the musical establishment, without the ideological commitment to nurturing Hebrew culture in America, were not so easily convinced. Jochsberger remembers the resistance: "I kept the recorder in my pocketbook . . . and would take it out and demonstrate my materials when I visited Jewish organizations" (quoted in Hershenson, 2001). She started *halil* classes in Herzliyah High School, the Hillel Foundation of Hunter College, and Brooklyn College. In 1952–53, she was teaching music classes in the Extension Division of the Jewish Theological Seminary and also at Yeshiva University. (Jochsberger was an assistant professor at the Cantors Institute and Seminary College of Jewish Music at JTS from 1954 to 1973 and an instructor in music education at the Teachers Institute of JTS from 1954 to 1968. She also taught at Yeshiva University in the Teachers Institute for Women from 1954 to 1968.)

In the introduction to the American version of *Hava N'chalela*, Jochsberger frames her rationale for using folk music and articulates her educational vision: "[Folk music] can be used by teachers to create musical associations to Israeli folkways, natural surroundings, the towns and cities, the Sabbaths and holidays, and thus to bring children both in Israel and in the Diaspora into more intimate contact with these aspects of culture in Israel" (Jochsberger, 1952). She asserts the authenticity of the *halil* in the teaching of *ahavat ha-aretz* (love of the land) while simultaneously imbuing the simple recorder with the status of high culture: "The recorder was a favorite instrument of the 16th and 17th centuries and came back into use in the beginning of the present century. It is very popular in Israel, for its poignant, slightly monotonous tones suit the Israeli folk song very well" (Jochsberger, 1952).

By 1952, Tzipora Jochsberger had organized the Hebrew Arts School (HAS), known then as the Hebrew Arts School of Music and Dance) with the support of the Hebrew Arts Foundation of the Histadrut Ivrit and the Department of Education and Culture of the Jewish Agency for Palestine. The school, which began with sixteen students, met in two classrooms at the Ramaz School. Jochsberger taught recorder, and Fred Berk taught dance. (The origins of the school became the basis for her master's thesis; see Jochsberger, 1957.) Lottie Davis served as chair of the school's advisory board and appealed to parents of Jewish day school students to send their children to the new venture (Davis, 2003). A letter from September 28, 1953, begins: "We are writing to you because we know of your special interest in Jewish education" (Davis, 1953). The Davis children, the Ettenberg children, and offspring of other members of the JTS community and alumni of Hanoar Haivri were heavily represented in the first classes of the school.

During those early years, Jochsberger was also teaching music and conducting the choir at the Society for the Advancement of Judaism (Mordecai Kaplan's Reconstructionist congregation.) As it grew, the school moved from Ramaz on the Upper East Side to West Sixteenth Street to the headquarters of the Histadrut Ivrit. After outgrowing that facility, the school moved to the Jewish Guild for the Blind, on West Sixty-fifth Street. At first, the school met only on Sundays; eventually it met on Sundays and Wednesdays.

For more than thirty years, Jochsberger was the driving force behind the

Hebrew Arts School. The school offered classes for adults as well as children, teacher-training classes for teenagers and professional development for teachers. In 1976, groundbreaking ceremonies celebrated Jochsberger's success in attracting major donors who would support the venture: a permanent building for the school in the heart of Lincoln Center, the Abraham Goodman House, which now serves as the anchor of the Kaufman Center. The center now features the successor to the Hebrew Arts School, the Lucy Moses School, two concert spaces, including the much admired Merkin Concert Hall, and a music library. It is also home to the Special Music School, a New York City public school devoted to musically gifted children. The vision is no longer the vision of the original enterprise. "Many changes have been made," Jochsberger asserts. "No doubt, much of the Jewish content has disappeared. However, the Jewish calendar is strictly adhered to, including Shabbat. How do I feel about it? Changes are inevitable, and who knows, perhaps one day with new leadership, there may be a return to the original intent of the institution" (personal communication, June 18, 2003).

Chronicling the Hebrew Arts School in 1985, Jochsberger recounts the impact of her brainchild:

> Its presence is felt throughout the country via the American Jewish Choral Festival, the Summer Institute of Jewish Arts Administrators, the Summer and Winter Festivals of Jewish Music, and through its many graduates who have become performers, composers, art therapists, educators, and enlightened audiences. In addition, thousands of its students, including adults who take part in the rich adult education programs the School offers, have made the arts an integral part of their lives. (Jochsberger, 1985, 13)

In 1986, Jochsberger returned to Israel where she has been composing music based on Hebrew sources, from the *siddur* (prayer book), the *Tanakh* (Hebrew scriptures), and from modern Israeli poetry. (She has also set some Edgar Allan Poe poems to music for voice and piano.) She is the founder and director of the Israel Music Heritage Project: A People and Its Music, which has produced a collection of music videos, another attempt to educate and build identity through music. Referring to the *eidot* (ethnic groups) in Israel, Jochsberger remarked, "One ethnic group knows very little about the music of another one" (Furstenberg, 1996, 35). The video library, containing ten volumes, features the music of Salamone Rossi, and of the Hassidic, Moroccan, Ashkenazi, Yemenite, and Sephardic communities, among others.

The Hebrew Arts School: Jochsberger's Vision

In several documents, Jochsberger spells out her vision for the Hebrew Arts School: in a statement she wrote on February, 27, 1968, for the Board of

Trustees of the Hebrew Arts School upon the occasion of their purchase of the land on West Sixty-seventh Street, in a description for *Music Journal* (October 1968), and in an article for the now-defunct *Pedagogic Reporter* (January 1985). The three documents complement one another. Reflecting on the history of the school, Jochsberger is proud of what she accomplished. "The vision remains a vision!" (personal communication, July 18, 2003).

Daniel Pekarsky (1997) describes a Jewish educational vision as necessitating an existential, intellectual, and spiritual dimension. Pekarsky's definition relies on a vocabulary similar to the one that Jochsberger (1985) employs. She evokes the image of Bezalel and the artisans who built the *mishkan* (sanctuary) in her discussion of the curriculum and scope of the Hebrew Arts School. She describes these biblical craftspeople as possessors of *hokhmah*: intellect, spiritual involvement, and creativity (10). All of the formulations of the vision of the Hebrew Arts School, as well as those embedded in Jochsberger's reflections to me and to others, contain the three elements Pekarsky describes.

EXISTENTIAL

Jochsberger's vision was anchored in a response to the loss of her parents and others like them. She suggests that her life was spared for the purpose of linking Jews to their musical heritage.

> I saw this problem: [European] Jews were murdered who didn't know about the beauty of Judaism. This preoccupied me. It could happen in the United States. In the U.S. there were thousands of Jews who knew nothing about Judaism. It was roiling within me. If something, *has v'shalom* [heaven forbid] would happen here, they should at least know the beauty of our culture. (Jochsberger, 2003a)

The loss created by the Holocaust both for herself and for her people echoes in Jochsberger's review of Eric Werner's *A Voice Still Heard: The Sacred Songs of the Ashkenazic Jews* (Jochsberger, 1977). She lauds the musicologist for the importance of the endeavor, not only for its comprehensive nature, but also for capturing the cultural and historical nuances of the music and its people: the interplay between sacred and secular, Jewish and non-Jewish. In her review, Jochsberger repeats an age-old theme: the power of music "beyond the limitations of language" (50), the power of music "to be the guardian and transmitter of the voices of generations past" (52). Music is the bridge to ethnic identification and a vital response to the memory of the dead. Her review ends with an acknowledgment that echoes the rationale for the Hebrew Arts School: "Dr. Werner's magnum opus is a most fitting memorial to the victims of the Holocaust. They perished but their voice is still heard" (52). This obligation to rescue and rediscover Jewish culture after the Holocaust was articulated by Marc Rottenberg, the chairman of the board of HAS in 1970: "The function of preserving, renewing, increasing, and passing on the millennial living tradition of creative Jewish cultural expression must be taken up by those who are left, chief among them ours — the largest surviving Jewish community in the world. This in essence is what the Hebrew Arts School for Music and Dance represents" (quoted in Jochsberger, 1970, 6).

Jochsberger had another opportunity to renew life in a nearly moribund Jewish population. She takes particular pleasure in her role in introducing Jews from the former Soviet Union, both as students and as teachers, to Jewish culture via the Hebrew Arts School. On June 10, 2003, I attended a concert at the Merkin Concert Hall featuring some of Jochsberger's compositions, including "Five Times Ten," a little suite for piano, written in honor of the fiftieth anniversary of the Kaufman Center. The delightful piece was played by two youngsters, students currently enrolled at the Lucy Moses School (the successor to the Hebrew Arts School), and the children of the first Russian student Jochsberger accepted for study. I couldn't help but notice the *kippah* (skullcap) on the boy, and at the reception that followed, I observed the *kippah* on his father, and that his mother was modestly dressed and wearing a hat. Were they some of Tzipora's success stories? Representatives of another Jewish community who found their way to meaningful Jewish lives through the arts?

In our correspondence after the concert, Tzipora asked, "By the way, did you notice the ten-year-old boy who with his sister, age 7, played my 'Five x Ten' — a Little Piano Suite, wearing a *kippa*?" (personal communication, June 19, 2003). I was delighted that we were both *kvelling*, and asked her to elaborate: Was their father observant when he studied with her? She responded: "The father of the little boy wearing a *kippa*, was a gifted piano student during the seventies called Oleg Rivkin. He came to us at the time when Jews from the Soviet Union arrived in the U.S. . . . . That Oleg, now a successful lawyer, has become religious, was a great surprise to me (personal communication, July 18, 2003).

The school met the existential needs of teachers as well as students. Jochsberger hired twenty Russian musicians for her faculty during the seventies, at the height of the emigration. In an interview with radio personality Robert Sherman during the June 10 concert, she told the audience about interviewing an émigré musician who knew no English. It was early summer. Tzipora warned her that any member of her faculty must be able to teach in English. The musician so wanted to become a part of this vibrant community that she promised she'd learn the language by September — and did. Jochsberger recalls "the Jewish aspect of the HAS also impressed assimilated American Jewish musicians who worked at the school" (personal communication, July 18, 2003).

INTELLECTUAL

Jochsberger (2003a) calls her pedagogy "learning by indirection." Her approach to achieving excellence is to capitalize on the innate curiosity of the child paired with the integrity of the subject matter. "When children are registered at the School, we are looking for their motivation for study in addition to their innate abilities" (Jochsberger, 1985, 11). She finds support for her uncompromising demand for excellence wedded to respect for the learner in Jerome Bruner (*The Process of Education*) one of the educational reformers of the post-Sputnik years. Bruner, who developed many science curricula at that time, advocated teaching intellectually challenging material in an age-appropriate manner, building curricula around the basic structure of the discipline. "Basic ideas that lie at the heart of science, and basic themes that give form to life and literature are as simple as they are powerful" (cited in Jochsberger, 1985, 11). Bruner recommends a spiral curriculum, revisiting the basic ideas of the discipline, and "excitement about discovery — discovery of previously unrecognized relations and similarities between ideas with a resulting sense of self-confidence in one's abilities" (cited in Jochsberger, 1985, 11).

Isa Aron, who attended the school in its early years, corroborates that sense of excitement. She remembers the school as being "small and *heymish*. I remember walking on flower pots as part of dance . . . and playing the overture to 'The Marriage of Figaro' on an alto recorder. I also played in a recorder quartet. But what I remember most is how much fun it was" (Aron, 2003).

SPIRITUAL

At the June 10 concert, Matthew Lazar, an eminent choral conductor and arranger of Jewish music, remarked that the school filled a unique niche in the community; there was no Jewish institution that believed that music could ennoble the soul. In the Hebrew Arts School, the spiritual and the cultural were intertwined. The school lived by the Jewish calendar, observing Shabbat and holidays. Jochsberger states,

> I wanted a school where Jewish identity was most important. At Hanukkah, I asked the students to bring *hanukkiyot* [candleholders] to the school. I brought extras for children who didn't have them. One mother told me that her child insisted that she buy him a *hanukkiyah*. He said, "If you don't get me a *hanukkiyah*, I will run away." (2003a)

Jochsberger's non-Jewish secretary recalls Hanukkah celebrations when Tzipora would call the entire staff into her office, where she enjoyed the luxury of a piano, to participate in candle-lighting and singing Hanukkah songs to Jochsberger's accompaniment (personal communication, July 18, 2003). "There were no grades, no competition. Only on *Purim* did we have a contest. You know, on *Purim* everything is upside-down. So then we had a competition with prizes. We gave awards for original compositions in music and dance" (Jochsberger, 2003a).

For Jochsberger, the music of the Jewish people was the key to Jewish identity and interconnected with the Hebrew language. Music of Jewish composers, Israeli folk music, music of the *eidot* (the diverse ethnic groups within Israel), and American Jewish music formed the subject matter of the Hebrew Arts School. The children were not the only beneficiaries. "When instrumental music is performed on the student's chosen instruments and listened to on recordings, Jewish music finds its way into the student's home and the entire family becomes exposed to it" (Jochsberger, 1985, 12). Sylvia Ettenberg (2003) remembers that her daughter and husband played *halil* duets for the school assemblies. Identity was inseparable from aesthetics. In discussing the accomplishments of the school, Jochsberger (1985) observed: "The students and the public are provided with rich experiences in the arts, exposing them to fine exhibits in the Art Gallery, concerts in the acoustically praised halls, and a Library and Listening Room that offer them opportunities to become fully acquainted with the music of the Jewish people" (13).

In the vision statement she drafted for the board of trustees in 1968, Jochsberger outlined an even more expansive role for the school as the nucleus of a department of creative arts and painting, a drama program, a department for the study of ancient instruments, a more extensive concert schedule, summer school and satellite programs, publications, educational television, professional development for Jewish communal educators, and outreach to community agencies. Her goal was to create a personal and cultural Jewish renaissance fueled by the arts.

> Group and individual work with the student is essential in order to make a lasting impression on the child so that the enjoyments of the arts may continue throughout life. He may want to make it part of his family life — and his life within the community. With highly developed tastes, he will make demands for raising standards. As a future performing or creative artist, he will be aware of the Jewish contribution to the arts; play works by Jewish composers; create dances on Jewish thematic materials; bring to life works by Jewish playwrights; choose Jewish themes as inspiration for paintings, etc. (Jochsberger, 1968a)

Although Jochsberger left for Israel without achieving all the program goals she had delineated in 1968, under her tenure, the school remained true to the earliest iterations of its founder's vision:

> To enrich the life of the individual, to develop his personality, to help him relate to other people and build confidence in his ability — this is the function of education in general. Education in the arts adds another dimension. It enriches the soul, sensitizes character, and gives one a chance to participate in the creative processes. It is man, the creator, who is mentioned in Genesis as having been created in God's image. Art makes it possible for every man to seek fulfillment in that it is the

immediate expression of his experiences and the bridge between senses and intellect. (Jochsberger, 1968b)

The school today, renamed the Lucy Moses School, regularly appears on the "Best Music School" lists in *New York Magazine*. Its constituency is no longer exclusively Jewish. In a concert I attended, the children were more likely to have Asian surnames than Jewish ones. (There was a large representation from the former Soviet Union in both the faculty and student body.) The coup of moving to Lincoln Center turned a mom-and-pop operation (in this case, all "mom") into an institution, and changed its character irrevocably.

Contexualizing Jochsberger's Vision

When I asked Tzipora what educational thinkers influenced her pedagogy, she answered without hesitation, "Summerhill." The reference, of course, is to A. S. Neill (1883–1973) and the boarding school in the village of Leiston, in Suffolk, England, about one hundred miles from London. When Neill founded the school in 1921, it stood in stark contrast to the British schools of its day, eschewing corporal punishment, rote learning, an authoritarian classroom atmosphere, and a rigid examination system. Summerhill was introduced to American audiences in the sixties, through the single-mindedness of Harold Hart, a school parent and publisher who devoted his resources to promoting Neill and his views to U.S. readers. Hart was so successful that Neill insisted he was better known in the United States than in the United Kingdom. I followed up with Tzipora: What aspects of Summerhill did she want to embed in her school? "Summerhill impressed me, for there the child's personality stood in the center. I always felt that the child is more important than the school and all it entails. For if one listens to [the child's] needs and his interests and acts upon them, one gets full motivation, which leads to successful learning, accomplishments as well as good attitudes" (personal communication, July 18, 2003). The centrality of the child was surely a fundamental tenet in Neill's philosophy. Introducing Summerhill to his American readers, he posits: "When my first wife and I began the school, we had one main idea: to make the school fit the child — instead of making the child fit the school" (Neill, 1960, 4). The philosophy of Summerhill was distilled from a slogan Neill learned from his mentor Homer Lane: "You must be on the side of the child" (Neill, 1972, 184).

However, Neill also shared his mentor's views on religion and religious education as suppressors of freedom. Regarding the Jewish and Christian Bibles, Lane noted: "The Old is always forbidding and threatening punishment, whereas the New preaches the gospel of Love and Liberty, and urges always toward the achieving of higher and higher things" (Lane, ([1928] 1969, 122–23). Neill, a neo-Freudian and one of Lane's analysands, reflected the prejudices of his time, a hostility to organized religion of any kind. "My highest card is my fear of religious training for the young. It is impossible to be taught religion without forming inhibitions and repressions" (Neill, 1962, 74). He was somewhat bemused by schools that "claimed the freedom of Summerhill," including a school that had a half-hour of compulsory religion every morning and a school that washed out kids' mouths with soap for swearing (Neill, 1972, 223). I suspect he would question how "Summerhillian" a school that celebrated Jewish holidays and observed *kashrut* and Shabbat could be.[3]

Although Jochsberger mentioned only Neill as a source of inspiration in our interview, the draft of her master's thesis is sprinkled with the names of the giants of progressivism: Rousseau, Dewey, Kilpatrick, Pestalozzi, and Tyler (Jochsberger, 1957). Each championed the child's innate curiosity and insisted that any educational venture must begin with the interests of the child. As Lawrence Cremin (1964), the great historian of American education, points out, the definition of progressive education had become so diffuse that it became an educational chameleon. Progressivism could encompass Neill's Freudian expressionism, vocational education, the project-method, experiential education, as well as Jochsberger's credo, the child-centered curriculum, the mantra of American education for fifty years.

What inspired the Hebrew Arts School is an amalgam of Jochsberger's personal response to the Holocaust and the progressive pedagogy she shared with the ideologues of Hanoar Haivri. Their philosophy of Jewish education and their commitment to nurturing Hebrew culture in America was the last chapter of the Benderly-Kaplan revolution in Jewish education. Kronish (1983) notes that in the Benderly era, Jewish educators appropriated the progressive lexicon of the American education of their day, a vocabulary shaped by Dewey and his followers, speaking of "the whole child," "the needs of the learners," "teaching children not subjects," and "real life experiences" (185). Although Kronish claims that Dewey's actual influence on these early reformers was more in style than in substance, the impact of the Benderly-Kaplan legacy on Jewish education was profound. Jochsberger (1957) cites Kaplan in her thesis:

> If Judaism is to be enabled to bring out the best in the Jew, the Jewish community must assume responsibility for stimulating among Jews an understanding and utilization of art, and indirectly, the creativity of Jewish artists. It must develop in Jewry the habit of expressing its emotional reactions to the circumstances of Jewish life esthetically. It must foster that reciprocal bond between the artist and his public which encourages the artist to create, by making him want to communicate his experience as a Jew, and will enable the lay Jew to perceive new values in Jewish experience by the magical power of art. (Kaplan, 1948, 355–56)

In the *Parent News* of January 1958, the editor, Helen Epstein, quoted Emanuel Gamoran, one of the Benderly boys and a member of the school's board of directors:

He keynoted the board's underlying philosophy which is the School beacon in the reversal of the words . . . "bringing the beauty of Greece into the tent of Shem." For the school it is also "bringing the beauty of Shem into the tents of Greece." As he spoke of the love and joy of the children for their work at the school, his love for his part in making the School grow shone in his eyes. (3)

This view is reflected in Leah N. Meir's recollections of her experience at the Hebrew Arts School. She remembers her lessons with Sophie Maslow in the late fifties, dancing both to Jewish themes and to "Swing Low, Sweet Chariot." Meir's parents were friendly with the Davises and the Ettenbergs; her maternal grandfather was Menachem Ribalow, the editor of *Hadoar*, published by the Histadrut Haivrit (Meir, 2003).

Dewey was not the revolutionary that Kaplan and Benderly were. He did not want to remake American society. On the other hand, Neill *was* a revolutionary: his goal was to change the stultifying British educational system. Jochsberger shared Neill's audacity, as did her original supporters, the "graduates" of Hanoar Haivri, who found in Jochsberger a means to achieve their goals: creating a vibrant Hebrew culture in America through learning and performing the arts.

This fortuitous meeting—Jochsberger's response to the Holocaust and the ideology of the Hebraist circle—launched and nurtured the fledgling Hebrew Arts School. Played against a background of American educational progressivism, these two forces merged in creating an exciting educational institution. It did not initially attract the students Jochsberger had anticipated. The first students were not Americans deprived of Jewish culture but the offspring of well-educated American Jews who wanted more for their children. In a statistical survey reflecting the background of the students of the 1956–57 year, 77 percent were day school students, representing ten schools. They were Bialik, the Yeshiva of Central Queens, Crown Heights Yeshiva, Soloveitchik, Ramaz, Manhattan Day School, Yeshiva Zichron Moshe, Kinereth, Shulamith, the Yeshiva of Flatbush. Fourteen out of sixty-three students attended public schools (Statistical Survey, 1957). Its first adherents were enchanted by the Hebraic aspect of the school; for later generations, it was the excellence of the music offerings and the caliber of the faculty that fueled the school's expansion and led to its current preeminence as a jewel in the Lincoln Center crown. During Robert Sherman's interview with Jochsberger (2003b), he asked what was in her mind when she founded the school. She said that she strove for excellence on every level: educationally, musically, and administratively. That legacy remains, though the luminous vision of Jewish renewal through Hebrew culture has been dimmed.

NOTES

Hava N'halela, with a *hey* (let us praise her) is a pun on Jochsberger's *halil* curriculum, *Hava N'chalela* (let's play the *halil*), with a *het*.

1. When Jochsberger made aliyah in 1938, she changed her name from Hilde to Tzipora and used H as her middle initial.

2. Bernice Frost is a composer and teacher who wrote a series of piano method books using international folk tunes.

3. From 1961 to 1965, David Ellison (2003) attended Kilquhanity, a sister school founded by Neill in Scotland. Ellison remembers the strong antireligious sentiments of the school at the time, such as protesting any intrusion of religion into civic life. He also remembers the frequency of faculty-student sexual liaisons.

REFERENCES

Aron, I. 2003. Interview with the author, December 17.

Bruner, J. 1960. *The Process of Education*. New York: Vintage Books.

Cremin, L. A. 1964. *Transformation of the School: Progressivism in American Education, 1876–1957*. New York: Random House.

Davis, L. 2003. Interview with the author, December 1.

———. 1953. Flyer to parents of day school children, September 28. Hebrew Arts School Archives, New York.

Ellison, D. 2003. Interview with the author, October 13.

Epstein, H., ed. 1958. *Parent News* (January). Hebrew Arts School Archives, New York.

Ettenberg, S. C. 2003. Interview with the author, November 10.

Furstenberg, R. 1996. Saved by the music. *Hadassah* 78.2 (October): 34–35.

Gardner, H. 1983. *Frames of Mind*. New York: Basic Books.

Handelman, S., and J. Saks, eds. 2003. *Wisdom from All My Teachers: Issues and Challenges in Torah Education*. Jerusalem: Atid/Urim Publications.

Hershenson, S. 2001. Musicologist gives rich legacy to Israel. JWeekly.com, January 12. www.jweekly.com/article/full/14863/musicologist-gives-rich-legacy -to-israel/.

Jensen, E. 1998. *Teaching with the Brain in Mind*. Alexandria, Va.: ASCD.

———. 2001. *Arts with the Brain in Mind*. Alexandria, Va.: ASCD.

Jochsberger, T. 1952. *Hava N'chalela*. New York: Shulsinger.

———. 1957. A proposed curriculum in the fundamentals of music: First and second years in the Hebrew Arts School. Draft of master's thesis written for her degree at Jewish Theological Seminary. In the Archives of the Hebrew Arts School, New York.

———. 1968a. Hebrew Arts School. Vision statement, typescript, February 27.

———. 1968b. Music schools of America: Hebrew Arts School for Music and Dance. Reprint from *Music Journal* (October): n.p.

———. 1970. Typescript. Jochsberger's personal files.

———. 1977. Review of *A Voice Still Heard The Sacred Songs of the Ashkenazic Jews*, by Eric Werner. *Jewish Spectator* 42 (Fall): 50–52.

———. 1985. The Hebrew Arts School: Music education for the young. *Pedagogic Reporter* 36 (January): 10–13.

———. 2003a. Interview with the author, June 5.

————. 2003b. Interview with Robert Sherman, June 10, Merkin Hall.

Kaplan, M. M. 1948. *The Future of the American Jews*. New York: MacMillan.

Klaff, S. 2003. Letter to Tzipora Jochsberger, July 27.

Kronish, R. 1983. John Dewey's influence on Jewish education in America: The gap between theory and practice. In *Studies in Jewish Education*, ed. Barry Chazan, 168–91. Vol. 1. Jerusalem: Magnes Press, the Hebrew University.

Lane, H. T. [1928] 1969. *Talks to Parents and Teachers*. With an introduction by A. S. Neill. New York: Schocken Books.

Leaf, H. 1989. *L'toldot tenuat HaNoar HaIvri b'amerika: Tkufat hamesh hashanim ha-rishonot*. In *Kovets Masad*, ed. R. Shulsinger-Shear Yashuv. Jerusalem: Irgun Hahanot "Masad" be-Yisrael ve-Igud bogre "Masad" be-Artsot ha Berit.

Meir, L. N. 2003. Interview with the author, November 24.

Neill, A. S. 1960. *Summerhill: A Radical Approach to Child Rearing*. With a foreword by Erich Fromm. New York: Hart.

————. 1962. *Hearts Not Heads in the School*. Ashford, Middlesex, U.K.: Cornerstone Press.

————. 1972. *"Neill! Neill! Orange Peel!"* New York: Hart.

Pekarsky, D. 1997. The place of vision in Jewish educational reform. *Journal of Jewish Education* 63 (Winter–Spring): 31–40.

Siegel, R. A., ed. 2002. *Commission Report on the Future of Jewish Culture in America: Preliminary Findings and Observations*. New York: National Foundation for Jewish Culture.

Statistical Survey, 1956–57. 1957. Typescript in Hebrew Arts School Archives.

10 : Sylvia C. Ettenberg
A Portrait in Practical Wisdom

1917–

Sylvia C. Ettenberg, circa 1946.
Photo by Moshe Ettenberg; courtesy of Sylvia C. Ettenberg

S ylvia Cutler Ettenberg was the force behind Kaplan's Teachers Institute (TI) of the Jewish Theological Seminary (JTS) and many of its most innovative educational initiatives in the post–World War II era: Camp Ramah, the Leadership Training Fellowship (LTF),[1] the Melton Research Center, and the Prozdor (a supplementary Hebrew High School). Although she never received the title Dean of the Teachers Institute, it was she who expanded and professionalized the school, integrating it into JTS, and transforming JTS in the process (Kaufman, 1997). In his excellent history of the Teachers Institute, Kaufman maintains that Ettenberg's association with men bearing the titles and degrees she lacked often obscured her achievements.

> Like so many other women who could not aspire to the rabbinate, she became instead a Jewish educator and an "educated layperson." Ettenberg was a Jewish woman who made a difference. In an age when women may become rabbis and scholars, the story of Sylvia Ettenberg and the Teachers Institute ought to remind us of the vital contribution of those who toil in the vineyards of Jewish education: the teachers (most of whom remain women). (620)

Using portraiture, the methodology popularized by Sara Lawrence-Lightfoot and Jessica Hoffman Davis (1997), I take up Kaufman's invitation to convey Ettenberg's milieu, personality and her accomplishments, placing her in the foreground of the canvas, rather than in the background, behind Moshe Davis and Seymour Fox. I also examine the constraints on her career and, responding to Kaufman's challenge, examine the role gender played in Ettenberg's long and varied professional journey.

Middleton (1993), drawing on the work of Foucault and Bourdieu, uses the term "intellectual genealogy" to examine the contexts that transformed the women she studies. Having mined those environments and experiences, she then draws "life histories" of her collaborators. A life history is subtly different from Lagemann's (1979) "educational biography"; it conjures up a reciprocal element, in which the subject *constructs* as well as *receives* the educational events of her life. For someone like Sylvia Ettenberg, who routinely elicits adjectives like forceful, indomitable, and indefatigable from those who know her, a conceptual framework that privileges *interaction with* as well as *response to* education is preferable. Building on interviews, artifacts, and the existing research literature, I draw a life history of Sylvia Ettenberg, placing her against a backdrop of American and Jewish history, educational history, and the Jewish Theological Seminary, reflecting on how she shaped those domains.

Sylvia Cutler began her love affair with Zionism and the Hebrew language through her father's matchmaking. Mordechai (Max) Cutler figures prominently in her narrative.

> I was born in East New York, in Brooklyn. . . . One side of the tracks was Brownsville, and the other was East New York. It was the better side of the tracks, but there was a lot of communication with both sides. My father — let's see — I would say he was a *maskil* [literally, enlightened one; someone well-read in Western culture who hoped to reinvigorate Hebrew as a modern language]. He was a very active Zionist. But that was not his work. . . . When he came here, he worked in millinery. . . . I must say he disliked it intensely and was quite unhappy about it. So his happiness came from all the Zionist activities that he had. He was an officer in the B'nai Zion group, which is still in operation now. And he was very active in the Parent Teacher's Association of the Talmud Torah that I went to. (Ettenberg, 2005a)

Isa Aron (2006), Sylvia's daughter, remembers her grandfather as a man who prized Jewish learning, "My grandfather died when I was seven, so I have very limited memories of him. I remember this very sweet man. . . . His great pleasure was to have me sit on his lap and read Rashi to him."

Aron knew her grandmother much better than her grandfather since her grandmother lived with the Ettenbergs after suffering a stroke in 1961. Aron (2006) describes Rochel Malkah (Amster) Cutler as more modest and retiring than her husband and recalls her reading Yiddish novels. Ettenberg refers to her mother as a homemaker who took in sewing to make ends meet, much to her husband's embarrassment. Sylvia and her younger sister, who also became a Jewish educator, were raised in a traditional home. When Ettenberg began to work at JTS and dashed into the house just before the Sabbath, her father asked, "Finkelstein *hob nisht kein shabbos*? [doesn't Finkelstein have a Sabbath?]" (Ettenberg, 2005a).

Her father looms large in Ettenberg's life history. When I call her a daddy's girl, she doesn't disagree, but stresses that he treated her sister in the same manner.

> SYLVIA ETTENBERG (S): Just a couple of other things about my
> house. My father had two daughters and not any males. He decided
> that we were going to learn and treated . . . us as if we were boys.
> So everything he might have done with boys. . . . He didn't know
> anything about . . . [pauses to find the right word]
> CAROL INGALL (C): Feminism?
> S: He didn't know what it was called, but it didn't matter. This was

the way he treated me. The result is, for example, my father, who was certainly not a sportsman, I recall very vividly, that I went to a game, a soccer game, because Ha'koah [an Israeli team] came from Israel to America. . . . And my father, who certainly didn't know what this game was, maybe he did, but not very much . . .

c: It was the *Tziyonut* [Zionism].

s: [Nodding, making sounds of agreement.]

c: Not the *mishak* [game].

s: [Sounds of agreement, laughing.] I remember vividly seeing soccer. . . . The result was that I still have an affinity for soccer.

I still remembering going to hear Bialik when he came to America, which I did not understand exactly but it was . . .

c: An adventure?

s: At that time all the Zionists were there. The same kind of thing with mass meetings and so on. We weren't [exactly] schlepped along; we were very pleased to be part of it. So my father felt that was his job, to expose us to everything, to take us to all these things. In my house, we had very little artwork. But we did have pictures of Herzl and Nordau. (Ettenberg, 2005a)

When I ask Ettenberg about her extended family, all the relatives she mentions are on her father's side. They merit a place in her narrative because of the *yihus* (status) conferred by their scholarship.

My father had very close relatives who were involved in Judaica and so forth. And one of my close cousins, my father's first cousin, was an Orthodox rabbi who was a great influence on me. He was young, he was handsome, he was very outgoing, and very much with it. And he was somebody who had a great influence because he was a bachelor for many years, and he practically lived in our house. . . . And his [sister's] . . . husband was a very knowledgeable guy. . . . I don't think he was a rabbi, I don't know what his work was . . . but it was a treat for me to visit with these people all the time. (Ettenberg, 2005a)

Coming from this kind of background, it is not surprising that Mordechai Cutler would want an intensely Hebraic, intensely Zionistic education for his daughters.[2] Ettenberg remembers her father "poring over the *protokol* [agenda] he had to write for every meeting" as secretary of the Parent Teacher Association of the Tiferet Yisrael Talmud Torah (Ettenberg, 2005a). She flourished in the school, which met two hours a day, five days a week, stimulated by teachers who were *maskilim*. She recalls: "It was really a very exciting school. And I immediately loved Hebrew, so Hebrew became my métier and I worked very hard in the tests that they gave. More so than the ones in the public school" (Ettenberg, 2005a). I asked her how she thought her classmates might remember her. She paused and spoke softly, "I don't know." Then, her voice getting louder, she continued. "I was an active student; I was not very quiet. And I was very competitive at that point, because I really wanted to get 99 on the *Nevi'im* test," she concluded, chuckling (Ettenberg, 2005a). It was at the Talmud Torah that Sylvia Cutler met her husband-to-be, Moshe (Morris). He joined her class after moving to New York from Ohio. Together they were involved in a web of extracurricular activities sponsored by the synagogue and school: The Boys Congregation and Sisterhood, youth groups, clubs, and sports (where she learned to play punch ball). She spent seven days a week in this environment, and says it was "a great influence on my life" (Ettenberg, 2005a). Some of the leaders of the clubs and youth groups were students at the Seminary; it was they who told her about JTS and suggested that she attend.

The focus of Sylvia Cutler's educational, cultural, and social life was the Talmud Torah, not her public school. In her sophomore year, Thomas Jefferson High School added Hebrew to the curriculum. They needed students, so she joined, immediately becoming the star of the class, involved in a co-curricular Hebrew club, becoming in the process very close to her teachers who were students at the Teachers Institute (TI). By her own admission, Ettenberg was an indifferent student in everything but Hebrew. Although she wanted to attend classes at JTS, she was neither sixteen nor a senior in high school. For a year she attended the Beis Midrash L'Morot (the teacher training school that evolved into Stern College) in Manhattan, where she studied with Rabbi Joseph Lookstein (1902–1979), the founder of the Ramaz School. After biding her time for a year, Sylvia, accompanied by her father, traveled to Manhattan for an interview at JTS with Professor Zvi Scharfstein (1884–1972). She was accepted to the TI during her senior year in high school and continued her general education at Brooklyn College. Brooklyn College never captured Ettenberg's imagination nor affection; it was a simply a place where she spent her afternoons. At the Teachers Institute, where she spent the bulk of her time, she found a thriving community, a place energized by Mordecai Kaplan (1881–1983) and his laboratory for Reconstructionist principles (Kaufman, 1997). Ettenberg (2006a) has few memories of Brooklyn College and of her professors there, but when I asked her which professors at TI made an impression on her, she replied, laughing, "All of them. I was really like a fish in water. Well, of course, we were very friendly: Halkin, Dinin, Scharfstein, Chertoff."

At the Teachers Institute, Ettenberg re-created her experience at the Talmud Torah, an interlocking network of curricular and co-curricular activities, with stimulating, like-minded friends, similarly enchanted by Jewish studies, Hebrew, and Jewish culture.

> I had a very interesting life at the Seminary. I really enjoyed my classes;
> I enjoyed my friends. I had very close friends from there, and I enjoyed

a lot of extracurricular work we did. It was at that point — I must have been about a junior — [that] Moshe Davis was in my class. And this was a very close friendship. We had a student organization, and we were very active. And that was what preceded Hanoar Haivvri [the Hebrew Youth organization associated with the Histadrut Ivrit]. For example, at the Teachers' Institute, we had also *hugim* [clubs]. And we had a *hug dramati* [dramatics club] there. And as students, we put on a play, which we took around to other cities. (Ettenberg, 2005a)

Entering the World of Jewish Education

Ettenberg began her long career in Jewish education while she was still a student at the TI. Many of the assumptions and attitudes that would characterize her professional practice took shape at this time, while she was still in her teens. She recalls her successes and her failures with good humor, like her first job as a seventeen-year-old, teaching at an Orthodox synagogue, Tiferet Ha'Gra (Gra is an acronym for the Vilna Gaon) in Brooklyn. She was teaching thirteen-year-olds, students only four years younger than she, and remembers the rabbi coming in "every fifteen minutes to see if I was still alive" (Ettenberg, 2005b). She supplemented her income by teaching Sundays for Henry R. Goldberg, a TI graduate who would become one of her first mentors and working summers at Camp Cejwin, where she found another significant mentor in Albert P. Schoolman (1894–1980), yet another TI graduate. Goldberg taught her a great deal.

> He taught me how to handle a class. There were problems and he would come in and help me. I mean there are problems in every class. A very funny incident happened. He once came into my classroom during the intercession [recess] and said, "You taught them a song, but you don't know music very well." Which was true. [Laughs.] (Ettenberg, 2005b)

Schoolman, a devoted disciple of Kaplan, hired her in 1934. She rose through the ranks, becoming a division head in 1944. Those experiences were crucial in formulating Ettenberg's vision for Camp Ramah. The Cejwin experience also proved to be a training ground for Ettenberg's problem-solving skills.

I asked Ettenberg to tell me about one of the challenges she faced at Cejwin and how she dealt with it. She described working in an all-male environment, a pattern in her career. There was an official camp mother, but she was the only staff member who interacted regularly with the campers. Ettenberg was hired as a division head during World War II, when most of the counselor pool was serving in the army. As the head counselor of Hadar, the younger boys camp, she had to supervise the only counselors available, yeshivah students. Schoolman had made it clear to these young men before they were hired that there would be no instructional swimming on Shabbat, but that they would be responsible for supervising recreational swimming. They agreed in the spring in order to secure employment, but tested Ettenberg when the summer season began.

> Hadar was in a valley, and it would have been miserable if [the boys] couldn't go swimming. . . . So I remember this very serious problem where [the counselors] didn't want to go out on patrol on Shabbat. . . . So we sat down and had it out. I said to them, "Listen. I looked it up, and the only reason not to go in swimming is because when you come out, you have to wring your bathing suit: *issur s'hitah* [squeezing or wringing is forbidden on the Sabbath]. So I'm ready to leave the campus grounds (I was the only woman there) [while you strip and I climb onto higher ground] and you guys can go in later. (Ettenberg, 2005b)

Faced with her ultimatum, go swimming nude, under her supervision, or swim with bathing suits that would require wringing, the counselors' resistance and rebellion evaporated. This anecdote foreshadows many instances of Ettenberg's willingness to tackle controversy and to choose tactics that were perfectly suited to disarm those who stood in her way. The anecdote is also emblematic because she never held a grudge. She mentions remaining good friends with those counselors, even hiring them later on to teach at JTS. "Nothing was ever personal. Everybody has their own *mishagas* [craziness]. I always worked within the boundaries of that *mishagas*" (Ettenberg, 2006b).

After graduating from the TI in 1937, Ettenberg began teaching at Cejwin, where she had been a camp counselor for several years. Comparing herself to her faculty colleague Deborah Pessin (1910–2001), noted author of Jewish textbooks, she informs me, "She was a terrific teacher, and I was not. I was a beginning — and not good — teacher." When I asked her to explain what she meant by "not good," Ettenberg identified her lack of creativity and her difficulties with classroom management. Due to a decline in student enrollment, the administration of Cejwin consolidated their faculty; as last hired, she was first fired. Desperately needing a job, Ettenberg took one in Staten Island teaching in a Jewish Community Center. Her responsibilities included adult education and outreach to a tuberculosis sanitarium, where she read Sholom Aleichem in Yiddish, drawing on the language she had learned to speak and read at home (Ettenberg, 2005b).

In 1938, Ettenberg began to teach at the Yeshivah of Flatbush, an opportunity that she embraced because it offered an intensely Hebraic environment. Required by the TI to fulfill a number of school observations (there was no official student teaching), the would-be teacher visited the classroom of a Miss Soyer (the sister of American social realist painters Moses, Raphael, and Isaac), "a superb teacher" (Ettenberg, 2005b). Ettenberg recalls, "I fell in love with the school" (Ettenberg, 2005b). Joining the Yeshivah of Flatbush faculty gave her an opportunity to put into practice all she had learned at the TI: to use the art she had learned with Temima Gezari, particularly working with clay in the classroom; the songs she had picked up from Judith Eisenstein (1910–1996), Mordecai Kaplan's daughter; and most appealing, teaching *Ivrit b'Ivrit* (Hebrew through immersion), a technique she had studied with Zvi Scharfstein (Ettenberg, 2005b).

Ettenberg doesn't downplay how much she had to learn: "I was a babe in the woods. I was on probation, and probably wasn't very good to begin with . . . when I first started. But I think he [the principal] hired me for two other reasons" (Ettenberg, 2005b). Her experience with Hanoar Haivri and the TI theater group, *Hapargod* (the Theater Curtain), was appealing to a principal looking to hire a drama teacher. Then too, she was studying for a master's in speech pathology at Columbia University's Teachers College. For one course she had to administer eighty intelligence tests. The principal at the Yeshivah of Flatbush, whom Ettenberg describes as a "noneducator," also thought he could use her to help settle a running dispute with the faculty. While both the administrator and the teachers agreed that not all children were capable of carrying a double program, the principal was willing to overlook the deficiencies of children who came from wealthy families. These tests might strengthen his case.

> Anyway, so . . . beginning with that year I gave the exam to incoming students, and I remember that there was a very interesting incident. We had an intercom [call] from the classrooms to his office. I gave the exam to somebody, and at that time I tried to tell him [the principal] that there's an area that we call the median. It was about 100, 110. I think it was 110, if I remember correctly. I still have the test in my closet because I don't clean my closets! [Laughter.] . . . At any rate, I called him to tell him that this young child that I interviewed had about 108. I just mentioned it to him. So his answer to me on the phone was, *"At lo yikhola l'ha'alot b'shtei nekudot?"* [You can't raise it by two points?] [More laughter.] That's to show you what I mean by [his] not being an educator. And I'll never forget that. (Ettenberg, 2005b)

Ettenberg would not be pushed around nor embarrassed by a "noneducator." While women are often accused of being reluctant to stand up for themselves, this was not the case with Sylvia Ettenberg. As in the incident with the *yeshivah bochurs* (the yeshivah students) who refused to swim on Shabbat, she knew exactly how to deal with an inappropriate principal who had crossed a boundary.

> That second year, I was on probation. He came into my class a few days before Sukkot, and he said to me, *Hem yod'im et habrakhot?* [Do they know the holiday blessings?] I didn't know what he was talking about, so I said, *Yed'u, yed'u.* [They'll know, they'll know.] So he started

screaming at me in front of the kids. *Sh'nei yamim lifnei ha'hag, v'at omeret she'yed'u?* [Two days before the holiday and you say that they'll know them?] I was left wooden, and I didn't answer. And during the intermission I discussed it with some of the teachers. Some of them were my mentors, and they said, "You just have to tell him that he can't do this to you." So I decided to be very brave, and I walked into his office. There were a couple of parents sitting there. I never spoke English to him, but I said to him, "I want to speak to you. The next time you walk into my class that way is when I have to walk out." So he said, *Eizeh safah at m'daberet?* [What language are you speaking?] And I said, *Ani rotzah she'hem yavinu.* [I want them—the parents—to understand.] So that was what broke the ice. (Ettenberg, 2005b)

In 1940, while she was teaching at the Yeshivah of Flatbush, Sylvia Cutler married her Talmud Torah and TI classmate Moshe (Morris) Ettenberg. A PHD in physics from New York University, Moshe Ettenberg did research at Sperry Gyroscope and Raytheon and taught at Brooklyn Polytech and City University. Isa Aron (2006) recalls her father as a polymath who played the cello, did calligraphy, led the JTS faculty Talmud group, and taught summer institutes in philosophy. Moshe Ettenberg died in 1991.

When the registrar of JTS, Israel Chipkin (1891–1955) called Ettenberg to teach at Beit HaYeled, the innovative day school for children dedicated to teaching *Ivrit b'Ivrit*, she was elated by the prospect.[3] Hired to teach Hebrew, Judaica, and all the general subjects, she would be the sole teacher in the classroom of "graduating" seven-year-olds. (As she discovered once she met the group, their general skills were on or above grade level, allowing her to devote most of her time to her first love, teaching Hebrew.) When she turned in her resignation at the Yeshivah of Flatbush, she unleashed the principal's anger. Although he called the head of the Hebrew Teachers Union and complained—"She was nobody; I made her a teacher and now she's leaving me"—Ettenberg holds no grudge. Remembering the incident more than sixty years later, she uses a phrase that comes up often in our interviews, "anyway, we remained friends." She notes that he would later send her students when she was running the TI (Ettenberg, 2005b).

Ettenberg spent close to two years teaching at Beit HaYeled, beginning in the 1944–45 academic year. She describes the institution "as growing out of our school" (Ettenberg, 2005b), meaning the Teachers Institute. Beit HaYeled, like TI for so many of its graduates in that era, like the Talmud Torah Ettenberg had attended as a youngster, was a "total environment" (Goffman, 1961; Peshkin, 1988). She reveled in the excellent faculty and staff, including Leah Klepper from JTS, Roma Gans from Teachers College, and the former registrar of JTS, Israel Chipkin, as principal. She spent her summers at Cejwin, in another total environment. She had begun to think about a career in camping; she was offered a position as assistant director of the Cejwin camp. She would have continued teaching at Beit HaYeled, a position that would allow her to grow in the camping field, were it not for a fateful phone call. During the 1945–46 year, she was asked to join the JTS community as registrar and faculty secretary of the Teachers Institute.[4]

> The recommendation was through Moshe Davis who was my close friend, but my interviews were with Kaplan and Finkelstein. . . . I had a dilemma. Here I was really preparing myself for some kind of future career in camping. I had a long talk with Dr. Schoolman, and I recall even today what he said: "When your alma mater calls you, you must respond." (Ettenberg, 2005b)

This vignette highlights three powerful elements in Ettenberg's intellectual biography: her early dedication to camping as a potent venue for Jewish education; her encouragement by mentors, almost all male; and her intense loyalty to JTS. Ever the professional, she spent a semester training her replacement at Beit HaYeled before beginning the next, and most rewarding, phase of her career.

Jewish Theological Seminary:
The Davis Partnership, 1945–1947

Moshe Davis (1916–1991), Ettenberg's close friend from their TI days, had continued his JTS education in its Rabbinical School. In 1942, he was asked to join the administration as registrar and lecturer in American Jewish history. In 1944, he was named the assistant to Mordecai Kaplan, the dean of the Teachers Institute. Within a year, he knew he would become Kaplan's successor and would need to find an associate, someone with whom he could work closely, who shared his views and vision of Jewish education. He did not have to look far. His good friend Sylvia Cutler Ettenberg would make a perfect ally.

Davis (1990b) knew how to "sell" his fellow TI classmate, Hanoar Haivri activist, and well-rounded Jewish educator to a wary all-male faculty and administration.

> I can tell you in the case of a person whom I have great affection for, Sylvia Ettenberg, how I prevailed on the faculty to have a young lady become a registrar. It was one thing what I said to the faculty. It was another thing what I said privately [while speaking to the administration]. I said, "Look, most of our students are girls. I don't understand them." And I told them, I said, "Look. I was in the elevator the other day with three young ladies. And one girl virtually fainted. There was nothing I could do! I need somebody who can cope with that kind of

problem." That's what I said. But to the faculty, of course, I said, "We need a personality . . ." I wouldn't say that was the only way I got Sylvia Ettenberg appointed, but I can say [it] was an important factor.

Ettenberg had never heard this story before I told it to her, but she agreed that Davis was a skilled politician who could quell resistance, even playing "the gender card" if necessary.

From 1945 to 1947, Ettenberg unleashed a sirocco of activity, designing with Davis the programs that would energize JTS and define the Conservative movement. Among them were Camp Ramah, Leadership Training Fellowship (LTF), Mador, and Atid, an early childhood program. In discussing her many accomplishments, I delve into a few in detail.

Ettenberg (2006a) speaks of Ramah as "my baby right from the beginning."[5] It was she who had the hands-on experience in Jewish camping, not Davis. Although Davis was a founder of Camp Massad through his involvement in the Histadrut Ivrit, his experience in camping was limited to having served as camp rabbi in several private Jewish camps (personal communication from Sylvia Ettenberg, August 16, 2006). It was Ettenberg who brokered the deal that would launch the first Camp Ramah in Wisconsin and energized the venture. A group of Conservative Jews in Chicago were ready to launch a camp that would meet their needs. At the same time, Ettenberg and Davis were contemplating a camp of their own, one that could become a cornerstone of Mordecai Kaplan's vision of a reconstructed American Jewry. Traveling to Chicago in a prop plane in mid-January 1947, Ettenberg sold the Chicagoans on the Ettenberg-Davis vision (Schwartz, 1987). The first flyer refers to "Camp Ramah, operated by the Council of Conservative Synagogues, Midwest Branch, United Synagogue of America, in cooperation with the Teachers Institute, Jewish Theological Seminary of America" (Camp Ramah flyer, 1947). It was Ettenberg (2006a) who convinced the Chicagoans that formal classes in Hebrew and Jewish education had to be a part of the camp culture and that when it came to Jewish education, only the TI could do the job. Accordingly, the first publicity included mandatory classes in Bible, Hebrew language and literature "directed toward fruitful, meaningful living in our present-day American-Jewish community" (Camp Ramah flyer, 1947). The camp emphasized the arts that were so appealing to Ettenberg in her Talmud Torah days, prominent in the activities of Hanoar Haivri, embraced by Kaplan at the TI, and promoted by the Hebrew Arts Committee of the Histadrut Ivrit led by Davis.

> Creative self-expression is stressed rather than mere mechanical repetition in Arts and Crafts. The usual camp-crafts and handicrafts are, of course, engaged in by campers, but in addition dancing (folk and creative movement); dramatics (including conceiving, writing, directing and acting of original productions); vocal and instrumental music

(such as Palestinian folk and liturgical music); appreciation of classical and Jewish music; Journalism and numerous other creative activities are an integral part of the Camp program. (Camp Ramah flyer, 1947)

When Davis (1990b) first heard Kaplan preach, he thought to himself, "This is the kind of person I want to be like; I was attracted to him completely, absolutely! It was love, respect, admiration, everything at first sight." He understood the new activities he developed with Ettenberg as an extension of Kaplan's dream for the TI, often dipping into Kaplan's vocabulary and retrieving "metamorphosis," "conscious Jewish renascence," and "Jewish peoplehood" to describe them (Davis, 1963, 1986). Ettenberg was drawing upon her experience of the confluence of Jewish, Hebraic, and Zionist activities of her Talmud Torah and the TI to promote a social ideal, to create a Jewish-Hebraist-Zionist Eden in America. Her years at Cejwin and the summer at Massad made her well aware of the power of camp as "an educational environment [that could] be a transformational change-agent . . . [creating] an eruption of awakening that serve[s] to change perspectives, open up a person's mind, and shake up the status quo" (Scialabba, 2006).

In an insightful article, Reimer (1989) compares Ramah to the kibbutz, both examples of social engineering, both "ideologically driven utopian experiments" (57). Reimer provides a definition of "utopian":

A social reality which could not be found elsewhere in the culture, which stood, value-wise, in contrast to the general culture, and which aimed to so impress that contrast in the minds of its participants (staff and campers) that they could no longer view their mundane lives as "normal." Ramah, like the kibbutz, represented an inherent critique of the surrounding culture (general and Jewish) which was not so much articulated as lived and felt. (58)

Josselit and Mittelman (1993) point out that American Jewish camping during the period between 1920 and 1950 was all about ideology: either assimilating into American life or encouraging ethnic persistence (16). Camps like Ramah were more "transgressive" and more utopian in their ideology (hooks, 1994), attempting to create an alternative to American values like competition and egalitarianism. Naomi Cohen (2003) claims, "the unspoken aim of its founders was to create a native American elite for the Jewish community" (39).

If education begins in disequilibrium, then ideological camps, whether they were promoting the Americanization of Jewish immigrants in the twenties or an American Hebrew renaissance in the forties, were sending their campers a message about moving away from their family of origin. The presence of a "camp mother" in these institutions is more than a palliative for homesickness. She also serves as a symbol of the new family that was being created at camp, an alternative to, if not a substitute for, the old, making Reimer's kibbutz analogy even more apt. Even a Jewish-lite camp like Alton, designed to prepare Jewish boys from Boston to compete in WASP America, held Friday night services in which the camp mother lit Shabbat candles (Ingall, 1997). What was unique about Ramah among the utopian camps like Achvah, Cejwin, and Yavneh was that it was a religious camp designed to instill a commitment to Conservative Judaism. For Ramah, Hebrew and Zionism were a means to an end, while for Massad, a camp to which it is often compared, "Hebrew and Zionism were [its] religion" (Fox with Novak, 1991, 17). As a religiously oriented camp, Ramah offered not only a new model of family for its campers, but also an alternative model for a new prayer community. That model was often far more exciting than the one provided by the Conservative synagogues that encouraged these youngsters to attend Ramah (Ackerman, 1997; Sales and Saxe, 2004). Referring to the culture created by Lou Newman, director of Camp Ramah in Wisconsin from 1951 to 1953, Shapiro and Cohen capture the ideological impact of Ramah on its campers in those early years: "It was the first generation of the young Jewish religious revolutionary who returned home to upset rabbis, parents, and friends by the very intensity of his religious beliefs and commitments" (1984, xi).

Ettenberg understood the power of a total environment to change perspectives by captivating the mind and imagination. She grew up in a series of interlocking environments; the Talmud Torah, the synagogue, the youth groups, and *hugim* (clubs) created a series of overlapping circles. Ramah, TI, LTF, Mador, and later, the Prozdor would replicate this web, together making a year-round environment, a greenhouse to make up for the deficits of the supplementary school. Ramah was launched as a place to grow leaders; the first promotional flyer offered a special program for LTF members. (LTF was founded in 1946 through Kaplan's and Davis' efforts.) Ramah would feed LTF, and LTF would produce counselors for Ramah through a counselor-training program, Mador. Those counselors would enroll in the TI and the Rabbinical School, some eventually becoming faculty members. JTS professors served as scholars-in-residence at the Ramah Camps where they sent their children. When JTS introduced a new graduate school, Ettenberg recruited students for it in the Ramah camps. When she and Seymour Fox ran the Melton Center for Research in Jewish Education, Ramah became a laboratory to test out new curricula. These first programs created a rich educational ecology that was unparalleled in the American Jewish community.

In 1947, Moshe Ettenberg received an invitation to teach at the new Weizmann Institute, which was about to welcome its first students. Sylvia Ettenberg took a leave of absence from JTS. The couple traveled around England and France, and visited with Sylvia's sister and husband in Germany. They were in Rome when the independence of the state of Israel was declared. The opening of the Weizmann Institute was delayed because of the War of Independence. Moshe Ettenberg was a lieutenant colonel in the Israeli Air Force, teaching his specialty, radar. Isa (Israela) was born in 1949. Sylvia Ettenberg missed her family and her job, and she worried about how difficult it was to raise a child in this early period of Israeli statehood. In 1949, the three Ettenbergs returned to New York. Their son David would be born there in 1955.

Jewish Theological Seminary:
The Davis/Goldin Years, 1950–1959

Upon her return from Israel, Ettenberg continued to expand the programs under the aegis of the Teachers Institute. Her educational endeavors resembled the musical genre of a theme and variations. A major theme was to offer others the Jewish universe she had experienced as a young person. The variation of the 1940s was Ramah and its offshoots; the variation of the fifties was Prozdor (literally, a hallway), like Ramah, an avenue to compensate for the limitations of the synagogue school. Another major theme was a passionate attachment to the Teachers Institute and the Jewish Theological Seminary. In the fifties, as in the forties, Davis was an ideal partner. It was he who helped change Finkelstein's initial icy response to Ramah by using a baseball analogy—the feeder system of Little Leagues to Minor Leagues to Major Leagues—to illustrate why an institution of higher learning had to be involved in youth programming (Kaufman, 1997, 830). In 1951, Davis became provost of JTS, well positioned to champion Ettenberg's projects, and Judah Goldin (1914–98) became the dean of TI.

That year Ettenberg launched the Prozdor as a preparatory school for the Teachers Institute. She knew firsthand of the vacuum it could fill; she well remembered having to study elsewhere until she was old enough to apply to the TI. Principals of Hebraist/Zionist yeshivot also pressured her to create a serious institution for their graduates to continue their Jewish education. She used the Prozdor for other purposes as well. Those who know her often used the term "talent scout" to describe her (Davidson, 2006; Holtz, 2006). Ettenberg (2006a) used the Prozdor to scout for players for the JTS team.

> Shlomo Feffer was one of our teachers—he was one of the first teachers in the Prozdor. A lot of people [cut] their teeth [at the Prozdor]. . . . Yochanan Muffs taught at the Prozdor, you know, when he was a "little boy." Sholom Paul taught at the Prozdor. . . . This was a very good training ground for them in the Prozdor. We were able to test them out.

Isa Aron (2006) remembers her Prozdor experience as "fabulous." "This was my mother's doing. She kept her eyes out for the young, sharp PHD, or not-yet-PHD, she thought would be good, and you'd get him in to teach in the Prozdor. So I had Muffs and Sarna . . . Avraham Holtz, all these people who went on to be great scholars. . . . They were my high school teachers."

In 1953, Ettenberg and Goldin began to resurrect an idea originally developed by Mordecai Kaplan, planning an undergraduate program that would allow students to take secular studies at Columbia School of General Studies while studying Judaica at JTS. They wrote about the venture in separate chapters for *The Education of American Jewish Teachers* (Janowsky, 1967). Goldin opened his chapter in a curmudgeonly tone, "We had best remember that even as much of what passes today (or any time) as liberal arts education is neither liberal nor artistic nor educational, so much of what passes today (or any time) as Hebrew teachers college is neither Hebrew nor teaching, nor is it enlightening" (119). Ettenberg provided the nuts and bolts in her chapter, describing the history of the venture, its curriculum, achievements, and comparisons to other combined programs. The Joint Program of List College celebrated its fiftieth anniversary in 2005.

In 1955, Moshe Davis made aliyah and began his long association with the Hebrew University. In 1959, Judah Goldin left JTS to join the faculty of Yale University. From the mid-fifties to the mid-seventies, Ettenberg held a variety of positions at JTS. "I served as registrar, as the dean of students, and the general cook! I'm laughing, but I really enjoyed it" (Ettenberg, 2006a). During the fifties, a talented educational theorist with a PHD from the University of Chicago attracted the attention of Louis Finkelstein. Seymour Fox (1929–2006) came to JTS to study at the Rabbinical School; he received ordination in 1956, becoming Assistant to the Chancellor in 1959 and eventually Dean of the Teachers Institute. While he was still a rabbinical student, he took over the supervision of Camp Ramah. Sylvia Ettenberg's association with Seymour Fox had begun.

The Jewish Theological Seminary: The Fox Years, 1954–1966

Fox may have been the titular head of Ramah, but even a ten-year-old could see who was really in charge. Aryeh Davidson (2006), Fox's nephew, remembers meeting Sylvia Ettenberg at Camp Ramah in Wisconsin in 1957.

> My parents were on staff and they wanted me to meet this very prominent educator and leader in Jewish education whom my father had known from his teenage years, . . . a woman currently responsible for Camp Ramah. And as a ten-year-old what struck me was that here in camp was a very attractive, stunning woman walking around with high heels. . . . I remember that my uncle, Seymour Fox, accompanied Sylvia. And in my life Seymour was this towering figure. But he made it clear that Sylvia was his boss.

If not exactly "the boss," Ettenberg was certainly the keeper of the flame, the person who could access the Ramah institutional memory and held the camps up to the lofty standards prized by the founding generation, chief among them, the primacy of the Hebrew language.[6]

INGALL

Seymour didn't think that [Hebrew] was very important. We laugh about it all of the time. I mean, he didn't think that that was the most important thing. . . . [It was] one of the things he . . . left . . . to me. I carried the banner of Hebrew, and we always laugh about it. He said, "If not for you . . ." And his Hebrew was not very good [at that time, before he made aliyah]. When he came to Israel, and he started to teach in Hebrew, he used to open his classes by saying, "If anybody corrects my Hebrew, they fail before I start." [Laughs.] (Ettenberg, 2006a)

In 1960, Fox created the Melton Research Center for Jewish Education at JTS. It was an attempt to treat Jewish education as a serious object of study, to bring the wisdom of the academy to the development of Jewish curricula, and to ratchet up the level of teaching in the Jewish synagogue school. In many ways, Fox was Benderly redux, a gifted thinker who generated more ideas than he could possibly implement. It was his idea to use the Ramah camps as laboratories to pilot the teaching of Melton curricula (Brown, 1997, 836). Kaufman (1997) refers to Melton Center in the Fox years as under the "unsung supervision of Sylvia Ettenberg" (618). Ettenberg (2006c) disagrees with that assessment:

No, this was not so. . . . He [Fox] was the dean at that point, and he became the overseer of Melton. It was not a conception that I had, but I immediately fell in with the thing, so I was a part of it. My oversight of Melton was only after he left. Then that came into my bailiwick. So I oversaw Elaine Morris, then Barry [Holtz] and Edy [Rauch].

Barry Holtz (2006), codirector of Melton with Edy Rauch from 1978 to 1994, recalls meeting Ettenberg just after he was hired by Fox, who had de-camped to the Hebrew University in 1966 but remained the titular head of Melton at JTS.

Sylvia was the boss. The real boss behind all of this stuff. I had heard about her. . . . I had never met Sylvia, even though I [had] heard legends about her, what a powerful figure she was, and all that stuff. . . . I was trying to get the lay of the land and how things worked. And it became clear to me, kind of rapidly, that Sylvia was the boss. . . . Everything important had to go through Sylvia. Everything connected to money had to go through Sylvia.

Assistant Dean of the Teachers Institute, 1966–1976

After Seymour Fox left for Israel, Sylvia Ettenberg was appointed assistant dean of the Teachers Institute, fulfilling all the responsibilities of the dean, but lacking the title. Ettenberg (2006a) describes those years:

So I ran the school from '66 to '76. I had a chairman of the faculty. First it was Bavli and Halkin but I set the agendas, and they were *my* alter egos, or as Moshe Held would run through the halls [and] call me, *balabusteh* [Yiddish for "mistress of the house"; it connotes a multitalented housewife]. I think that was the most endearing term that I ever had because he said it with much love.

She used her keen ability to read people and analyze problems to work with the faculty. Barry Holtz (2006) recalls her healthy attitude toward some of the luminaries on the JTS faculty. Unlike Seymour Fox, whose "yeshivish" upbringing led to his putting the great men up on a pedestal, "Sylvia by contrast had a much more jaundiced eye." Regarding a great Talmudist, Holtz remembers her saying: "He thought he was an expert in everything. He could give you advice on the stock market. He thought to himself, 'Since I'm a genius in Talmud, I must be a genius about the stock market.' Feh!" While Ettenberg always treated scholars with great respect, Holtz adds, "she also viewed them as 'they're kind of in their little academic cages, and they don't exactly know the real world. I know the real world.'" Ettenberg (2006a) recalls working with these men, many of them her former teachers: "I was very close with Halkin. And I used Halkin in the proper way. He was the chairman of the faculty. If I had a problem with a faculty man, I called up Halkin, and we decided how to handle it. But I was the one to detect the problems that he didn't know, and I was the one who had to solve them. That was my role."

Her years of experience as a practitioner interacting with students gave Ettenberg a gift for understanding what teaching and learning should be within a given educational context. Isa Aron (2006) recalls her mother sharing stories about working with faculty members who failed to connect with their students and fielding complaints from those students.

> The typical story goes: "The students were complaining, and so I called this person in, and we had this conversation and I did this, and I did that. . . ." She understood in an era where, I don't think most of the people in the institution really cared, or didn't bother to understand, that it was important that the students learn, not just that the faculty teach.

Dean of Educational Development, 1976–1988

In 1976, Ivan Marcus replaced Ettenberg as the dean of the undergraduate school (now List College). Ettenberg was awarded the title of Dean of Educational Development. Throughout her interviews, with me and with others, Ettenberg makes it clear that titles really did not matter to her. She knew she lacked the requisite degrees. Ever the realist, she understood that she had neither the time nor the inclination to pursue a doctorate. "It was easier for me, personally, to sacrifice the academic work. It's wrong, but that was my preference. I couldn't have handled all of [those] things" (Ettenberg, 2006a).

The deanship was a portmanteau including the coordination of the Melton Center, Camp Ramah network, Prozdor, and LTF, and liaison with numerous organizations including the United Synagogue of Conservative Judaism's Commission on Jewish Education, Educators Assembly, Council on Jewish Education, Solomon Schechter Principals Council, Association of Institutions for Higher Learning in Jewish Education, National Board of License, and Joint Placement Committee (with the Jewish Educators Association). In addition, she coordinated the Department of Education, designing new courses, answering all queries and correspondence, initiating long-range planning, overseeing all awards and prizes, and as a lecturer in the department, supervising an internship in administration for principals. She also advised master's and doctoral level students, and recruited students for education and other programs. It was she who recruited thirty-five students for the new Graduate School of JTS at various Ramah camps (Ettenberg, 2006a). In 1989, Ettenberg was awarded an honorary doctorate from JTS and named lecturer emerita of Jewish education.

Reflections on a Life History

Ettenberg's achievements are either underappreciated or overshadowed by her male colleagues who wrote about them (Lerner, 1971; Davis, 1963, 1986; Fox, 1997, 2003). Because she wrote very little, and because she was such a team player, Ettenberg never countered the impression that she, like so many women before and after her, was merely an extension of the powerful men with whom she worked.

IDEAS OR IMPLEMENTATION?

Even David Kaufman (1997), in his history of the Teachers Institute, while calling for more attention to Ettenberg's role in the JTS story, describes her partnership with Davis as combining "the creativity of the one with the practicality of the other" (613). Such a description ignores the fact that Sylvia was as much an ideologue as Davis was when it came to trying to create a Hebrew renaissance in America. It took a utopian imagination to establish Ramah. Sylvia's "baby" was born out of the shadows of the Holocaust and the rise of Zionism; its name, suggested by her teacher Hillel Bavli, suggests a rebirth of a decimated community (Schwartz, 1987).[7]

Education is a practical discipline, straddling theory and practice. Ettenberg told William Kennedy (1994), "An educator must have the theoretical background. He can't be just a practitioner." Her colleague Fox (2003) maintains that vision cannot be separated from implementation, that the field of education demands that theory be translated (253). To create a dichotomous relationship between educational theory and practice is specious; it parallels the artificial separation of intellect from affect (Scheffler, 1991). In the

Nicomachaean Ethics, Aristotle (1998) differentiates between philosophical wisdom and practical wisdom. Throughout her life, Ettenberg privileged practical wisdom, an interest in ideas in the service of action over abstract ideas. An educator to her very core, she sums up her credo in one sentence: "If education should reflect society, our task as Jewish educators is to create that society" (personal communication, May 17, 2006).

ACHIEVEMENTS AND CONSTRAINTS

I have found the work of the anthropologist-sociologist Pierre Bourdieu helpful in broadening my perspective on Ettenberg's life history, particularly his work on social practice and its manifestations in the academy. I have tried to capture Ettenberg's unusual gifts, her practical wisdom, while also describing the old boys club that was JTS, an institution trying to shed its image as "Schechter's yeshivah." How much could she accomplish when status at JTS was determined by one's scholarship, the subject matter one taught, and access to the chancellor? Where status was symbolized by where one sat in the JTS synagogue, which did not allow mixed seating? (See Goldberg [1997] for an anthropological study of JTS before the women's movement.) However, even in this highly stratified, degree-conscious, all-male arena, Ettenberg *did* succeed. She was able to ride upward in an elevator she constructed, albeit not to the topmost floors. I am trying to walk a fine line between voluntarism and determinism. What Ettenberg accomplished through her drive, institutional loyalty, and skills was remarkable for a woman without advanced degrees in a prefeminist era in this particular setting. Bourdieu's use of habitus, capital, and field provides a conceptual theory for better understanding the successes, compromises, and obstacles in Ettenberg's life history (Bourdieu and Passeron, 2000). Bourdieu's theory sheds light on what constitutes competence in a "visible social world of practice" during a forty-five-year period (cited in Jenkins, 1991, 67).

By "habitus," Bourdieu means dispositions embodied in a certain individual. Like Lagemann's (1979) "educational biography" or Middleton's (1993) "intellectual biography," habitus, acquired through experience and socialization, predisposes actors to certain activities. Habitus seems to mean traits, character, and skills. (It is hard to pin Bourdieu down on clear definitions.) One's life history is the interaction of habitus, "a subjective reality," with the environment, which Bourdieu understands as an "objective reality." A career can be viewed as a negotiation between one's talents, skills, and abilities and the limitations and opportunities of what Bourdieu calls a given "field": a structured system of social positions (cited in Jenkins, 1992, 80, 85). One's place in the field is determined by various kinds of capital: economic, social, cultural, and symbolic (Bourdieu and Passeron, 2000). In an academic institution, economic capital plays a minor role. Ettenberg possessed a bountiful reservoir of cultural, social, and symbolic capital.

Her rich Judaica background and Hebrew skills — encouraged by her father and formally taught in her Talmud Torah and later in her beloved Teachers Institute — were valuable commodities at JTS, especially to Mordecai Kaplan and his disciples (Mintz, 1997). Her cultural capital was enhanced by her command of Hebrew. No one dared speak to her in English (Ettenberg, 2006a). Her social capital lay in her ability to size up people and situations, including her skill at recognizing potential; her unflagging energy; and most of all, complete loyalty to JTS. Moshe Ettenberg's honored position on the JTS faculty also added to her social capital (Goldberg, 1997), which Bourdieu defines as "having valued relations with significant others" (cited in Jenkins, 85). Isa Aron (2006) muses:

> My mother attained her position because she was incredibly competent, but I think that probably her position was bolstered in the same way that the executive male needs the woman who . . . puts on beautiful dinner parties. Having a husband who could *daven musaf* [lead a section of the prayer service] was a nice perk for my mother. It paved the way that my father was so conversant in these circles and could hold his own.

Ettenberg's practical wisdom made her an invaluable colleague. In an all-male culture, Ettenberg held her own; she says of herself, "I was one of the boys" (Ettenberg, 2005a). I describe her (to Ettenberg's amusement) as "out-guying the guys." She had no fear of confrontation and instinctively knew what weapons from her well-stocked arsenal to select in disarming an opponent. With the swimming-averse *yeshivah bochurs*, she one-upped them on *halakhah* (Jewish law). When the intellectual, academic dean of the TI, Judah Goldin complained about the artwork of Temima Gezari's art students decorating the windows of a JTS building and asked her to remove them, she told him to do it himself (Ettenberg, 2006a). Ettenberg recalls a time when during a tempestuous meeting "the boys" called a break and proceeded to come to a solution in the men's room. "When they came back and said, 'We got it solved,' I said, 'You know, the next time that happens, I'm coming in there'" (Ettenberg, 2006a).

In maneuvering her way around the restraints of the JTS "field," Ettenberg, although a singularly beautiful woman, never used "womanly wiles" as a political strategy. (She does, however, admit to flirting with her first class of thirteen-year-olds as an inexperienced seventeen-year-old teacher [Ettenberg, 2005a]). However, there was a time when she used traditional gender roles to wrest a salary increase from Finkelstein. Salaries were highly variable for men, as they were for the few women, all of whom with the exception of Ettenberg were in clerical roles. Both Fox and Goldin had advocated for her unsuccessfully; "Finkelstein was not going to give a 'woman' the kind of salary he offered a man" (Kennedy, 1994). Ettenberg went directly to Finkelstein and told him she needed money for a babysitter on Sundays and evenings. When he refused and asked what she would do, she responded that Moshe would babysit. "So what happens to his own research?" he asked. Ettenberg told him, "It's out the window" (Kennedy, 1994). Finkelstein registered his horror at the prospect of a promising academic career stunted by childcare responsibilities. "He cannot be your babysitter. You're interfering with his work!" and granted her the raise, first extracting a promise that she wouldn't ask for another raise for two years (Ettenberg, 2006a).

Ettenberg did a considerable amount of "heavy lifting" for Team JTS. When Moshe Davis was disturbed at a student's choice in neckwear, he sent her to tell him that hand-painted ties with bathing beauties weren't appropriate for a future rabbi. It was she who became the go-between during the Massad-Ramah flag brouhaha in 1950. Goldin had refused to fly the flag of the fledgling state of Israel and created a more "Jewish" flag to be flown in the Wisconsin camp.

> Massad people sent some of the *farbrente* [fiery] idealists up in an airplane and they bombarded Wisconsin with leaflets about that. It was [a] big *sha'aruriyah* [scandal]. It was terrible. And of course, Jay was upset; everybody was upset. I, being the go-between, I called Shlomo [the director of Massad] and I said, "That's impossible, how did that thing happen?" . . . He talked with the board, and they sent us a letter of apology. (Ettenberg, 2006a)

Aryeh Davidson (2006) recalls Ettenberg asking him to take over a project that fell in the domain of another faculty member.

> ARYEH DAVIDSON (A): And I would say, "I can't do that. They'll be offended. They'll be hurt." And she would say, "Don't worry; I'll take care of it."
>
> C: So were people angry at you?
>
> A: They weren't angry at me; they were angry at her. She took a lot of the heat. She would be the bad guy, and I came out clean. She didn't mind. She'd say, "I'll be the bad guy." It was part of the job.

Although Ettenberg had to wait a long time for the salary and the titles she deserved, it is a mistake to imagine her as lacking symbolic capital, a term Bourdieu uses to describe prestige and social honor (cited in Jenkins, 1992, 85). Quoting Hobbes who observed, "reputation of power is power," Bourdieu might be describing Ettenberg's hold over the TI, even though she may not have been the titular head (Bourdieu, 1988). Davidson (2006) discusses Ettenberg's cultural capital and its limits:

> Here's a woman who grew up in a Hebraist, Zionist world, who developed a certain degree of mastery in those areas, was committed to

those ideals, for what ever reason could not have reached in that age the crowning achievements of the men around her. She couldn't go to Rabbinical School; she couldn't get a doctorate. And on a certain level, she made her peace with that, and said, "How can I contribute in terms of practice?" . . . She was very satisfied to run the show under the wings of these towering figures. As long as she had the autonomy she didn't have to get . . . [pause] . . . top billing.

In *Homo Academicus*, Bourdieu (1988) describes the compromise made between the habitus and the field. He notes that academics adjust their ambition and goals so that they end up only "wanting" what they can realistically achieve, labeling it as "rejection of the inaccessible or the choice of the inevitable" (11). This description applies to Ettenberg's accommodation to the world of JTS.

Feminism

Ettenberg has a complex relationship with feminism. She has difficulty defining it precisely. Isa Aron (2006), her daughter, notes, "She's often said to me that because of the women's movement, she got a raise later in life. Her salary was made commensurate with male dean salaries. But she always adds, 'But I would never . . . I was never a feminist. I would never have agitated. . . .' But she did appreciate it."

I suspect that if Ettenberg were to read the revisionist feminism of bell hooks (2000), she might find many points of agreement. The first generation of feminists, according to hooks, was myopic about issues of class and race, and self-absorbed in their "common oppression" by men and in their victimhood as women. At no time did Ettenberg see men as the enemy; at no time did she see herself as a victim. She was what hooks would call a "liberal individualist," who competed, and succeeded, in a man's world (hooks, 2000, 9). Ettenberg agrees completely with the issue of equal pay for equal work and readily admits that she was grateful to feminism for evening out some of the worst inequities in her title and salary. She quips, "I didn't learn to be offended because of the Women's Movement. The Women's Movement taught me that I should have been offended!" (Ettenberg, 2006a).

While Ettenberg does not approve of changing the liturgy to include the matriarchs as well as the patriarchs, she didn't change her name when she got married in 1940. She continued to call herself Sylvia Cutler. "Why did I do it? Not because of the Women's Movement. I had another problem. . . . I think I had mentioned it to you at some point. There were two of us in our family, both girls, and I felt that my family's name should be . . . that my father had done so much. I felt I should . . . and Moshe [it] never bothered." Having said this, she hastens to add, "You know why I changed it? And I never resented it. Finkelstein said, 'It's not nice for your husband'" (Ettenberg, 2006a).

However, she speaks of tackling Lieberman (the distinguished Talmudist on the JTS faculty) on the issue of Judith Hauptman (currently a member of the Talmud faculty of JTS and the first woman to receive a PHD in Talmud) taking advanced Talmud courses in the Rabbinical School (Kennedy, 1994). She also defended and voted for women's ordination, and fought for the expansion of the roles of young women in prayer services at Ramah. Barry Holtz (2006) tells a wonderful story that illustrates both Ettenberg's stance on the girls' participation in prayer and her practical wisdom. "You know, we had a *p'sak din* [a rabbinic ruling] from Rabbi Klein that all cheeses are kosher. So [I asked Ettenberg,] how come at Ramah they only serve kosher cheese? And her reply to me was, 'I traded it for *aliyot* for women.'"

Ettenberg's scrapbooks are full of testimonials that refer to her dedication to Hebrew and Zionism, her commitment to JTS, the Teachers Institute, and her crowning achievement, the founding of Ramah. When I asked her what she would like to be remembered for, she responded predictably, in her collegial manner: she would like to be remembered for her association with the shapers and builders of the Conservative movement. But there are some who would suggest that it is time for her to move into the spotlight on her own. They would applaud the sentiments expressed by Paula Hyman, former dean of List College and currently a professor of Jewish history at Yale. Writing on the occasion of Ettenberg's receiving the Distinguished Service Alumna Award from the Alumni Association of JTS, Hyman (1985) says: "Sylvia Ettenberg has ... been an important role model for women at the Seminary. She was among the first to prove that women could achieve positions of authority and influence in a Jewish institution of higher learning." Sylvia Cutler Ettenberg may not have intended to be a standard-bearer for women, but that too is part of her remarkable legacy.

NOTES

1. The national director of LTF was appointed by JTS and overseen by the TI. "For most of the group's thirty-five year history, he was directly supervised by Sylvia Ettenberg, the indomitable longtime TI associate dean who was an alumna of both Cejwin and Massad" (Brown, 1997, 827).

2. When Ettenberg was a young woman, a friend sent her a copy of what he hoped would be the great American Hebrew novel. It was "very modern, and dealt with psychology, sexuality in the family." She read it, put it on the family bookshelves, and forgot about it. Her father picked it up and read it. He returned it to his daughter, saying, "For this he has to use *lashon hakodesh*? [the holy language]" (Kennedy, 1994).

3. For an account of this unusual laboratory school organized by Ivriah to teach Hebrew and general subjects to children ages three to seven, see Heller and Gelb (1948).

4. The position of registrar was not clerical. Ettenberg recalls that Louis Finkelstein's

first appointment at JTS was in this capacity (Ettenberg, 2005b). It was also an entry point for her good friend Moshe Davis. Similarly, secretary of the faculty of the TI, as much as it too sounds like a clerical title, was an administrative position. As Ettenberg repeatedly told me, "Titles didn't matter to me. It was probably foolish, but it never bothered me what the position was" (Ettenberg, 2006a).

5. For a fuller history of the founding of Ramah, see Schwartz (1987) and B. Cohen (1989).

6. Although Finkelstein was originally wary of the Ramah idea, he changed his mind. Ettenberg remembers his saying, "Only one camp? Only two camps? If we have 37 camps, then it will make a difference" (Ettenberg, 2006a).

7. Thus said the Lord: A cry is heard in Ramah—wailing, bitter weeping—Rachel weeping for her children. She refuses to be comforted for her children who are gone. Thus said the Lord: Restrain your voice from weeping, your eyes from shedding tears; for there is a reward for your labor, declares the Lord. They shall return from the enemy's land. And there is hope for your future (Jeremiah 31: 15–17).

REFERENCES

Ackerman, W. I. 1977. Becoming Ramah. In *Ramah: Reflections at Fifty. Visions for a New Century*, ed. S. A. Dorph, 3–24. New York: National Ramah Commission.

Aristotle. 1998. *The Nicomachean Ethics*. New York: Oxford University Press.

Aron, I. 2006. Interview with Carol K. Ingall, June 7.

Bourdieu, P. 1988. *Homo Academicus*. Cambridge: Polity.

Bourdieu, P, and J. C. Passeron. 2000. *Reproduction in Education, Society, and Culture*. London: Sage.

Brown, B. 1997. It's off to camp we go. In *Tradition Renewed: The Making of an Institution of Jewish Higher Learning*, ed. J. Wertheimer, 823–54. Vol. 1. New York: JTSA.

Camp Ramah Flyer. 1947. Chicago: Council of Conservative Synagogues.

Cohen, B. I. 1989. A brief history of the Ramah movement. In *The Ramah Experience: Community and Commitment*, ed. S. C. Ettenberg and G. Rosenfield, 3–16. New York: JTSA in cooperation with the National Ramah Commission.

Cohen, N. W. 2003. *The Americanization of Zionism, 1897–1948*. Waltham, Mass.: Brandeis University Press.

Davidson, A. 2006. Interview with Carol K. Ingall, July 27.

Davis, M. 1963. *The Jewish People in Metamorphosis*. Syracuse: Syracuse University.

———. 1986. *Jewish Distinctiveness within the American Tradition: The Eretz Yisrael Dimension as Case Illustration*. Syracuse: Syracuse University.

———. 1990a. Interview with Mychal Springer, January 28. Typescript. Ratner Archives.

———. 1990b. Interview with Mychal Springer, February 27. Typescript. Ratner Archives.

Ettenberg, S. C. 1967. The changing image of the combined program. In *The Education of American Jewish Teachers*, ed. O. I. Janowsky, 123–28. Boston: Beacon Press.

———. 2005a. Interview with Carol K. Ingall, July 6.

———. 2005b. Interview with Carol K. Ingall, September 15.

———. 2006a. Interview with Carol K. Ingall, February 16.

———. 2006b. Interview with Carol K. Ingall, May 17.

———. 2006c. Interview with Carol K. Ingall. July 27.

Fox, S. 2003. The art of translation. In *Visions of Jewish Education*, ed. S. Fox, I. Scheffler, and D. Marom, 253–95. Cambridge: Cambridge University Press.

Fox, S., with W. Novak. 1997. *Vision at the Heart: Lessons from Camp Ramah on the Power of Ideas*. New York: Mandel Institute and the Council for Initiatives in Jewish Education.

Goffman, E. 1961. *Asylums: Essays on the Social Situation of Mental Patients and Other Inmates*. New York: Anchor Books.

Goldberg, H. E. 1997. Becoming history: Perspectives on the seminary faculty at mid-century. In *Tradition Renewed: The Making of an Institution of Jewish Higher Learning*, ed. J. Wertheimer, 353–437. Vol. 1. New York: JTSA.

Goldin, J. 1967 *Japhet in Shem's Tents*. In *The Education of American Jewish Teachers*, ed. O. I. Janowsky, 111–21. Boston: Beacon Press.

Heller, M., and L. Gelb. 1948. The Beth Hayeled school. *Jewish Education* 20(1): 53–57.

Holtz, B. 2006. Interview with Carol K. Ingall, July 27.

hooks, b. 1994. *Teaching to Transgress: Education as the Practice of Freedom*. New York: Routledge.

———. 2000. *Feminist Theory: From Margin to Center*. Cambridge, Mass.: South End Press.

Hyman, P. 1985. Letter to Sylvia C. Ettenberg.

Ingall, M. A. 1997. My beautiful summer at Camp Alton. [October.] www.ralphmag.org/alton.html.

Janowsky, O. I., ed. 1967. *The Education of American Jewish Teachers*. Boston: Beacon Press.

Jenkins, R. 1992. *Pierre Bourdieu*. London: Routledge.

Josselit, J. W., ed. With K. S. Mittelman. 1993. *A Worthy Use of Summer: Jewish Summer Camping in America*. Philadelphia: National Museum of American Jewish History.

Kaufman, D. 1997. Jewish education as a civilization: A history of the Teachers Institute. In *Tradition Renewed: The Making of an Institution of Jewish Higher Learning*, ed. J. Wertheimer, 567–621. Vol. 1. New York: JTSA.

Kennedy, W. B. 1994. Oral history of Sylvia C. Ettenberg. Typescript.

Lagemann, E. C. 1979. *A Generation of Women: Education in the Lives of Progressive Reformers*. Cambridge, Mass.: Harvard University Press.

Lawrence-Lightfoot, S., and J. H. Davis. 1997. *The Art and Science of Portraiture*. San Francisco: Jossey-Bass.

Lerner, S. C. 1971. Ramah and its critics. *Conservative Judaism* 25(4): 1–28.

Middleton, S. 1993. *Educating Feminists: Life Histories and Pedagogy*. New York: Teachers College Press.

Mintz, A. 1997. The divided fate of Hebrew and Hebrew culture at the seminary. In *Tradition Renewed: The Making of an Institution of Jewish Higher Learning*, ed. J. Wertheimer, 83–103. Vol. 1. New York: JTSA.

Peshkin, A. 1988. *God's Choice: The Total World of a Fundamentalist Christian School*. Chicago: University of Chicago Press.

Reimer, J. 1989. Changing educational strategies at Ramah. *The Ramah Experience: Community and Commitment*. New York: JTSA in cooperation with the National Ramah Commission, 57–61.

Sales, A. L., and L. Saxe. 2004. *How Goodly Are Thy Tents: Summer Camps as Jewish Socializing Experiences*. Waltham, Mass.: Brandeis University Press.

Scheffler, I. 1991. *In Praise of the Cognitive Emotions and Other Essays in the Philosophy of Education*. New York: Routledge, Chapman, and Hall.

Schwartz, S. R. 1987. Camp Ramah: The early years, 1947–1952. *Conservative Judaism* 40(1): 12–41.

Scialabba, K. 2006. Outthinking the media: Lessons from a tennis master. *Religious Education* 101(2): 261–91.

Shapiro, A. M., and B. I. Cohen. 1984. *Lilmod u'l'lamed: Studies in Jewish Education and Judaica in Honor of Louis Newman.* New York: KTAV.

Index

"friendly visitors," 28
Frost, Bernice, 202n2

Gallas, Karen, 178
Gamoran, Carmi, 103
Gamoran, Emanuel, 14, 77–79, 93n14, 99,
    101–2, 201; educational philosophy,
    104–8; retirement and death, 112
Gamoran, Hillel, 102–3, 112, 114
Gamoran, Judith Halperin, 98–99, 103
Gamoran, Mamie Goldsmith, 1, 10, 14,
    98–115; *Days and Ways: The Story of
    Jewish Holidays and Customs*, 106;
    early history, 100–104; family history,
    98–99; *Hebrew Spirit in America*, 103;
    Hillel's Calendar, 107; *Hillel's Happy
    Holidays*, 105, 123, 177; memoir, 98;
    old age and death, 113–14; *With Singer
    and Sage*, 103; *Talks to Jewish Teach-
    ers* (with E. Gamoran), 98, 100, 105,
    107–8, 110–12; *Voice of the Prophets*,
    103
Gans, Roma, 212
Gardner, Howard, 175, 189
Geiger, Abraham, 4
gender issues: Ettenberg and, 209–12,
    223–25; Sherman and, 159–60
gender roles: and Benderly trainees,
    69–71; Brickner and, 69–71; and
    Teachers Institute, 14; in Weilerstein's
    Ten and a Kid, 130–31. *See also* Sister-
    hoods for Personal Service
German language, 101
Gezari, Daniel, 173–74
Gezari, Temima (Fruma Nimtzowitz),
    1, 10, 14–16, 160, 166–85, 211, 223;
    as artist, 171–73; artistic philosophy,
    177–79; at BJE, 170–71; and *Brush and
    Color*, 175–76; and children's art exhi-
    bitions, 179–81; early history, 166–67;
    and feminism, 174–75; *Footprints and
    New Worlds*, 176; *Jewish Kindergarten*
    (with Pessin), 175; legacy of, 182–85;
    marriage and family, 173–74;
    Palestine's Past, Present, and Future
    (mural), 171–73; pedagogy, 181–82;
    teacher training, 167–69; as TI faculty
    member, 169; *Traveling to Rocky

Point (oil painting), 174; *Woman of
    Valor* (mosaic), 173; writings, 175–77
Gezari, Zvi, 173
Ginsburg, Asher, 147
girls clubs, 101
Giroux, Henry, 16, 158
Goldberg, Harvey, 159
Goldberg, Henry R., 208
Goldberg, Israel, 10
Goldfarb, Samuel, 168
Goldin, Judah, 181, 217–18, 223
Goldsmith, Matilda Bauer, 101
Gordon, A. D., 145
Gordon, Ayala, 173
Gottschalk, Alfred, 69
goyische kop, 135
Grant, L. D., 162
Gratz, Rebecca, 4
Greenberg, Eliezer, 129
Greenberg, Hayim, 191–92
Greene, Maxine, 179, 189
Grimm Brothers, "Tom Thumb," 124
Grossman, Ovadiah, 145
Grossman, Sarah Weinstein, 144
Grossman, Shlomo, 144–45
Grossman, Shoshana, 145
guest lecturers, in settlement houses, 39

"habitus," 222
Hadassah, 15, 120, 148; American Zionist
    Medical Unit, 162n2; archives, 99;
    Braverman and, 79–81; Brickner and,
    65; conventions, 47–48, 57; Education
    Committee, 57; first constitution, 47;
    focus on education, 48–49, 56–58;
    Gamoran and, 113–14; mission in
    Palestine, 47, 57; Sampter and, 46–59;
    and Zionism, 53
Hadassah chapters: and education
    programs, 57; and Hadassah School of
    Zionism, 56
Hadassah Community College (Israel),
    Libbie Braverman Scholarship Fund
    in Memory of Sigmund Braverman, 91
Hadassah Leadership Academy, 58
Hadassah Magazine, 113
Hadassah Medical Organization, 56–57
Hadassah School of Zionism, 47–59

Weilerstein's works, 138; as target of settlement house program, 29–32
Muffs, Yochanan, 217
multiculturalism, 137
multiple intelligences, 175, 189
murals, 171–73
Museum of the City of New York, 180
music, based on Hebrew sources, 194
music education: Braverman and, 87, 89; Jochsberger and, 189–202; Sherman and, 158; at Teachers Institute, 168
mussar (pietistic Jewish literature), 7

National Board of License, 221
National Council for Jewish Education, 76
National Council of Jewish Women (NCJW), 148; and Esther Hellman Settlement House, 30; and immigrant aid, 27–28
National Federation of Temple Sisterhoods, 67
National Foundation for Jewish Culture, 189
Neill, A. S., 199–201, 202n3
New Jerusalem Conservatory and Academy of Music, 192
Newman, Lou, 216
Northern Exposure (TV series), 135
Nuland, Sherwin, 2, 20

Ohio Michigan Indiana Religious School Teachers' Association, 95n55
Olitzky, Kerry M., 104
Oppenheimer, Arthur, 153
oral histories, from settlement house attendees, 29
ordination of women: Brickner and, 70; Ettenberg and, 226; Weilerstein and, 131
Organization for Rehabilitation through Training, 180
Orthodox schools, and art education, 189
Orthodoxy, Braverman and, 77
Outlook, 121, 124

Palestine: Braverman and, 79–83; Brickner's travels in, 67–68; Gamoran's travels in, 102–3; Hadassah and, 47, 57; Sampter and, 58; Sherman's residence in, 147–48
Palestine Academy of Music, 190–91
Palestine Jewish Colonization Association, 144
Palmer, Parker, 152
parodies, written by students, 154–56
Pascoe, Peggy, 27
passion, and excellence in teaching, 154–56
Passover, 105
Paul, Sholom, 217
pedagogy: based on primacy of Hebrew language and culture, 1; child-centered, 199–200; of Feineman, 41; feminist, 156; of Gezari, 181–82; Hebraist-nationalist, 18, 20; of Jochsberger, 195–99; progressive, 17, 20–21; of Sherman, 143, 149–51
Pekarsky, Daniel, 195
performing arts education, 87–89
personal service, 25, 30–31
Pessin, Deborah, 109, 175, 210
Pestalozzi, 167, 200
Pevsner, Bella, 120
philanthropists, Jewish female, 25
philosophy of art, Gezari and, 177–79
Pioneer Women, 48–49
pluralism, American, and Jewish particularism, 136
Poetry Society, 50–51
portraiture, as methodology, 205
positivism, 17
Prep School for Girls No. 3 (New York), 166–67, 182
preservation efforts, 129
professionalism: among educators, 17; Braverman and, 85; Brickner and, 64–65; in social work, 34
progressive education, 21n1, 183, 189, 200; Braverman and, 86; Gamorans and, 111; Sampter and, 50–51, 55
progressivism, 13–14, 20; and Zionism, 51–52
protofeminism, in Weilerstein's *Ten and a Kid*, 130–31. *See also* feminism
Prozdor, 205, 217–18, 221

public schools, 20
Purim, 105, 170, 197
Puritans, 3
purity and pollution, in Jewish identity,
    135–36

Raanana Club, 158
Ramaz Academy (New York), 125
Ramaz School, 193, 201
Rauch, Edy, 219
rebbetzin: Brickner as, 66; Weilerstein as,
    119, 122
Reconstructionism, 15, 167, 171, 193, 208
Reconstructionist, 113
Reconstructionist Foundation, 176
Reform Judaism, 4–6; Braverman and,
    77–78; Brickner and, 64–71; in work of
    Gamorans, 105–8; and Zionism, 79
refugees, Jewish, 80–81
Reimer, J., 215
residence club, 33
revisionist historians, and settlement
    house movement, 41–42
Ribalow, Menachem, 201
Richman, Julia, 13
Rivera, Diego, 171–72
role modeling: in settlement house move-
    ment, 26–29, 37; Sherman and, 158
Rose, Bernard, 119, 121
Rose, Tillie Berger, 119–21
Rosen, Ben, 111
Rosenberg, Rose R., 156
Ross, Lucille, 144, 151–52
Rossel, Seymour, 110
Roth, Cecil, 176
Roth, Philip, 129
Rothchild, Adelaide M., 31
Rottenberg, Marc, 195–96
Rousseau, Jean-Jacques, 200
Rubel, Hadassah, 181–82

Sabbath observance, in settlement
    houses, 38
Sabbath schools, 64
Safian, Elizabeth, 133
salaries, for JTS teachers, 159–60
Sampter, Jessie, 1, 13–14, 16, 47–59;
    background, 50–51; *Book of the*

Nations, 58; *Course in Zionism*, 47,
    55–56; as educator, 55–56, 59; *Emek*,
    58; move to Palestine, 58; *Seekers*, 50;
    as Zionist, 52–53
Sampter, Rudolph, 50
Sampter, Virginia, 50
San Francisco, Emanu-El Sisterhood for
    Personal Service, 25–42
San Francisco Symphony, 31
Sarna, J. D., 108–9
Schachter, Lifsa, 178
Scharfstein, Zvi, 208, 211
Schechter, Solomon, 12, 149
Schiff, A., 184
Schiff, Jacob, 8
Schindler, Alexander M., 98
Schoolman, Albert P., 209
Schoolman, Bertha, 67
Schorsch, I., 160
Schutz, Alfred, 149
Schwab, Joseph, 154
Schwartz, Shuly Rubin, 122
Scult, Mel, 70
Second Great Awakening, 4
Seekers Club, 50–51
Segal, Hyman, 61n49
self-government, in settlement houses, 38
self-promotion, Braverman and, 90–91
Seminary School of Jewish Studies, 143,
    149, 161
settlement house culture, 26–29
settlement house movement, 13, 25–42;
    and revisionist historians, 41–42
settlement houses, 25–26; curriculum in,
    27; as "model homes," 26–29, 37–42
Shapiro, A. M., 216
Shapiro, Chava, 159
Shearith Israel congregation, 3; school,
    3–4
Sherman, A. Joshua, 143–44, 146, 151,
    154, 158–60
Sherman, Anna G., 1, 14–16, 70, 143–62;
    as "Benderly girl," 70; early history,
    144–49; and excellence in teaching,
    152–58; health issues, 147–49, 153; as
    Hebrew teacher, 143, 145–46, 151–58;
    pedagogy, 143, 149–51
Sherman, Earl Mayo, 147, 149, 153

Hebrew-language, 83–84; McGuffey Readers, 6–7; Pike's *Catechism and Scripture Lessons*, 4; publication of, 65; Zionist, 54–56'

Thomas Jefferson High School, 208

Tiferet Ha'Gra (Brooklyn), 208

Tiferet Yisrael Talmud Torah, 207–8

total environment, Jewish camp as, 216

tough love, Weiner and, 35

"traditional Conservative," 124–25

"Try a Little Kindness!" (art exhibition), 180

Tu B'shevat, 106

typewriter, Hebrew, 65, 72n4

tzedakah, 132

UAHC-CCAR Joint Commission on Jewish Education, 78

Union of American Hebrew Congregations (UAHC), 102–3, 112; *Talks to Jewish Teachers* (Gamoran and Gamoran), 98

Union of Reform Judaism, 99

Unitarianism, 50–51

United States, history of Jews in, 2–8

United Synagogue for Conservative Judaism, 112; Commission on Jewish Education, 221; Women's League, 148

unity, Jewish, Gamorans and, 105–6

University of California, 31

University of Cincinnati, 65

Unterberg, Israel, 172

Uptown Jews, of New York, 7

Uris, Leon, *Exodus*, 141n53

values, Jewish: in art education, 180; in *Dick: the Horse That Kept the Sabbath*, 127–28; in K'tonton stories, 125

Varnhagen, Rahel, 159

Vella, Jane, 157

vocation, and excellence in teaching, 152–54

Volk, Libbie, 39–40

volunteerism, as "personal service," 30–31

Wald, Lillian, 13, 25

Warburg, Frieda Schiff, 146, 148–49

Weilerstein, B. Reuben, 119, 128

Weilerstein, Deborah, 123, 131

Weilerstein, Herschel, 118, 121

Weilerstein, Reuben, 118

Weilerstein, Sadie Rose, 1, 14–16, 118–38; *Adventures of K'tonton*, 118–19, 124–25, 132; *Dick: the Horse That Kept the Sabbath*, 126–28, 136; *K'tonton in Israel*, 132–35; *K'tonton in the Circus*, 135–36; *K'tonton on an Island in the Sea*, 131; *Molly and the Sabbath Queen*, 126; as *rebbetzin*, 119, 122; as storyteller, 120–21; *Ten and a Kid*, 128–31; *What Danny Did*, 121; *What the Moon Brought*, 126; as writer, 121–23

Weiner, Grace, 1, 13–14, 44n21; and role modeling, 28, 41–42; as social worker, 25–26, 33–37. *See also* Emanu-El Sisterhood for Personal Service (San Francisco)

Weizmann Institute, 216–17

Werner, Eric, 195

Wertheimer, J., 18

Western Reserve University, 77

white slavery, 32–33

Wise, Isaac Mayer, 6

Wise, Stephen, 11, 66

Wissenschaft des Judentums, 160

women: and Hebrew-language study, 146; on JTS faculty, 169; ordination of, 70, 131, 226

Women's League for Conservative Judaism, 124

working girls, as target of settlement house programs, 29–30

World Union for Progressive Judaism, 68

World War I, settlement houses and, 37–38

World War II, 80, 191, 209

World Zionist Congress, 80

Wright, Merle St. Croix, 50–51

Yemin Orde Youth Village (Israel), 173

Yeshiva of Central Queens, 201

Yeshiva of Flatbush, 201, 210–12

Yeshiva University: Azrieli Graduate School, 184; Museum, 184; and music education, 193

Yeshiva Zichron Moshe, 201
Yiddish Institute for Jewish Research, Vilna, 129
Yiddishkeit, Braverman and, 77
Yiddish language, in Weilerstein's works, 137
Young, Ruth Breslow, 123
Young Israel movement, 11
Young Judaea, 53–54, 65
Young Women's Hebrew Association (YWHA), 33, 54, 146
youth, Jewish, and exchange programs, 81
Youth Aliyah, 79

zakhor (remember), as biblical injunction, 129

Zangwill, Israel, *Melting Pot*, 52
Zborowski, Mark, 129
Zion, Harriet, 175, 177
Zionism, 2, 18; Americanized, 51–52; Braverman and, 77, 79–83; breadth of, 51; Brickner and, 64; cultural/spiritual, 8–9; and ethnic cohesion, 132; Gamorans and, 106; Sampter and, 47–59; Sherman and, 151; T. Rose and, 119–20; Weilerstein and, 132–35. *See also* Hadassah School of Zionism
Zionist Organization of America (ZOA), 48
Zionist organizations, and Americanization, 132
Zipperstein, Steven, 129
z'khut hakibush, 144–45

—